D0586189

A Field Guide in Colour to
WILD FLOWERS

A Field Guide in Colour to

WILD FLOWERS

By Dietmar Aichele

Illustrated by

Marianne Golte-Bechtle

English version first published 1975 by
Octopus Books Limited
59 Grosvenor Street, London W1

Reprinted 1976, 1977, 1978, 1979, 1980

The original German edition was published by
Franckh'sche Verlagshandlung, Kosmos-Verlag, Stuttgart
under the title of 'Was blüht denn da? In Farbe'

© Copyright first edition 1973, second edition 1975,
Franckh'sche Verlagshandlung,
W. Keller & Co., Stuttgart

Translation © 1975 Octopus Books Limited

ISBN 0 7064 0474 2

Printed in Czechoslovakia
5/4/033/51-06

Introduction

This book has been written to help the flower lover who is not scientifically trained, but wishes to be able to identify and to learn a little more about the plants which are likely to be found commonly both near at home and when on holiday. The author, Dr. Alois Koch, himself an amateur, worked for over twenty-five years to produce this book, and his work was continued after his death by Professor W. Kreh and Professor W. Fischer, while botanical nomenclature has been brought up to date by Dr. Dietmar Aichele who has also completely revised the book, following the latest classification.

As an amateur, Dr. Koch understood the problems likely to be encountered by the layman and evolved a method of identification using obvious features rather than the more usual botanical keys. Colour is the first step to identification, the book being divided into six sections, one for each flower colour which will be met with. These main sections are then divided into smaller groups by taking the habitat in which the flower is found, for example woodland, marsh or roadside. These are in their turn divided into four subgroups according to the structure of the flowers. Of these the first three cover plants with symmetrical flowers, having up to four, five and more than five petals respectively. The fourth group is of those with irregularly shaped flowers regardless of the number of petals. Where there is any possible source of confusion, the most easily understood course has been followed. An obvious example is the daisy family (Compositae). To the botanist, the head of a daisy is a cluster of many tiny flowers, but to the layman it appears to be a single flower with many petals, and it has been treated in this fashion here, coming into the subgroup of flowers with more than five petals. The symbols used in the text for these subgroups are small outline flowers, and these are to be found at the top of each page and also in the left-hand margin if a new subgroup begins in the middle of a page. Perhaps the greatest advantage of the system used in this book is that having worked through the alternatives described, the pages containing the descriptions and illustrations are automatically reached without the need for a separate key or system of numbering. This makes for great simplicity and ease of use. To confirm identification made and to add further details, the text contains additional information. Where possible this has been condensed to allow as many facts to be included as space permits and a number of abbreviations are used. The letters 'IM' stand for identification marks listing points which serve to distinguish the plant readily from others which are similar. 'D' is followed by a more detailed description. The technical terms used in these descriptions are all illustrated in the introduction. Against 'H' is to be found information about the habitat of the plant and against 'AI' any additional information including the plant's economic value — if any — whether it is edible or poisonous, its uses in medicine and the nature of its life-cycle (whether it is annual, biennial or perennial).

Altogether 750 different species are keyed, described and named, and all are illustrated in colour by the accurate drawings of Marianne Golte-Bechtle which add greatly to the attraction and value of the book. Where plants are likely to be found in more than one colour, or in more than one habitat, they are included in both relevant sections. As 750 species by no means cover all the plants to be found in any one country, a careful selection has had to be made. Ferns have not been included, neither have grasses nor most sedges and rushes as these are not easy for a beginner to identify with their more complex structure and lack of colourful petals. The more specialized plants of highland and mountain have also been omitted and the book concentrates upon the many flowering plants of the lowlands which are likely to be noticed by the beginner, especially the many attractive 'weeds' which have followed European man wherever he has settled around the world. The success of this book in fulfilling the aim of its author, that is to provide a basic handbook for the reliable identification of flowers, can be gauged by the fact that it is now in its thirty-sixth edition.

Gillian Beckett, B. A.

Hints on the use of the book

The tables on pages 20—21 help you to identify plants quickly. You need only answer the following simple questions.

Questions: 1. What is the flower colour of the plant in question?
2. To what habitat group does the place where you found the plant belong?
3. Is the flower radially symmetrical?

If the answer to 3 is yes, then how many petals or corolla segments do the flowers have? Is the plant bilaterally symmetrical?

Now look up in the table of habitat subgroups the one which is appropriate in terms of the answers given. Then compare the plant you have found with the coloured illustrations on the plate to which you have been led. The descriptions under IM and D should help you to ensure its identification.

Example: You have found a violet[1] flowered plant on the edge of a wood in an alpine region. It has 6 petals. The synopsis tables lead you to the habitat group 'Violet — Woods, Thickets, Hedgerows' and to the subgroup 'radially symmetrical flowers with more than 5 petals', which in turn takes you to pages 342—345. As a quick glance shows, the leaves of the plant are not fully developed but nevertheless are quite clearly recognizable as being pinnate. Therefore the plant we are trying to identify can only be the Pasque Flower.

[1]) It is not always possible to arrive at an immediate conclusion as to whether a particular plant has 'violet', 'blue' or 'pink' flowers. I have tried to indicate the flower colour as it is likely to be interpreted by the majority of observers. All species which could equally well be considered to have 'violet' or 'blue', or 'pink' or 'violet' have been listed under both alternatives. There are, however, regional variations in flower colour, such that some species which normally have obviously 'blue' flowers, may sometimes have 'violet' ones. If for this reason you fail to identify a plant, you are advised to turn to the next most likely colour under which the plant might be considered.

Diagrammatic representation
of most important technical expressions

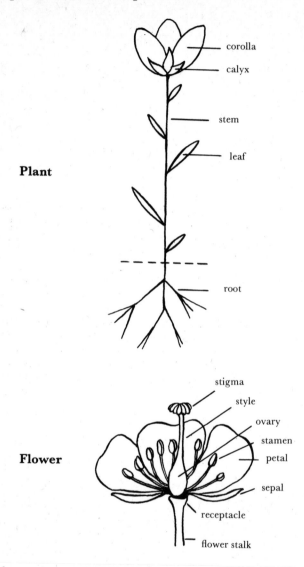

Plant

corolla

calyx

stem

leaf

root

Flower

stigma

style

ovary

stamen

petal

sepal

receptacle

flower stalk

Inflorescences

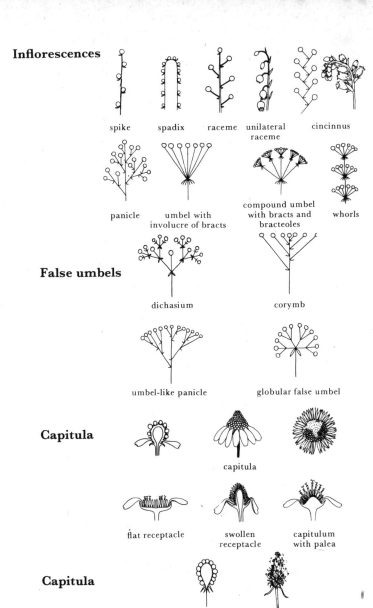

spike   spadix   raceme   unilateral   cincinnus
                                raceme

panicle   umbel with   compound umbel   whorls
            involucre of bracts with bracts and
                                 bracteoles

False umbels

dichasium   corymb

umbel-like panicle   globular false umbel

Capitula

capitula

flat receptacle   swollen   capitulum
                    receptacle   with palea

Capitula

capitula

9

Flowers

Corolla

polypetalous

Corolla

gamopetalous

flat   campanulate

Corolla

bilaterally symmetrical

labiate   violaceous   papilionaceous

ligulate

tubular

ray florets on outside   pendulous   flower with corona
disc florets in the centre   flower

Pistil

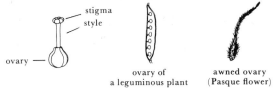

stigma
style
ovary

ovary of
a leguminous plant

awned ovary
(Pasque flower)

Stamen

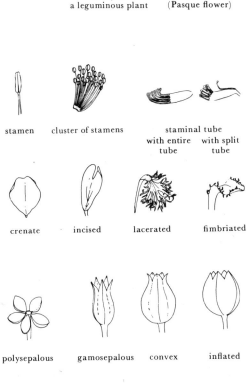

stamen   cluster of stamens

staminal tube
with entire   with split
tube   tube

Petal

crenate   incised   lacerated   fimbriated

Calyx

polysepalous   gamosepalous   convex   inflated

veined   with scales   two-lipped   outer calyx

11

Fruits and fructifications

legume

follicle

operculate capsule

non-operculate
capsule

drupe

nut

winged achene

samara

achene with pappus

berry

compound fruit
of strawberry

pod

biloment

siliquas

erect pods

horizontally
placed siliquas

12

Stem

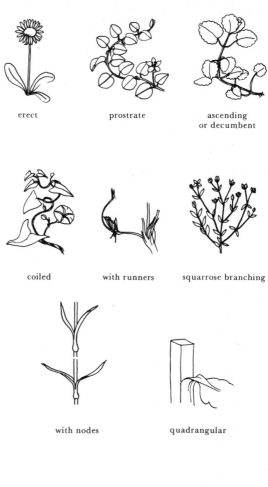

erect

prostrate

ascending
or decumbent

coiled

with runners

squarrose branching

with nodes

quadrangular

winged

ribbed

Leaves

rosette of leaves

subtending leaves

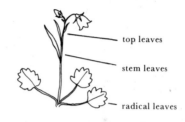

top leaves

stem leaves

radical leaves

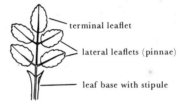

terminal leaflet

lateral leaflets (pinnae)

leaf base with stipule

compound leaf

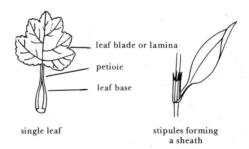

leaf blade or lamina

petiole

leaf base

single leaf

stipules forming
a sheath

Arrangement of leaves

alternate   distichous

opposite and decussate   whorled

Attachment of leaves

stalked or petiolate   sessile   with sagittate base
embracing stem

Leaf axils

offshoot or runner
in leaf axil   dwarf shoot
in leaf axil   bud in leaf
axil

Leaf blades

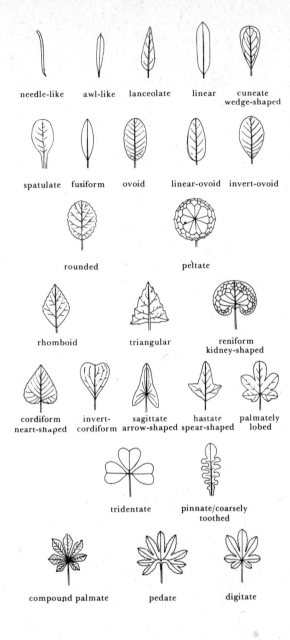

needle-like   awl-like   lanceolate   linear   cuneate
wedge-shaped

spatulate   fusiform   ovoid   linear-ovoid   invert-ovoid

rounded   peltate

rhomboid   triangular   reniform
kidney-shaped

cordiform   invert-   sagittate   hastate   palmately
neart-shaped   cordiform   arrow-shaped   spear-shaped   lobed

tridentate   pinnate/coarsely
toothed

compound palmate   pedate   digitate

Leaf blades (continued)

pinnate

pinnate with unpaired terminal leaflet

pinnate with terminal tendril

paired pinnate

paired pinnate with terminal point

stipules with tendrils

Leaf margin

margin entire

serrate

doubly serrate

dentate

dentate-serrate

spiny serrate

crenate

undulate

coarsely serrate

Venation

pinnate venation

net venation

parallel venation

Subterranean parts
of plant

taproot

swollen taproot

rhizome/rootstock

tuber

root tuber

bulbous tuber

bulb

bulb cut in half

18

Abbreviations and symbols

IM : Identification marks
 D : Description
 H : Habitat
AI : Additional information
 M : Monocotyledonous plant
 P : Polypetalous plant
 G : Gamopetalous plant
 ⊙ : Annual plant
 ⊙ : Biennial plant
 ♃ : Perennial plant
 † : Poisonous plant
(†) : Slightly poisonous plant

Flower forms

 = Flowers with up to 4 petals

 = Flowers with 5 petals

 = Flowers with more than 5 petals or ray florets

 = Bilaterally symmetrical flowers

Synopsis of the tables

❶ Shepherd's Purse *(Capsella bursa-pastoris)*
Brassicaceae (Cruciferae)

20—40 cm

IM: Flowers in loose racemes, with terminal cymes. Fruits triangular to cuneate or heart-shaped, upright, broadest at the top.

D: Stem branched. Basal rosette of leaves. Basal leaves dentate. Upper leaves entire.

H: Weedy places in fields, gardens and vineyards and on embankments, waste ground and along paths. Grows on sandy, loamy and gravel soil, rich in nitrogen.

AI: P; ☉; ⊙

The common name of the plant is derived from the purse-like shape of the fruit. Occasionally Shepherd's Purse is attacked by a fungus and then appears to be dusted with a white powder. Medicinal plant, containing choline and acetylcholine.

❷ Field Penny Cress *(Thlaspi arvense)*
Brassicaceae (Cruciferae)

15—30 cm

IM: Ovaries at most 3 times as long as broad. Fruit 10—18 mm long, broadly winged and deeply dissected dorsally. Stem angular. Plant glabrous.

D: Inflorescence racemose. Stem leaves sessile, linear, broadly toothed, with sagittate base, bright green. Locules many-seeded.

H: Weedy places, particularly in vegetable fields, vineyards and gardens; more rarely on wasteland and rubbish dumps and in cornfields. Predominantly on porous, loamy soil, rich in nutrients.

AI: P; ⊙

The common name refers to the shape of the fruits. The plant contains mustard oil and has a sharp taste.

❸ Shepherd's Cress, Common Teesdalia *(Teesdalia nudicaulis)*
Brassicaceae (Cruciferae)

8—20 cm

See p. 42 See p. 42

❹ Common Whitlow Grass *(Erophila verna; Draba verna)*
Brassicaceae (Cruciferae)

5—10 cm

IM: Petals indented over about $\frac{1}{3}$ of their length. Ovary at most 3 times as long as broad. Stem leafless. Leaves in flat rosettes.

D: Inflorescence racemose. Leaves lanceolate.

H: Weedy places in vegetable fields and on waysides, on dry and partially dry turf, less frequently on gravel tracks; likes a nitrogenous soil with a preference for coarse, granular, sandy soil.

AI: P; ⊙

The plant grows on rather unproductive soil.

❺ Procumbent Pearlwort *(Sagina procumbens)*
Caryophyllaceae

2—5 cm

IM: Mostly 4, occasionally 5 petals; plant procumbent.

D: Pedicel grows out of leaf axil and after flowering turns back on itself. The branches bend upwards and root at the nodes. The leaves are very short, narrowly linear and pointed at the top.

H: Weedy places in fields, waysides, near springs and on river banks; likes compact, non-chalky loams. Indicator of moisture.

AI: P; ♃

22

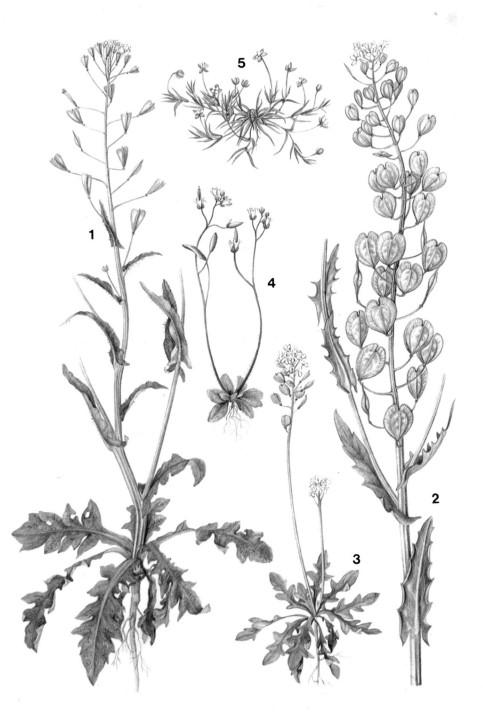

❶ **Perfoliate Penny Cress** *(Thlaspi perfoliatum)*
Brassicaceae (Cruciferae)
5—20 cm See p. 42

---

❷ **Pepperwort** *(Lepidium campestre)*
Brassicaceae (Cruciferae)
15—30 cm
IM: Flowers in racemes, inconspicuous. Ovary at most 3 times as long as broad. Fruit strongly compressed, oval, broadly winged near the top. Locules one-seeded. Pedicel mostly hairy. Stem leaves with cordate or sagittate bases which clasp the stem.
D: Leaves undivided, toothed, often wavy at the edge. Lower leaves linear, narrower towards the petiole, with soft hairs.
H: Weedy places in fields and waste ground with a liking for nutrient-rich, loamy soils, in a warm situation.
AI: P; ⊙ ; ⊙
Old medicinal plant. It sometimes gets mixed with Clover seed and thus springs up in places from which it has been absent for a long time.

---

❸ **Hoary Cress** *(Cardaria draba ; Lepidium draba)*
Brassicaceae (Cruciferae)
20—50 cm
IM: Flowers in dense false umbels, fragrant. Ovary at most 3 times as long as broad. Fruit strongly compressed, heart-shaped. Locules one-seeded. Peduncle glabrous. Middle and upper stem leaves with cordate or sagittate bases clasping the stem.
D: Umbel-like panicles. Stem usually erect and somewhat angular. Lower leaves stalked.
H: Weedy places along verges, embankments and wasteland. Likes a stony, rather chalky soil and prefers dry habitats.
AI: P; ♃
The seeds of Hoary Cress have a sharp taste (mustard oil) and were at one time used as a condiment.

---

❹ **Garlic Mustard, Jack-by-the-Hedge** *(Alliaria petiolata ; A. officinalis)*
Brassicaceae (Cruciferae)
20—100 cm
IM: The plant gives off a smell of garlic when rubbed.
D: Inflorescence a false umbel. Stem erect. Leaves undivided; the lower leaves kidney-shaped or heart-shaped with long petioles, coarsely crenate; upper leaves heart-shaped to ovoid, broadly toothed.
H: Copses, margins of open, moist woodlands, wasteland, sometimes on roadside verges. Likes porous soil rich in nutrients and nitrogen.
AI: P; ⊙
Contains mustard oil (hence common name); old medicinal plant.

---

❺ **Hoary** *or* **Hairy Rockcress** *(Arabis hirsuta)*
Brassicaceae (Cruciferae)
15—60 cm
IM: Ovary more than 3 times as long as broad. Leaves undivided with heart-shaped or sagittate bases clasping the stem. Plant hairy.
D: Flowers in a single inflorescence. Stem very densely covered with hairs.
H: Dry and semi-dry turf, dry mountain pastures, roadside verges, also on heaths. Likes chalky soils, rich in nutrients.
AI: P; ⊙ — ♃

24

❶

30—100 cm

Hedge Bedstraw *(Galium mollugo)*
Rubiaceae
IM : Tips of petals drawn out into a fine point. Stem quadrangular.
D :   Panicles. Flowers white or ivory colour. Leaves linear to invert-ovoid, with prickles; mostly in whorls of 8.
H :   Meadows, pastures, roadside verges, hedgerows; likes nutrient-rich, loamy soils with a preference for nitrogenous soils.
AI : G : 2↳

❷

30—130 cm

Cleavers, Goosegrass, Sticky Willie *(Galium aparine)*
Rubiaceae
IM : Inflorescences in leaf axils longer than the leaves. Stem quadrangular, climbing by means of stiff hairs.
D :   Flowers white or greenish white. Leaves cuneate, prickly. Coarse hairs are present on the leaf margins and in the middle of the underside of the leaf and these can be felt if a finger is stroked over the leaves. The whorl consists of 6—8 members.
H :   Weedy places in fields, gardens, vineyards, on wasteland, in thickets, hedgerows and in woodland, particularly the edges. Likes a moist, nitrogenous and loamy soil, rich in nutrients.
AI : G ; ⊙

❸

30—60 cm

Wild Radish *(Raphanus raphanistrum)*
Brassicaceae(Cruciferae)
IM : Flowers pale yellow or white, with dark yellow or purple veins. Sepals erect. Ovary and fruit more than 3 times as long as broad. Fruit strongly constricted between seeds.
D :   Umbel-like inflorescence. Stem with stiff hairs. Lower leaves lyre-shaped, upper leaves lanceolate.
H :   Weedy places in fields, more rarely in gardens and on waste ground. Likes non-chalky, loamy soil; also found on sandy soil and is an indicator of superficial soil acidity.
AI : P ; ⊙
This species is in all probability the wild ancestor of the cultivated radish. Radish is a corruption of the Latin word *radix* (root).

❹

15—30 cm

Hoary Plantain *(Plantago media)*
Plantaginaceae
See p. 44

See p. 44

❺

5—60 cm

Ribwort, Narrow-leaved Plantain *(Plantago lanceolata)*
Plantaginaceae
IM : Spike short. Flowers inconspicuous. Stamens white, subsequently turning brown.
D :   Stem grooved. Leaves lanceolate, forming a rosette.
H :   Meadows, pastures, roadsides and paths, also on wasteland. Likes a sandy or loamy soil, rich in nutrients, particularly nitrogen.
AI : G ; 2↳
An old medicinal plant containing mucilage. The seeds contain aucubin, which is a weak poison.

1

2

3

4

5

❶
5—15 cm
Wild Strawberry *(Fragaria viridis)*
Rosaceae
See p. 44

❷
8—60 cm
Common Chickweed *(Stellaria media)*
Caryophyllaceae
IM: Hairs on stem confined to a single, easily recognizable row. 3 styles present.
D: Flowers terminal. Leaves opposite; lower leaves petiolate, upper leaves sessile, oval with a pointed tip.
H: Weedy places, particularly in vegetable fields and in gardens, but also on waste ground. Likes nitrogenous soils.
AI: P; ☉
     Common Chickweed contains saponin and is an old medicinal plant.

❸
15—30 cm
Lesser Stitchwort *(Stellaria graminea)*
Caryophyllaceae
IM: Petals cleft to the base, 3—5 mm long (i.e. about as long as the calyx). 3 styles present. Bracts small, membranous.
D: Dichotomous false umbel; branches often geniculate. Stem quadrangular, flaccid. Leaves opposite, sessile, linear-lanceolate.
H: Dry meadows, mountain pastures, more rarely in weedy places in fields. Likes a loamy or rather sandy, calcifugous soil.
AI: P; ♃

❹
5—20 cm
Umbellate Stitchwort *(Holosteum umbellatum)*
Caryophyllaceae
IM: Flowers in umbels. Petals finely toothed.
D: False umbel. Pedicel bends back after flowering. Leaves sessile, oval, obtuse. Lowest leaves linear-lanceolate. Plant as a whole bluish green.
H: Weedy places in fields and on verges. Likes sandy and loamy soils.
AI: P; ☉

❺
10—30 cm
Field Mouse-ear Chickweed *(Cerastium arvense)*
Caryophyllaceae
See p. 46

❻
10—50 cm
Mouse-ear Chickweed *(Cerastium fontanum; C. caespitosum; C. vulgatum; C. holosteoides)*
Caryophyllaceae
IM: Petals at most divided over $\frac{1}{3}$ their length, usually only indented. Styles 4—5. Near the flowering shoots are some flowerless branches.
D: False umbel. Stem prostrate, decumbent or erect, densely hairy or glabrous. Leaves linear-ovoid or lanceolate.
H: Meadows, occasionally also in weedy places in fields. Likes a moist, loamy soil rich in nutrients.
AI: P; ♃
     The scientific name of the genus (Greek *keras* = horn) is derived from the horny, curved fruit capsule which occurs in some species.

❼
5—25 cm
Sand Mouse-ear Chickweed *(Cerastium semidecandrum)*
Caryophyllaceae
See p. 44

❶

5—20 cm

Thyme-leaved Sandwort *(Arenaria serpyllifolia)*
Caryophyllaceae
IM: Petals entire, shorter than the calyx. 3 styles.
D: Flowers in the leaf axils, stalked. Stem branched, decumbent. Leaves opposite, very small, oval, sessile. Plants glabrous or markedly hairy.
H: Dry turf, wayside verges, crevices in walls, weedy places in cornfields. Likes dry, sandy or stony soil.
AI: P; ⊙
Plant contains saponin.

❷

10—50 cm

Corn Spurrey *(Spergula arvensis)*
Caryophyllaceae
IM: Short shoots grow out from the leaf axils. The leaves on these shoots apparently verticillate. Petals entire.
D: Terminal false umbels. Stem with swollen nodes. Leaves linear or awl-like, with a ventral, longitudinal furrow.
H: Weedy places in vegetable fields and cornfields, also on sandy paths. An indicator of acid soil.
AI: P; ⊙
Formerly was cultivated as a fodder plant for cattle.

❸

30—60 cm

Common Soapwort *(Saponaria officinalis)*
Caryophyllaceae
See p. 274

❹

20—100 cm

White Campion *(Silene alba; Melandrium album)*
Caryophyllaceae
IM: Petals deeply cleft into two. Calyx inflated, markedly hairy, with 10 ribs.
D: Sometimes there are 3 flowers in the leaf axils. Flowers unisexual, the females with 5 styles. Leaves opposite; upper leaves lanceolate-ovoid.
A similar species is the Night-flowering Campion *(Silene noctiflorum)*. Flowers of this latter species are, however, bisexual and have 3 styles. It grows in weedy places in cornfields and likes a loamy soil.
H: Weedy places in fields, on wasteland and verges. Likes warm habitats.
AI: P; ⊙; ♃
Both species are pronounced night-flowering plants. The flowers become fully open in the evening and begin to exhale their scent. Moths serve as pollinators.

❺

20—50 cm

Bladder Campion, White Bottle *(Silene vulgaris; S. cucubalus; S. inflata)*
Caryophyllaceae
See p. 46

❻

10—50 cm

Knotweed, Knotgrass *(Polygonum aviculare)*
Polygonaceae
IM: Flowers axillary. Stem prostrate.
D: Flowers green with a white or red border. Stem branched, with the branches bearing leaves up to the apex.
H: Weedy places in fields and on waste ground, roadside verges, field paths. Likes a nitrogenous soil.
AI: P; ⊙
Knotweed contains up to 1 % dry weight silicic acid. An old medicinal plant. Has also been used as a tea admixture.

1

2

3

4

5

6

❶

20—80 cm

Pale Polygonum, Pale Persicaria, Pale Knotgrass *(Polygonum lapathifolium)*
Polygonaceae
See p. 274

---

❷

15—50 cm

Corn Gromwell, Bastard Alkanet *(Lithospermum arvense)*
Boraginaceae
IM: Leaves with one vein, coarsely hairy.
D: Flowers small. Stem simple or branched. Leaves linear-lanceolate.
H: Weedy places, particularly in cornfields, more rarely in vegetable fields. Likes
      loamy soils.
AI: G; ⊙
      The root contains a red dye, which was formerly used as a rouge.

---

❸

5—15 cm

White Stonecrop *(Sedum album)*
Crassulaceae
See p. 86

---

❹

15—50 cm

Field Eryngo *(Eryngium campestre)*
Apiaceae (Umbelliferae)
IM: Flowers in almost spherical umbels. Leaves with strong spines.
D: Involucre of umbel spiny, often with a bluish tinge. Leaves alternate, lower
      ones divided, the upper ones amplexicaulate; young leaves undivided. Stem
      leaves pinnate with 3 pinnae.
H: Dry and semi-dry turf, also on wayside verges. Likes shallow, stony, calcareous
      soil in warm situations.
AI: P; ♃
      This plant is suited to dry situations since it has tough, leathery leaves and also
      a root system which goes down to a depth of 2 m. An old medicinal plant.
      Contains saponin.

---

❺

1—2 m

Hemlock, Mother Die *(Conium maculatum)*
Apiaceae (Umbelliferae)
IM: Flowers in umbels; umbels with 7—20 rays. Involucre of umbel with 4 leaves,
      but involucral leaves only occur on the outside of the umbels. Stem with
      a bluish bloom with red spots towards the base, glabrous. Leaves bi- to
      quadripinnate, glabrous. Plant smells of mice.
D: Compound umbels. Leaf tips serrate.
H: Weedy places on waste ground, along paths, in fields and gardens. Likes
      a moist, loamy soil and warm conditions. Nitrogen indicator.
AI: P; ⊙; †
      This plant contains the very poisonous alkaloid coniine in all its organs, but
      particularly in the seeds. In ancient times the Greeks prepared a poisonous
      drink from the unripe seeds which those who were sentenced to death by the
      State were compelled to drink. Socrates died from such a drink.

---

❻

30—170 cm

Rough Chervil *(Chaerophyllum temulum)*
Apiaceae (Umbelliferae)
See p. 76

❶

50—100 cm

Greater Burnet Saxifrage *(Pimpinella major; P. magna)*
Apiaceae (Umbelliferae)
IM: Flower head an umbel. Umbel of 9—15 slender branches which are quad-
   rangular before the flowers open. Involucre of bracts absent. Bracteoles absent,
   or of 1 or 2 segments. Stem sharply quadrangular, sulcate. Leaves simple
   pinnate.
D: Umbel compound. Stem glabrous. Leaves dark green, somewhat lustrous.
   Leaves give off an unpleasant smell on being rubbed.
H: Meadows, roadside verges, alpine meadows. Likes a rather moist, loamy and
   nitrogenous soil.
AI: P; ♃
   Old medicinal plant; contains ethereal oils, tannins and the substance pimpinellin, which has a burning taste.

❷

30—100 cm

Caraway *(Carum carvi)*
Apiaceae (Umbelliferae)
See p. 52

❸

10—100 cm

Fool's Parsley *(Aethusa cynapium)*
Apiaceae (Umbelliferae)
IM: Flower head an umbel. Umbel of 10—20 branches. Involucre of bracts absent.
   Only 3 bracteoles are present on the outside of the secondary umbels. Petals
   only 1—2 mm long.
D: Umbels compound. Leaves bi- or tripinnate. Resembles Parsley.
H: Weedy places on waste ground, along paths and in vegetable fields, more
   rarely in cornfields and gardens. Likes a porous, nitrogenous soil, often found
   in large stands.
AI: P; ⊙; †
   Fool's Parsley contains the very poisonous alkaloid coniine in small quantities.
   Eating the plant can lead to fatal poisoning. This plant differs from true Parsley
   in having much more shiny leaves and in its exudation of a garlic-like smell
   when its leaves are rubbed.

❹

30—60 cm

Wild Carrot *(Daucus carota)*
Apiaceae (Umbelliferae)
IM: Flower head an umbel; usually there is a blackish purple flower in the middle
   of the umbel.
D: Umbels compound; initially they resemble a bird's nest, later they become
   flat, and when in fruit they revert to the bird's nest shape. Stem hairy, sulcate,
   hollow. Leaves bi- or tripinnate.
H: Semi-dry verges, meadows, wayside verges, weedy places and waste ground.
   Likes a dry, sandy or stony soil where there is little other vegetation.
AI: P; ⊙
   Wild form of the cultivated Carrot; contains ethereal oils and, in the root,
   17 mg/100 g provitamin A (carotene), together with vitamins of the B group.

❺

50—200 cm

Wood Angelica *(Angelica sylvestris)*
Apiaceae (Umbelliferae)
See p. 76

❻

30—150 cm

Cow Parsnip, Hogweed, Keck *(Heracleum sphondylium)*
Apiaceae (Umbelliferae)
See p. 52

1

2

3

4

5

6

❶ **Goutweed, Ground Elder, Herb Gerard, Bishop's Weed**
(Aegopodium podagraria)
Apiaceae (Umbelliferae)
30—100 cm   IM: Flowers in flat, compound umbels. Umbel with 12—18 rays. Bracts and bracteoles absent. Leaves simple, or doubly tripartite.
D: Stem hollow, glabrous. Leaflets linear-ovoid, deeply serrate.
H: Lowland forest, canyon forest, moist deciduous or mixed woodland, thickets, parkland, weedy places, particularly in gardens. Likes soil which is moist with ground water, loamy and rich in nitrogen.
AI: P; ♃
The leaves have been used as a 'wild' vegetable. Plant was employed to soothe rheumatism and gout (Latin *podagra* = gout). It was crushed and placed on the affected part of the body. So far no active principle has been recovered, although the seeds contain an ethereal oil.

❷ **White Mullein** *(Verbascum lychnitis)*
Scrophulariaceae
50—130 cm   See p. 48

❸ **Thorn Apple** *(Datura stramonium)*
Solanaceae
30—100 cm   IM: Flowers 5—8 cm long, funnel-shaped, erect.
D: Flowers terminal or on a terminal fork. Stem erect, glabrous. Leaves petiolate, sinuously toothed, with an unpleasant smell.
H: Weedy places along roadsides, on the outskirts of villages, waste ground, on walls and embankments. Likes a porous soil, rich in nitrogen.
AI: G; ⊙; †
The name Thorn Apple is derived from the thorny capsule. The flowers open between 7 and 8 p.m. and in rainy weather remain shut. The plant is pollinated by moths. It contains a very poisonous alkaloid, used medicinally.

❹ **Black Nightshade** *(Solanum nigrum)*
Solanaceae
30—100 cm   IM: Flowers similar to those of the potato; stem glabrous or slightly hairy.
D: Racemes with few flowers. Stem branched. Leaves alternate, with long stalks, ovoid in shape and with a lobed margin.
H: Weedy places in vegetable fields; in gardens, on walls and waste ground. Likes a warm, nitrogen-rich, loamy soil.
AI: G; ⊙; †
Black Nightshade contains a poisonous alkaloid. It smells faintly repulsive.

❺ **Common Bryony, White** *or* **Red Bryony** *(Bryonia dioica)*
Cucurbitaceae
50—300 cm   See p. 72

❻ **Lesser** *or* **Field Bindweed** *(Convolvulus arvensis)*
Convolvulaceae
30—100 cm   See p. 218

❼ **White Convolvulus, Greater Bindweed** *(Calystegia sepium : Convolvulus sepium)*
Convolvulaceae
150—300 cm   See p. 74

36

❶

3—10 cm

Common Daisy *(Bellis perennis)*
Asteraceae (Compositae)
  See p. 54

❷

10—20 cm

Star of Bethlehem *(Ornithogalum umbellatum)*
Liliaceae
IM: Umbellate inflorescence. Peduncle up to 8 cm long.
D: Petals with a green stripe down the back. Leaves first appear in the autumn. They have a white stripe down the middle. Bulb without bulblets.
H: Weedy places in vegetable fields and particularly in vineyards, less frequently in thickets and copses. Likes a nitrogen-rich soil and prefers deep, porous and loamy soils to others.
AI: M; ♃

❸

15—30 cm

Wild Chamomile *(Matricaria chamomilla)*
Asteraceae (Compositae)
IM: Flowers in paniculate capitula; on the outside are the white ray florets, in the middle the yellow disc florets. Receptacle hollow, without paleae. Leaves slender, double pinnate. Plant has a strong aromatic smell.
D: Ray florets bent downwards in older flowers. Stem erect, branched, hollow.
H: Weedy places, particularly in cornfields and along verges. Likes a soil rich in nutrients, particularly nitrogenous material; somewhat calcifugous.
AI: G; ☉
Medicinal plant; flowers rich in ethereal oils.

❹

25—60 cm

False Chamomile, Scentless Mayweed *(Tripleurospermum inodorum;*
Matricaria maritima; M. inodora)
Asteraceae (Compositae)
IM: Flowers in paniculate capitula; on the outside are the white ray florets, in the middle the yellow disc florets. Receptacle medullate, without paleae. Leaves slender, double, tripinnate. Plant smells somewhat aromatic.
D: Stem erect, branched at the top.
H: Weedy places in fields, on waste ground, along paths and occasionally among road rubble. It is found on a variety of soils, even those poor in nitrogen.
AI: G; ☉; ♃
In contrast to the last species contains very few ethereal oils.

❺

20—50 cm

Corn Chamomile *(Anthemis arvensis)*
Asteraceae (Compositae)
IM: Flowers in capitula; on the outside are the white ray florets, on the inside the yellow disc florets. Receptacle with paleae. Leaves pinnate.
D: Leaflets linear-lanceolate, undivided or with 1—3 teeth, green, with soft hairs.
H: Weedy places in fields and by the wayside. Likes a nitrogenous, but acid soil.
AI: G; ☉
The Corn Chamomile contains ethereal oils.

❻

15—50 cm

Yarrow, Milfoil *(Achillea millefolium)*
Asteraceae (Compositae)
  See p. 238

❶

10—90 cm

Small-flowered Galinsoga *(Galinsoga parviflora)*
Asteraceae (Compositae)
IM: Flowers in capitula, which are collectively arranged in false umbels; on the outside of the capitula are the ray florets, on the inside the yellow disc florets. Leaves undivided, dentate, opposite.
D: A maximum of 5 ray florets. Stem branched.
H: Weedy places in vegetable fields, also on waste ground, or along wayside verges. Likes a porous, nitrogenous soil (e.g. sandy soil).
AI: G; ☉
The Small-flowered Galinsoga is a plant which originated from the Peruvian Andes.

❷

30—100 cm

Canadian Fleabane, Erigeron *(Conyza canadensis; Erigeron canadensis)*
Asteraceae (Compositae)
See p. 82

❸

30—60 cm

White Deadnettle *(Lamium album)*
Lamiaceae (Labiatae)
IM: Plant nettle-like, but without stinging hairs.
D: 5—8 flowers in axillary whorls. Stem square in section. Leaves opposite and decussate, stalked, crenate-serrate.
H: Weedy places on roadsides, on waste ground, walls and embankments, seldom in fields. Likes a nitrogenous soil.
AI: G; ♃
Flowers rich in nectar and visited particularly by long-tongued bumblebees. Old medicinal plant. It contains mucilage, tannins and ethereal oil.

❹

15—30 cm

Hollow Wort, Hollow Corydalis, Hollow Fumitory *(Corydalis cava)*
Papaveraceae
See p. 224

❺

10—30 cm

Common Eyebright *(Euphrasia stricta; E. officinalis)*
Scrophulariaceae
See p. 58

❻

30—130 cm

White Melilot *(Melilotus albus)*
Fabaceae (Leguminosae)
IM: Flowers in long, narrow, erect racemes. Leaves pinnate with 3 teeth.
D: Stem erect, branched. Leaflets invert-ovoid, dentate. Dry plant smells of Woodruff.
H: Weedy places on roadsides, among road rubble and on stony wasteland. Likes stony, but also loamy nitrogen-rich soils.
AI: P; ☉
The smell of Woodruff is due to the presence of coumarin which is chemically bound in the plant, but is released on drying. If White Melilot is present in moist hay, coumarin is released, and can prevent blood coagulation in animals which consume the hay.

❶ **Common Whitlow Grass** *(Erophila verna; Draba verna)*
Brassicaceae (Cruciferae)

5—10 cm See p. 22

---

❷ **Shepherd's Cress, Common Teesdalia** *(Teesdalia nudicaulis)*
Brassicaceae (Cruciferae)

8—20 cm
IM: Small terminal racemes. The two outer petals are almost twice as long as the inner ones. Stem mostly unbranched.
D: Leaves form a basal rosette. They are lyre-shaped and pinnatifid. The stem usually has one or two stem leaves.
H: Weedy places in cornfields, dry turf, verges, dunes; an indicator of sandy soils. Prefers poor soils, lacking plant nutrients; calcifugous.
AI: P; ☉

---

❸ **Cuckoo Flower, Lady's Smock, Milkmaids** *(Cardamine pratensis)*
Brassicaceae (Cruciferae)

30—60 cm
IM: Ovaries more than 3 times as long as broad. Leaves pinnate.
D: Racemes. Stem hollow, almost circular in section. Basal léaves form a rosette, unpaired pinnate. Leaflets round; terminal leaflet often larger than the others. Stem leaves pinnate with linear segments.
H: Damp meadows, moist places in deciduous, mixed and coniferous woodland, fen woodland and mountain pastures. Likes a loamy soil, saturated with ground water.
AI: P; ♃
This plant is often covered with 'cuckoo spit' or 'frog spit' which is produced by leaf-hopper larvae. These suck juice from the stem and this, when mixed with air, gives the familiar froth. See also Ragged Robin, p. 230. The plant is rich in mustard oil and vitamin C.

---

❹ **Perfoliate Penny Cress** *(Thlaspi perfoliatum)*
Brassicaceae (Cruciferae)

5—20 cm
IM: Petals 2—3 mm long. Ovary at the most 3 times as long as broad. Fruit 4—6 mm long, slightly winged; locules many-seeded. Stem round. Stem leaves blue-green, mainly with an entire margin and a heart-shaped base, sessile. Plant glabrous.
D: The flowers are arranged in a raceme. Plant without barren shoots.
H: Dry and semi-dry turf, roadside verges, weedy places in warm fields and vineyards. Likes a calcareous loess or loam soil. Abundant in those places where it occurs.
AI: P; ☉
Name: see Field Penny Cress, p. 22.

---

❺ **Hoary** *or* **Hairy Rockcress** *(Arabis hirsuta)*
Brassicaceae (Cruciferae)

15—60 cm See p. 24

---

❻ **Hedge Bedstraw** *(Galium mollugo)*
Rubiaceae

30—60 cm See p. 26

❶

15—40 cm

Marsh Bedstraw *(Galium palustre)*
Rubiaceae
IM: Leaves in whorls of 4. Each leaf has a single vein. Stem rough, with backward pointing prickles.
D: Diffuse panicles. Stem quadrangular, prostrate or decumbent. Leaves dark green, linear, rounded at the tip.
H: Margins of stagnant or slow-running water, reed beds, ditches, river banks, also in wet meadows and wet alpine mat. Likes a soil rich in humus and saturated with ground water. Prefers peaty or loamy soils.
AI: G; ♃

❷

5—60 cm

Ribwort, Narrow-leaved Plantain *(Plantago lanceolata)*
Plantaginaceae
See p. 26

❸

15—30 cm

Hoary Plantain *(Plantago media)*
Plantaginaceae
IM: Stem 2—5 times as long as the flower spike. Leaf blades at least 4 times as long as the petioles.
D: Short, thick spikes. Flowers inconspicuous. Anthers reddish violet, long. Leaves form a rosette; margins entire.
H: Semi-dry turf, meadows, pastures, paths, verges, sports fields. Likes a rather calcareous, loamy soil, rich in nutrients.
AI: G; ♃
Old medicinal plant containing mucilage.

❹

5—15 cm

Wild Strawberry *(Fragaria viridis)*
Rosaceae
IM: Flowering stem with 3—10 flowers, erect. Petals not crenate, touching each other. Upper side of leaves with silky hairs. Plant usually devoid of runners or with short runners.
D: Petals ivory. Plant similar to the Wood Strawberry but somewhat smaller.
H: Dry thickets, light woodland, semi-dry turf, verges. Likes a porous, calcareous soil.
AI: P; ♃
The berries of this Wild Strawberry taste rather insipid. Contrasts of temperature, particularly heat and even extreme dryness of the soil do not harm it in the least. Nevertheless, in places where it occurs it is often overgrown by other plants. It therefore prefers open areas which it can colonize.

❺

10—50 cm

Mouse-ear Chickweed *(Cerastium fontanum; C. caespitosum; C. vulgatum; C. holosteoides)*
Caryophyllaceae
See p. 28

❻

5—25 cm

Sand Mouse-ear Chickweed *(Cerastium semidecandrum)*
Caryophyllaceae
IM: Petals cleft about $\frac{1}{3}$ along their length. 4—5 styles. All shoots bear flowers.
D: Cymes. Stem erect or decumbent. Leaves opposite, lanceolate-ovoid.
H: Dry turf, verges. Likes warm, chalky loams and is an indicator of porous, sandy soils.
AI: P; ☉

❶ **Field Mouse-ear Chickweed** *(Cerastium arvense)*

10—30 cm
Caryophyllaceae
IM: Petals more than 8 mm long, i.e. twice as long as the sepals, grooved up to $\frac{1}{4}$ of their length. Plant covered with short hairs.
D: Cymes. Barren stems often form thick mats. Leaves opposite, linear-lanceolate.
H: Weedy places in fields, clefts in walls, on roadside verges and in semi-dry turf. Likes a porous, chalky soil.
AI: P; ⧾

❷ **Lesser Stitchwort** *(Stellaria graminea)*

15—30 cm
Caryophyllaceae
See p. 28

❸ **Bladder Campion, White Bottle** *(Silene vulgaris; S. cucubalus; S. inflata)*

20—50 cm
Caryophyllaceae
IM: Petals cleft about $\frac{1}{3}$ along their length. Calyx inflated, with a network of veins and 20 main veins.
D: Loose cymes. Stem erect or decumbent, not sticky. Leaves opposite, elliptical or lanceolate, pointed, glabrous.
H: Weedy places in fields, on verges, in semi-dry turf and open, dry places in woodland. Likes warm, nitrogenous, somewhat calcareous soils.
AI: P; ⧾
The Bladder Campion secretes abundant nectar in its flowers. It is pollinated by moths. The plant contains saponin.

❹ **Nottingham Catchfly** *(Silene nutans)*

30—60 cm
Caryophyllaceae
See p. 72

❺ **Meadow Saxifrage** *(Saxifraga granulata)*

15—40 cm
Saxifragaceae
IM: Bulbils present at the base of the stem. Petals without any coloured spots.
D: Cymes with relatively few flowers. Stem with few leaves, erect and covered with sticky hairs. Basal leaves with long petioles, reniform, lobate-crenate. Stem leaves cuneate, cleft into 2—5 segments.
H: Meadows, semi-dry turf, more rarely in light woodland. Prefers a loamy soil, somewhat calcifugous.
AI: P; ⧾
Name: see Mountain Saxifrage, p. 86.

❻ **Greater Wood Anemone** *(Anemone sylvestris)*

15—50 cm
Ranunculaceae
IM: Flowers single (rarely in pairs) growing out of a whorl of leaves. Diameter of flower up to 7 cm, petals up to 3 cm long, hairy on the outside. Style without tails. Basal leaves present (they first begin to unfold at the time of flowering).
D: Usually 2—6 basal leaves, palmate with 5 lobes, covered with white hairs.
H: Dry, open woodland, semi-dry turf. Likes a porous, chalky soil, rich in nutrients.
AI: P; ⧾; †
Contains protoanemonine and saponin. Poisonous.

❶ **Narcissus-flowered Anemone** *(Anemone narcissiflora)*
Ranunculaceae

30—60 cm
IM: Umbels of 3—8 flowers. Petals only 1—1.8 cm long; glabrous on the outside.
D: Inside of petals white, outside with a reddish blush. Many flowers have 6 petals instead of the usual 5. Leaf whorl sessile. Lower leaves divided into 3—5 segments.
H: Alpine tussocks and semi-dry turf.
AI: P; ♃; †

The plant contains the poisonous protoanemonine in all its parts.

❷ **White Dogbane** *(Cynanchum vincetoxicum; Vincetoxicum officinale)*
Asclepiadaceae

30—60 cm
See p. 72

❸ **White Mullein** *(Verbascum lychnitis)*
Scrophulariaceae

50—130 cm
IM: Stamens white and woolly. Stem sharply quadrangular at the top, powdery. Upper sides of leaves glabrous, lower sides powdery white.
D: Racemes. Lower leaves stalked, upper leaves ovate-lanceolate, sessile.
H: Dry turf, semi-dry turf, thickets, roadside verges, road rubble, clearings in woods, edges of woods. Likes a calcareous soil in warm situations.
AI: G; ⊙

❹ **Spiked Rampion** *(Phyteuma spicatum)*
Campanulaceae

30—100 cm
IM: Basal leaves about as long as wide, deeply heart-shaped.
D: Flowers in untidy heads, white or blue; curved upwards before they open.
H: Deciduous woodland, mixed woodland, more rarely in coniferous woodland, mountain pastures. Likes a porous, mull soil, rich in nutrients and rather moist.
AI: G; ♃

❺ **Pyrenean Bastard Toadflax** *(Thesium pyrenaicum; T. pratense)*
Santalaceae

15—30 cm
IM: Petals at the time of fruiting (observe the lowest flowers) rolled just at the tip. Upper leaves rough at the edge.
D: Double raceme. There are 3 tiny bracts under each flower. Flowers mainly with 5 lobes; the inner ones white, the outer green. Leaves alternate. There are many similar species, but all are rare and difficult to distinguish.
H: Semi-dry turf and sparse meadows. Somewhat calcifugous.
AI: P; ♃

❻ **Purging Flax, Cathartic Flax** *(Linum catharticum)*
Linaceae

8—30 cm
IM: Petals not crenate, 4—5 mm long, yellow at the base.
D: Loose panicles. Stem slender, with squarrose branching at the top. Lower leaves opposite, upper leaves often alternate; leaf margins entire.
H: Semi-dry turf, moist, unmanured meadows, reed beds, heath. Likes soils which are wet in winter and dry in summer.
AI: P; mostly ⊙; †

At one time this plant was used as a purgative in medicine, hence the name Purging Flax. The plant contains tannin and the poisonous alkaloid linin.

❶

5—20 cm

Thyme-leaved Sandwort *(Arenaria serpyllifolia)*
Caryophyllaceae
   See p. 30

❷

5—15 cm

White Stonecrop *(Sedum album)*
Crassulaceae
   See p. 86

❸

1—2 m

Meadowsweet *(Filipendula ulmaria)*
Rosaceae
IM: Leaves simple pinnate. Leaflets 3—5 cm long in 2—5 pairs.
D: Flowers in branched cymes, strongly scented, often with 6 petals. Stem leafy. Leaflets large, serrate, the terminal one cleft into 3—5 segments. Undersides of leaflets with white hairs.
H: Wet meadows, wet heath, moist mountain pastures, lowland woods. Likes sandy or loamy soils providing they are wet.
AI: P; ♃; (†)
   Contains a slightly poisonous glycoside.

❹

70—130 cm

Wild Chervil *(Anthriscus sylvestris)*
Apiaceae (Umbelliferae)
IM: Flowers in umbels. Umbel with 8—16 rays. Involucral bracts absent or confined to 1 or 2. Bracteoles ciliated. Petals round or only slightly crenate. Bottom of stem with coarse hairs, but usually no spots. Leaves 2—3 pinnate.
D: Umbels compound. Stem quadrangular.
H: Meadows, more rarely thickets, and the edges of woods. Likes a moist soil. Indicator of nitrogen. Often grows in masses where fields have been freshly manured, giving a very characteristic appearance to the meadows.
AI: P; ♃

❺

30—100 cm

Greater Astrantia *(Astrantia major)*
Apiaceae (Umbelliferae)
IM: Flowers in unusual umbels. Bracts as long as the umbel. Leaves palmately divided.
D: Umbel small and surrounded by conspicuous, whitish bracts. Stem only slightly branched. Leaflets serrate.
H: Deciduous woodland, mixed woodland, valley woodland and canyon forest, mountain woodland and pastures. Likes a calcareous, porous, loamy soil. An indicator of chalky and limestone soils.
AI: P; ♃

❻

15—50 cm

Burnet Saxifrage *(Pimpinella saxifraga)*
Apiaceae (Umbelliferae)
IM: Flowers in umbels. Umbel with 6—15 rays. No bracts. Bracteoles absent or only 1—2 present. Stem circular in section, finely furrowed. Leaves simple pinnate.
D: Umbels compound. Stem with few leaves at the top.
H: Dry and semi-dry turf, heaths. Likes a dry, rather shallow, porous, stony soil in warm situations.
AI: P; ♃
   An old medicinal plant, which contains ethereal oils, tannins and a sharp-tasting substance, pimpinellin, as well as other coumarinic compounds.

2

6

5

4

1

3

❶

30—100 cm

Caraway *(Carum carvi)*
Apiaceae (Umbelliferae)
IM: Flowers in umbels; umbels with 8—16 rays. Leaves bi- or tripinnate. Lowest pinnae of the upper stem leaves are situated at the base of the leaf sheaths.
D: Compound umbels. Leaves exude an aromatic smell when rubbed.
H: Meadows, particularly those of foothills and lower mountains, roadside verges. Likes a rather moist, porous soil, rich in nutrients, particularly nitrogen.
AI: P; ⊙
Root edible. Fruits used as a condiment (caraway seeds). They contain 3—7% ethereal oil, which gives them their typical taste. In small quantities the plant aids digestion.

❷

30—100 cm

Mountain Hog's Fennel, Mountain Celery *(Peucedanum oreoselinum)*
Apiaceae (Umbelliferae)
IM: Flowers in umbels; umbels with 15—25 rays. Bracts and bracteoles numerous. Stem round, finely furrowed. Leaves tripinnate, the lowest ones being 30—40 cm long. Pinnae at right angles or an obtuse angle to the rachis.
D: Compound umbels. Leaves have a strongly aromatic smell.
H: Dry woods and copses, also on semi-dry turf. Likes a shallow, sandy or stony soil in a warm situation.
AI: P; ♃
Old medicinal plant which contains ethereal oil (smell) and coumarinic compounds. The juice of the plant can sometimes cause inflammation of the skin, if the parts of the body wetted by the sap are exposed to the light.

❸

30—150 cm

Cow Parsnip, Hogweed, Keck *(Heracleum sphondylium)*
Apiaceae (Umbelliferae)
IM: Flowers in umbels. Umbels with 15—30 rays. Involucre of bracts absent or reduced to less than 6. Bracteoles numerous. Marginal flowers enlarged. Stem grooved, with stiff hairs. Leaves tri- or quadripinnate; lower leaves up to 50 cm long. Plant has an unpleasant smell.
D: Umbels compound. Flowers often with pale greenish or pinkish tinge.
H: Light, damp, mixed or deciduous forest, valley woodland, thickets, meadows and weedy places generally. Likes a damp, porous, nitrogenous soil.
AI: P; ♃
This plant is highly variable and has been split up into several subspecies which are difficult to distinguish. Good rabbit fodder. Contains ethereal oil and furocoumarin, which can cause inflammation of the skin if areas which have come into contact with the juice are exposed to sunlight. Old medicinal plant.

❹

30—60 cm

Wild Carrot *(Daucus carota)*
Apiaceae (Umbelliferae)
See p. 34

❺

15—50 cm

Field Eryngo *(Eryngium campestre)*
Apiaceae (Umbelliferae)
See p. 32

❻

50—100 cm

Greater Burnet Saxifrage *(Pimpinella major; P. magna)*
Apiaceae (Umbelliferae)
See p. 34

❶ **Spring Snowflake** *(Leucojum vernum)*

10—30 cm

Amaryllidaceae

IM: All 6 petals alike.

D: Stem with 1 or 2 flowers, which are scented. Petals with green splashes at the tips. Leaves narrow, somewhat fleshy, not hoary.

H: Damp meadows, thickets, woodland. Likes a loamy soil. Very rare but numerous where it occurs.

AI: M; ♃; †

The stamens drop the pollen at the slightest impact. The plant contains a poisonous alkaloid.

❷ **White Crocus, Spring Crocus** *(Crocus albiflorus)*

8—15 cm

Iridaceae

See p. 332

❸ **Unbranched Lily Spiderwort** *(Anthericum liliago)*

30—70 cm

Liliaceae

See p. 80

❹ **Branched Lily Spiderwort** *(Anthericum ramosum)*

30—100 cm

Liliaceae

See p. 80

❺ **White False Hellebore** *(Veratrum album)*

50—150 cm

Liliaceae

IM: Very difficult to distinguish from the Yellow Gentian before the flowers open, because of the shape of the leaves and the form of growth. Leaves opposite and possessing a strong smell. Rootstock tuberous.

D: Flowers in a terminal panicle; white on the inside, green on the outside.

H: Alpine pasture (common), manured moorland and valley woodland (rare). Likes a soil ·vhich is calcareous and nitrogenous.

AI: M; ♃; †

This plant does not flower until after several years' vegetative growth. It contains two poisonous substances, protoveratrine and veratrine, which act as irritants to the nerve endings in the skin. The veratrum alkaloids are, therefore, nerve poisons. In the old days the plant was used in the preparation of poison for arrows. It is also poisonous to insects and was at one time employed in preparations against lice.

❻ **Common Daisy** *(Bellis perennis)*

3—10 cm

Asteraceae (Compositae)

IM: No possibility of confusion with other species.

D: Flowers in capitula, which occur singly on a leafless stalk. On the outside are white, or white flushed with pink, ray florets, on the inside yellow disc florets. Leaves form rosettes, invert-ovoid to spatulate, crenate.

H: Meadows, pastures, verges, fieldpaths. Very common.

AI: G; ♃

The flowers of the Common Daisy can survive in dry air at temperatures as low as −15°C without suffering damage. The inflorescence behaves like a single flower and closes up at night and in wet weather. In addition it turns towards the sun. An old medicinal plant; the flowers contain saponin, ethereal oil, tannins, mucilage and alkaloids.

❶

30—60 cm

Marguerite, Moon Daisy, Ox-eye Daisy *(Leucanthemum vulgare;*
Chrysanthemum leucanthemum)
Asteraceae (Compositae)
IM: No possibility of confusion with other species.
D: Flowers in solitary, terminal capitula, the outside ray florets white, the inside disc florets yellow. Stem erect. Lower leaves with long petioles, invert-ovoid to spatulate, crenate; upper leaves sessile, serrate.
H: Semi-dry turf, meadows, dry thickets and light, dry woodland. Grows on a variety of soils.
AI: G; ♃

❷

15—50 cm

Yarrow, Milfoil *(Achillea millefolium)*
Asteraceae (Compositae)
See p. 238

❸

30—70 cm

Sneezewort *(Achillea ptarmica)*
Asteraceae (Compositae)
IM: Flowers arranged in cymose capitula. The outside of the flower consists of 8—13 ray florets, which surround the disc florets. Leaves undivided, linear-lanceolate, serrate.
D: Capitula about 1.5 cm in diameter. Flowers ivory-coloured. Stem with many leaves.
H: Wet meadows, hollows, banks of rivers. Likes loamy soils saturated with ground water. An indicator of wet ground.
AI: G; ♃
    An old medicinal plant. The root contains a substance with a sharp taste, the identity of which is not yet known.

❹

8—25 cm

Mountain Everlasting, Mountain Cat's-ear *(Antennaria dioica;*
Gnaphalium dioicum)
Asteraceae (Compositae)
See p. 258

❺

20—40 cm

Wood Cudweed *(Gnaphalium sylvaticum)*
Asteraceae (Compositae)
See p. 82

❻

30—40 cm

Stemless Carline Thistle *(Carlina acaulis)*
Asteraceae (Compositae)
IM: No possibility of confusion with other species.
D: Capitula 5—10 cm in diameter. Only the inner brownish-white disc florets are present. The inner bracts are long and white and simulate ray florets. Stem prostrate or decumbent. Leaves mostly rosette-like, more rarely on the stem, deeply pinnatifid, with prickly tips and undersides covered in a cobweb-like mass of hairs.
H: Semi-dry turf, heaths, meadows. Likes a dry, stony soil in warm situations.
AI: G; ♃
    The white bracts are hygroscopic (water attracting) and move inwards towards moist air, so keeping out dry air from the centre of the flower.

❼

30—80 cm

Dropwort *(Filipendula vulgaris; F. hexapetala)*
Rosaceae
See p. 82

❶
20—40 cm

Lesser Butterfly Orchid *(Platanthera bifolia)*
Orchidaceae
    See p. 84

❷
15—60 cm

Mountain Clover *(Trifolium montanum)*
Fabaceae (Leguminosae)
    See p. 84

❸
20—50 cm

White Clover, Dutch Clover *(Trifolium repens)*
Fabaceae (Leguminosae)
IM: Flowers clearly stalked, pure white in colour. Calyx with 10 veins. Stem prostrate, creeping and rooted in places. Leaflets glabrous on the undersides.
D: Flowers in ovoid heads, fragrant. Leaflets cuneate or invert-ovoid, with heart-shaped points.
H: Meadows, pastures, garden lawns, lawns in parks and sports fields. Likes a nitrogenous soil and resists trampling.
AI: P; ♃

❹
8—30 cm

Hare's-foot, Field Clover *(Trifolium arvense)*
Fabaceae (Leguminosae)
IM: Inflorescence cylindrical. Flowers white at first, then developing a pinkish tinge. Calyx stout and with long hairs. Sepals longer than petals.
D: Stem decumbent or erect. Leaflets linear-lanceolate.
H: Dry turf, on porous, sandy soils; calcifugous; likes a warm situation.
AI: P; ⊙
An old folk-herb. As a fodder plant Hare's-foot is worthless; it tastes bitter and is tough.

❺
20—60 cm

Mountain Woundwort *(Stachys recta)*
Lamiaceae (Labiatae)
    See p. 84

❻
10—30 cm

Common Eyebright *(Euphrasia stricta; E. officinalis)*
Scrophulariaceae
IM: Flowers 0.7—1 cm long. Calyx and adjacent leaves without glandular hairs, but with awns.
D: Spikes. Flowers white or whitish violet, with a yellow fleck on the lower lip. Stem erect. Leaves opposite, ovoid, crenate-serrate.
H: Semi-dry turf, meadows, verges. Likes a sandy soil.
AI: G; ⊙; (†)
Hemiparasite. For name and poisonous nature see Meadow Eyebright below.

❼
5—25 cm

Meadow Eyebright *(Euphrasia rostkoviana)*
Scrophulariaceae
IM: Calyx and adjacent leaves with glandular hairs.
D: Spikes. Lower lip bilobed, with violet stripes and a yellow fleck. Stem decumbent, usually branched. Leaves opposite, ovoid, crenate-serrate.
H: Meadows, semi-dry turf. Somewhat calcifugous.
AI: G; ⊙; (†)
Hemiparasite. Contains aucubin (cf. Red Rattle, p. 278), tannins and ethereal oil. An old medicinal plant. Previously, and probably occasionally even today, this plant was used for the treatment of eye complaints (hence the name).

❶   **Lords-and-Ladies, Wild Arum, Cuckoo-pint, Wake Robin, Jack-in-the-Pulpit** *(Arum maculatum)*
Araceae
15—50 cm   See p. 362

❷   **May Lily** *(Maianthemum bifolium)*
Liliaceae
5—15 cm
- IM: No possibility of confusion with other species.
- D: Flowers in paniculate racemes, with 4 petals. There are 2, more rarely 3, heart-shaped, petiolate leaves on the stem. Leaves opposite.
- H: Deciduous woodland, mixed woodland and coniferous woodland. Likes a loamy soil and is an indicator of light and often only surface acidity.
- AI: M; ♃; †
  The May Lily contains the same toxic substance as Lily-of-the-Valley (a digitalis glycoside).

❸   **Cuckoo Flower, Lady's Smock, Milkmaids** *(Cardamine pratensis)*
Brassicaceae (Cruciferae)
30—60 cm   See p. 42

❹   **Large Bittercress** *(Cardamine amara)*
Brassicaceae (Cruciferae)
5—30 cm
- IM: Anthers purple violet. Ovary and fruit more than 3 times as long as wide, flattened. Stem medullated.
- D: Racemes. Leaves frequently tinged with violet or pink. Stem pentagonal in section. Basal leaves do not form a rosette; they are unpaired pinnate. Leaflets ovoid or round to linear. Stem leaves vary from simple to double pinnate.
- H: Grows around springs and near streams, in hollows, where there is a seepage on stony mountain sides and in valley woodland. Likes a wet soil rich in nutrients; somewhat calcifugous.
- AI: P; ♃
  Contains oil of mustard, a bitter substance (hence its name) and considerable amounts of vitamin C. An old medicinal plant. May be gathered together with other cresses to form a 'wild' salad. Tastes less sharp, but more bitter than Watercress.

❺   **Garlic Mustard, Jack-by-the-Hedge** *(Alliaria petiolata; A. officinalis)*
Brassicaceae (Cruciferae)
20—100 cm   See p. 24

❻   **Glabrous Rockcress, Tower Mustard** *(Arabis glabra; Turritis glabra)*
Brassicaceae (Cruciferae)
50—150 cm
- IM: Ovary more than 3 times as long as broad. Leaves with entire margins and bluish bloom; all, except perhaps the basal leaves, glabrous.
- D: Racemes. Stem erect, unbranched. Basal leaves often quite stunted at flowering time. Stem leaves sagittate, with a base which clasps the stem.
- H: Dry thickets, edges of woodland, clearings in woods, light, dry woodland. Likes a stony, calcareous soil in a warm situation.
- AI: P; ⊙
  Tower Mustard, and the scientific name, *Turritis,* refer to the tower-like, stiff, erect, growth of the plant. Formerly this species was used as a medicinal plant, although what the active principles it contains are — other than a small amount of vitamin C — is not yet known.

❶ **Baneberry, Herb Christopher** *(Actaea spicata)*
Ranunculaceae
30—60 cm
IM: Flowers in single ovoid racemes. Leaves with 3 leaflets — double pinnate; when rubbed they give off a sharp and unpleasant smell.
D: Terminal and lateral racemes. Flowers small, with 4 sepals and 4 petals. Petals double-ternate. Leaflets ovoid-lanceolate.
H: Mountain forest, canyon forest, mixed woodland, deciduous woodland. Likes porous, stony, well-drained soils.
AI: P; ♃; †
Flowers form abundant pollen and are visited by beetles and Orthoptera. Old medicinal plant. Seeds and berries contain unknown poisonous substance. The Latin generic name refers to the Greek legend of Actaeon surprising Artemis whilst she was bathing. She changed him into a stag as punishment and Actaeon's own deerhounds tore him to pieces, as they had eaten the berries of baneberry and become mad. Formerly the plant was used against bubonic plague.

❷ **Gypsy Wort** *(Lycopus europaeus)*
Lamiaceae (Labiatae)
20—100 cm
See p. 90

❸ **Woodruff** *(Galium odoratum; Asperula odorata)*
Rubiaceae
10—30 cm
IM: Stem quadrangular. Leaves in whorls of 6—8, dark green.
D: Cymes on long stalks. Flowers funnel-shaped. Stem usually erect. Leaves lanceolate, rough at the edge and on the midrib. The plant has a strong and characteristic smell.
H: Deciduous and mixed woodland, less common in coniferous forest. Likes a porous, loamy soil, rich in plant nutrients.
AI: G; ♃
The plant contains coumarinic compounds, which release coumarin as the plant dies down, thus giving the characteristic smell of Woodruff. An old medicinal plant. The flowers were also used in posies, but if too much Woodruff were present the coumarin could cause headaches.

❹ **Wood Bedstraw** *(Galium silvaticum)*
Rubiaceae
30—130 cm
IM: Peduncles bend over before the flowers open. Stem round, with 4 fine ribs. often with a pinkish tinge (cf. Woodruff above). Leaves, at least on the undersides, bluish green.
D: Loose panicles. Stem erect. Leaves linear-lanceolate, with white terminal prickles, rough at the edges, in whorls of 6 to 8.
H: Deciduous and mixed woodland, mountain forest. Likes a rather moist, loamy, calcareous soil.
AI: G; ♃

❺ **Cleavers, Goosegrass, Sticky Willie** *(Galium aparine)*
Rubiaceae
30—130 cm
See p. 26

❻ **Alpine Enchanter's Nightshade** *(Circaea alpina)*
Onagraceae (Oenotheraceae)
5—15 cm
See p. 250

---

❶

20—50 cm

Common Enchanter's Nightshade *(Circaea lutetiana)*
Onagraceae (Oenotheraceae)
See p. 250

---

❷

15—30 cm

Christmas Rose *(Helleborus niger)*
Ranunculaceae

IM: Flowers single, separate. Stem with 1—3 leaves at the top. Basal leaves evergreen.
D: Flowers often with a pink tinge, and by the end of the flowering period they turn greenish. Basal leaves palmate (with 4—9 segments), leathery, serrate.
H: Mountain forests. Likes a calcareous, stony soil, rich in humus.
AI: P; ♃; †
Poisonous, as a result of containing a digitalis glycoside and saponin. The powdered dry rootstock irritates the mucous membranes and is a constituent of many sneezing powders.

---

❸

8—15 cm

Wood Sorrel *(Oxalis acetosella)*
Oxalidaceae

IM: Flowers with long peduncles; leaves Clover-like.
D: Petals white with violet veins and with a yellow fleck at the base.
H: Deciduous woodland, mixed woodland, coniferous forest. Likes a rather acid soil, rich in humus. Shade-loving.
AI: P; ♃;(†)
Wood Sorrel contains oxalic acid and oxalate in its leaves (cf. scientific name of genus) and attains its full assimilation rate at $\frac{1}{10}$ the intensity of normal daylight. The leaflets drop in strong sunlight and after repeated touching.

---

❹

15—50 cm

Greater Wood Anemone *(Anemone sylvestris)*
Ranunculaceae
See p. 46

---

❺

5—25 cm

White Tormentil *(Potentilla alba)*
Rosaceae

IM: Flowers 2—2.5 cm in diameter. Basal leaves mostly digitate with 5 leaflets; undersides of leaves with a white sheen.
D: Usually 3 flowers to each flower stem. Peduncles long. Stem decumbent to erect. Distal part of leaflets with 1—5 teeth.
H: Dry thickets, hedgerows and open, dry woodland. Calcifugous.
AI: P; ♃

---

❻

5—10 cm

Strawberry-leaved Potentilla *(Potentilla sterilis; P. fragariastrum)*
Rosaceae

IM: One or two flowers to the peduncle, which is flaccid. Petals crenate, not touching each other (in contrast to Wood Strawberry, p. 66).
D: Petals 4—7 mm long, broadly invert-ovoid. Sepals somewhat shorter than petals. Stem erect, hairy. Leaves like those of the Strawberry, often bluish green, hairy.
H: Deciduous and mixed woodland, coniferous forest. Likes a soil rich in humus and nutrients. Calcifugous and an indicator of acid soil.
AI: P; ♃

1　　2

3

4

5　　6

①

8 — 15 cm

Wood Strawberry *(Fragaria vesca)*
Rosaceae
IM: 3 – 10 flowers to the peduncle, erect. Petals not crenate, touching each other. Hairs on peduncle erect. Upper sides of leaves without silky hairs. Plants usually with runners.
D: Lateral leaflets sessile, the middle one with a short stalk.
H: Deciduous and mixed woodland, open coniferous forest, clearings, woodland paths. Likes a rather moist soil.
AI: P; ♃
Berries edible and with pleasant taste, rich in sugar (about 8% of the fresh weight). The Wood Strawberry in the Middle Ages served as a symbol of temptation. Hieronymus Bosch treated it as such in his paintings. People who languished after the fruit changed into monsters, symbolizing those lacking in virtue. The leaves contain tannins and can be used as a substitute for China tea.

②

5 — 15 cm

Wild Strawberry *(Fragaria viridis)*
Rosaceae
See p. 44

③

10 — 30 cm

Musk Strawberry *(Fragaria moschata)*
Rosaceae
IM: 3 — 10 flowers to the peduncle, erect. Petals not crenate, touching each other. Hairs on peduncle horizontal.
D: Petals 5 — 10 mm long, pure white. Flower like that of the Wood Strawberry (see above), although somewhat bigger.
H: Edges of woods, moist thickets. Likes a soil rich in nutrients.
AI: P; ♃
The berries of the Musk Strawberry taste very aromatic. Formerly the plant was commonly cultivated in gardens, but with the availability in the last few decades of the large cultivated varieties of strawberry, the practice has decreased. Of the wild strawberries this species is the one most affected by climate. It will not withstand marked changes of temperature, particularly night frost in late spring.

④

10 — 25 cm

Stone Bramble, Stone Blackberry *(Rubus saxatilis)*
Rosaceae
IM: Inflorescence an erect, cymose raceme. Leaves ternate.
D: Compound fruit made up of loosely aggregated, red drupelets. Vegetative reproduction by runner-like stolons. Leaflets invert-ovoid, serrate.
H: Deciduous and mixed woodland, coniferous forest. Likes a porous, calcareous soil, rich in humus. Quite abundant in those localities where it occurs.
AI: P; ♃

⑤

15 — 40 cm

Meadow Saxifrage *(Saxifraga granulata)*
Saxifragaceae
IM: Bulbils at the base of the stem. Petals without coloured spots.
D: False umbels with few flowers. Stem with few leaves, erect and covered with sticky hairs. Basal leaves with long stalks, kidney-shaped, crenate with lobes. Stem leaves cuneate, with 3 — 5 lobes.
H: Meadows, semi-dry turf, rarely in light woodland. Somewhat calcifugous. Prefers a loamy soil.
AI: P; ♃

❶

4 — 10 cm

One-flowered Wintergreen *(Moneses uniflora ; Pyrola uniflora ; Pirola uniflora)*
Pyrolaceae
IM: Flowers solitary, somewhat diffuse, 1.5 — 2.5 cm in diameter.
D: Solitary flowers on leafless stems; flower drooping with strong scent. Leaves form a basal rosette, evergreen, leathery, rounded-spatulate.
H: Mixed and coniferous woodland. Likes a porous, dry, loamy and somewhat acid soil.
AI: G; ♃
The scientific name of the genus *Pyrola* refers to the similarity between the leaves of this plant and those of the pear *(pyrus)*.
An old medicinal plant, containing aucubin in the leaves.

❷

15 — 20 cm

Serrated Wintergreen *(Orthilia secunda ; Pyrola secunda ; Pirola secunda ; Ramischia secunda)*
Pyrolaceae
IM: Unilateral racemes. Stem leaves longer than the campanulate flowers.
D: Flowers drooping. Stem erect. Leaves evergreen, leathery, ovoid, weakly crenate.
H: Mixed and coniferous woodland. Likes a porous, dry, loamy and slightly acid soil. Quite abundant in those localities where it does occur.
AI: G; ♃
Name: see One-flowered Wintergreen, above.

❸

10 — 30 cm

Intermediate Wintergreen *(Pyrola media ; Pirola media)*
Pyrolaceae
IM: 3 — 15 flowers in a multilateral raceme. Style projects beyond the rim of the campanulate flower.
D: Petals 6 — 8 mm long, strongly curved, and inclined towards each other. Stem erect. Leaves evergreen, round to ovoid, slightly crenate, leathery.
H: Deciduous and mixed woodland, coniferous forest. Likes a dry, slightly acid, porous, stony and loamy soil.
AI: G; ♃
Name: see One-flowered Wintergreen, above.
Although the flowers of this species are fragrantly scented, they attract few insects. Seed production is usually dependent on self-pollination.

❹

15 — 30 cm

Greater Wintergreen *(Pyrola rotundifolia ; Pirola rotundifolia)*
Pyrolaceae
See p. 256

❺

10 — 20 cm

Common Wintergreen, Lesser Wintergreen *(Pyrola minor ; Pirola minor)*
Pyrolaceae
IM: 4 — 16 flowers in a multilateral raceme. Style does not project beyond the rim of the campanulate flower.
D: Flowers drooping. Style straight. Stem usually decumbent. Leaves form basal rosette; they are ovoid, evergreen, leathery and crenate.
H: Deciduous and mixed woodland, coniferous forest. Likes a dry, slightly acid, porous, loamy soil.
AI: G; ♃
Name: see One-flowered Wintergreen, above.
Seed production sparse. Flowers are mostly self-pollinated or pollinated by flies and beetles.

❶ **Wood Goatsbeard** *(Aruncus vulgaris; A. dioicus; A. silvester)*
Rosaceae

90—200 cm   IM: Plants mostly dioecious. Inflorescence many-flowered panicle. Individual flowers small. Leaves bi- or tripinnate, up to 1 m long.

        D: Male inflorescence ivory coloured; female inflorescence pure white. Stem erect, simple, glabrous. Leaflets ovoid, pointed at the tip, double serrate.

        H: Canyon and mountain forest. Likes a dry, somewhat stony soil, rich in humus and moist through seepage.

       AI: P; ♃

          This species has such light seeds that they are not only carried by the wind but on convection currents set up by sunlight heating the soil surface. One seed weighs only 0.00008 g. Old medicinal plant. The seeds contain saponin, the leaves an organic cyanide compound in small amounts.

❷ **Meadowsweet** *(Filipendula ulmaria)*
Rosaceae

1—2 m   See p. 50

❸ **Greater Stitchwort** *(Stellaria holostea)*
Caryophyllaceae

15—30 cm   IM: Petals only cleft as far as the middle, 10—15 mm long, which is twice as long as the sepals. 3 styles. Upper leaves slender.

        D: Forked cymes. Stem quadrangular at the base. Leaves opposite, sessile, linear or linear-lanceolate, pointed at the tip.

        H: Deciduous and mixed woodland, more rarely coniferous forest and thickets. Found particularly on loamy, rather sandy soils.

       AI: P; ♃

❹ **Water Stitchwort, Water Chickweed** *(Myosoton aquaticum; Malachium aquaticum; Stellaria aquatica)*
Caryophyllaceae

20—100 cm   See p. 94

❺ **Wood Stitchwort** *(Stellaria nemorum)*
Caryophyllaceae

15—30 cm   IM: Petals deeply cleft into two, twice as long as the sepals. 3 styles.

        D: Stem with runners, flaccid, hairy towards the top. Lower and middle leaves petiolate, heart-shaped, pointed at the tip. Plant appears somewhat hyaline.

        H: Valley woods, mixed and deciduous woodland, coniferous forest. Likes porous, loamy, moist soil. Calcifugous.

       AI: P; ♃

❻ **Trinervate Sandwort** *(Moehringia trinervia)*
Caryophyllaceae

15—30 cm   IM: 5 (or 4) petals. Leaves with only 3 veins, rarely 4 or 5.

        D: Flowers emerge from the leaf axils, petiolate. Petals shorter than the sepals. Stem prostrate, decumbent or erect. Leaves ovoid, pointed; the lower leaves petiolate, the upper ones sessile.

        H: Deciduous and mixed woodland, coniferous forest. Likes a rather moist, loamy soil, rich in nutrients. Indicates surface acidity. Abundant where it occurs.

       AI: P; ♃

          The scientific name of the genus is in honour of Dr P. H. Moehring (1720—92), a physician and botanist from Gdansk.

❶

20—50 cm

Bladder Campion, White Bottle *(Silene vulgaris; S. cucubalus; S. inflata)*
Caryophyllaceae
    See p. 46

❷

30—60 cm

Nottingham Catchfly *(Silene nutans)*
Caryophyllaceae
IM: Petals deeply cleft. Calyx with 10 veins. Flowers drooping.
D: Umbellate panicles. Stem with soft hairs towards the base and sticky, glandular hairs (hence name) at the top. Lower leaves spatulate and petiolate; upper leaves opposite, lanceolate, sessile or almost sessile.
H: Semi-dry turf, heaths, dry woodland and thickets, rocky debris. Likes a warm, porous soil and is indifferent to plant nutrients.
AI: P; ♃
Night flowering. The flowers begin to exhale their scent at dusk and are pollinated by moths.

❸

50—130 cm

White Mullein *(Verbascum lychnitis)*
Scrophulariaceae
    See p. 48

❹

30—100 cm

Spiked Rampion *(Phyteuma spicatum)*
Campanulaceae
    See p. 48

❺

30—60 cm

White Dogbane *(Cynanchum vincetoxicum; Vincetoxicum officinale)*
Asclepiadaceae
IM: No possibility of confusion with other species.
D: Flowers in axillary cymes, 5—15 mm in diameter. Stem erect, occasionally spiralling at the top. Leaves opposite, with short petioles, heart-shaped to elongate.
H: Dry woods and thickets, stony landslips, rocky places, more rarely in semi-dry turf. Likes a shallow, stony soil, rich in plant nutrients and calcareous.
AI: G; ♃; †
The flowers possess a special pollination mechanism. The nectar-seeking insect thrusts its proboscis into the narrow throat of the flower, from which it can only disengage itself by withdrawing the pollinia on its proboscis. Many insects thrust their proboscis so firmly into the throat of the flower that they die in their attempts to withdraw. The fruiting plants bear seeds with hairy heads. Dogbane contains the poisonous vincetoxin in all its parts.

❻

50—300 cm

Common Bryony, White *or* **Red Bryony** *(Bryonia dioica)*
Cucurbitaceae
IM: Flowers dioecious. Stem climbing.
D: Cymous inflorescences in the leaf axils. Male flowers with long peduncles, female flowers with short peduncles. Leaves 5-lobed, rough.
H: Weedy places on wasteland, along paths, in hedgerows and on walls, but also in thickets, clearings and near the edge of woodland. Likes a porous, chalky and loamy soil. Calcicolous.
AI: G; ♃; †
A medicinal plant which contains glycosides, tannins and alkaloids.

❶

150—300 cm

White Convolvulus, Greater Bindweed *(Calystegia sepium; Convolvulus sepium)*
Convolvulaceae
IM: Flowers 3.5—6 cm long, growing out of the leaf axils, and without any pink stripes. Flowers scentless.
D: Stem coiling. Leaves alternate, petiolate, sagittate at the base.
H: Valley woodland, moist thickets, edges of woodland, by ponds and streams, also in hedgerows and along paths. Likes a wet, loamy soil, rich in nutrients and nitrogen.
AI: G; ♃
    The flowers of the White Convolvulus close in cloudy weather and during rain, but otherwise can be open both by day and night. The twisting of the stem takes 1¾ hours to complete a rotation. The leaves of the plant contain a cardiac glycoside and tannins. A medicinal plant.

❷

70—130 cm

Wild Chervil *(Anthriscus sylvestris)*
Apiaceae (Umbelliferae)
    See p. 50

❸

5—50 cm

Wood Sanicle *(Sanicula europaea)*
Apiaceae (Umbelliferae)
IM: Flowers in capitulate umbels. Involucral bracts very small. Leaves compound palmate.
D: Umbels compound. Stem leafless or with 1 or 2 small leaves. Leaves serrate.
H: Deciduous, mixed or coniferous woodland. Likes a moist, loamy soil.
AI: P; ♃
    The scientific and common names are derived from the Latin word *sanare* (to cure). In the Middle Ages (it was known in the 12th century) Sanicle was used as the preferred medicament for treating wounds. The plant contains saponins, tannins and an alkaloid. Today it is no longer used as a medicinal plant.

❹

30—100 cm

Greater Astrantia *(Astrantia major)*
Apiaceae (Umbelliferae)
    See p. 50

❺

1—1.8 m

Bulbous Chervil, Tuberous Cow Parsley *(Chaerophyllum bulbosum)*
Apiaceae (Umbelliferae)
IM: Flowers in umbels with 15—20 glabrous rays. No involucral bracts. Bracteoles 4—6, with non-ciliate edges. Petals cleft almost into halves. Only the basal part of the stem flecked with red and bearing stiff hairs. Stem round, with bluish bloom. Leaves tri- or quadripinnate.
D: Umbels compound. Leaflets of the upper leaves narrowly linear. Root with a bulbous swelling.
H: Valley woodland, weedy places on the banks of rivers and in water meadows. Likes a porous, calcareous soil, saturated with ground water.
AI: P; ⊙; (†)
    The plant contains the poison chaerophyllin in its leaves but not in the rootstock, which is very rich in starch. In the Middle Ages this plant was cultivated for its tuberous roots which were used as we now use potatoes. Their flavour is like that of sweet chestnuts. Those who might be inclined to eat this plant are advised that it closely resembles the very poisonous umbelliferous plants such as Hemlock and is therefore best avoided.

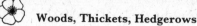

❶ **Rough Chervil** (*Chaerophyllum temulum*)
30—170 cm   Apiaceae (Umbelliferae)
IM: Flowers in umbels. Umbels with 6—12 rays, covered with rough hairs. Involucral bracts absent or reduced to 1—2. Bracteoles ciliated at the border. Petals cleft almost in halves. Stem with red flecks and stiff hairs, angular. Leaves double pinnate.
D: Umbels compound. Stem thickened below the nodes. Leaves pale green. Leaflets lobed.
H: Valley woodland; light, rather damp, deciduous and mixed forest, thickets, clearings. Likes a porous soil. Indicator of nitrogen.
AI: P; ⊙; ⊖; †
This plant contains the poisonous substance chaerophyllin. Animals which have eaten it tend to stagger about.

❷ **Goutweed, Ground Elder, Herb Gerard, Bishop's Weed**
(*Aegopodium podagraria*)
30—100 cm   Apiaceae (Umbelliferae)
See p. 36

❸ **Cow Parsnip, Hogweed, Keck** (*Heracleum sphondylium*)
30—150 cm   Apiaceae (Umbelliferae)
See p. 52

❹ **Mountain Hog's Fennel, Mountain Celery** (*Peucedanum oreoselinum*)
30—100 cm   Apiaceae (Umbelliferae)
See p. 52

❺ **Hog's Fennel, Milk Parsley** (*Peucedanum palustre*)
50—150 cm   Apiaceae (Umbelliferae)
IM: Flowers in umbels. Umbels with 20—30 rays. Bracts and bracteoles numerous. Stem grooved. Leaves bi- to quadripinnate. Leaf lobe linear.
D: Umbels compound. Stem hollow, often red; young stem has a milky sap.
H: Reed beds, banks of rivers and lakes, marshy woodland. Likes a muddy or peaty soil, which is occasionally submerged.
AI: P; ⊙
Old medicinal plant. Contains ethereal oil and a bitter substance in the roots.

❻ **Wood Angelica** (*Angelica sylvestris*)
50—200 cm   Apiaceae (Umbelliferae)
IM: Flowers in umbels with 20—40 rays. Bracts absent or reduced to 1—3, bracteoles numerous. Stem round, hollow, with a whitish bloom. Leaves bi- or tripinnate, the lower ones longer than 50 cm.
D: Umbels compound, with rounded secondary umbels. Leaflets 1.5—3 cm wide, serrate. Leaf sheaths inflated.
H: Fen woodlands, damp meadows, thickets and weedy places along paths, in gardens, and on banks of rivers and ponds. Likes loamy soil saturated with ground water.
AI: P; ♃; (†)
The common and scientific name of the genus (Latin *angelus* = angel) is derived from the legend that medicinal plants must have been shown to mankind by the angels. Angelica contains ethereal oil, which in high concentrations may be poisonous, and also furocoumarin.

❶ **Snowdrop** *(Galanthus nivalis)*
Amaryllidaceae
8—20 cm   IM: Petals of 2 kinds; the 3 outer ones white, the inner ones smaller and greenish.
      D: Only one flower to the peduncle. Leaves 2, basal, narrow, fleshy, ridged.
      H: Valley woodland, mixed deciduous woodland, canyon forest. Likes a saturated, loamy soil, rich in humus and plant nutrients. Found as a garden escape.
      AI: M; ⵊ
          The green patches on the inner petals are nectar guides and possess scent glands. They smell more strongly than the rest of the flower and serve to orientate the pollinating insect.

❷ **Spring Snowflake** *(Leucojum vernum)*
Amaryllidaceae
10—30 cm   See p. 54

❸ **Wood Anemone** *(Anemone nemorosa)*
Ranunculaceae
15—25 cm   IM: Flowers emerge singly from a whorl of leaves at the top of the stem. Petals glabrous or slightly hairy. Flowers 1.5—4 cm in diameter.
      D: Flowers often tinged with pink, particularly on the outside of the petals. There is a single, digitate, basal leaf growing out of the rootstock.
      H: All kinds of woodland and thickets. Likes a loamy soil.
      AI: P; ⵊ; †
          Contains the poisonous substances anemonine and protoanemonine.

❹ **European Trientalis, Chickweed Wintergreen, Seven Star**
(Trientalis europaea)
Primulaceae
10—20 cm   See p. 98

❺ **Ramson, Wild Garlic** *(Allium ursinum)*
Liliaceae
15—30 cm   IM: Leaves like those of Lily-of-the-Valley; smell strongly of Garlic when rubbed.
      D: False umbels with many flowers. Flowers snow white. Stem triangular.
      H: Mixed woodland, beech woods and valley woodland, parks, thickets. Likes a porous, moist soil, rich in humus and plant nutrients. Often forms dense stands covering a considerable area.
      AI: M; ⵊ
          This plant contains ethereal oils with unpleasant smelling sulphur compounds.

❻ **Lily-of-the-Valley** *(Convallaria majalis)*
Liliaceae
15—25 cm   IM: No possibility of confusion with other species.
      D: Unilateral racemes, with drooping flowers having a strong perfume. Usually 2 (more rarely 1 or 3) basal leaves. Creeping rootstock.
      H: Woods of various kinds, alpine mats. Likes a warm, porous soil. Forms dense stands in the localities where it occurs.
      AI: M; ⵊ; †
          Contains (particularly in the leaves and flowers) a heart poison (digitalis glycoside) which makes it of use in medicine. It is water soluble and may be extracted from water in vases where flowers have stood. The berries of the plant are also very poisonous.

❶ **Solomon's Seal** *(Polygonatum multiflorum)*
Liliaceae
30—60 cm IM: Stem round.
D: Racemes or solitary flowers in leaf axils. Berries at first red, later blue-black. Leaves in 2 rows, alternate.
H: Beech woods and mixed deciduous woodland, more rarely in coniferous woodland. Likes a calcareous, porous, loamy soil, rich in humus.
AI: M; ♃; †
Solomon's Seal is pollinated by bumblebees. As the entrance to the corolla is narrow, pollination is only possible in the case of long-tongued bees. Although the flowers of this plant are normally hermaphrodite, unisexual flowers occasionally occur. In this latter case, male flowers are commoner than female. The plant contains the same poisonous substance (digitalis glycoside) as does the Lily-of-the-Valley.

❷ **Angular Solomon's Seal** *(Polygonatum odoratum; P. officinale)*
Liliaceae
30—50 cm IM: Stem angular.
D: Usually there is a single flower in the leaf axil. Flowers scented. Leaves in 2 rows, alternate.
H: Dry, sunny slopes in mixed deciduous woodland or associated with coniferous woodland, also in thickets and copses. Likes a calcareous, porous or sandy soil.
AI: M; ♃; †
The Angular Solomon's Seal contains the same poisonous substance (digitalis glycoside) as the last species. This is the 'magic root' of stories and legends, which was reputed to open doors and cause water to spring forth out of rocks.

❸ **Whorled Solomon's Seal** *(Polygonatum verticillatum)*
Liliaceae
30—70 cm IM: Leaves in 3—8 membered whorls.
D: Flowers in leaf axils. Leaves narrow, lanceolate.
AI: M; ♃; †
This species contains the same poisonous substance (digitalis glycoside) as the other members of the genus.

❹ **White False Hellebore** *(Veratrum album)*
Liliaceae
50—150 cm See p. 54

❺ **Unbranched Lily Spiderwort** *(Anthericum liliago)*
Liliaceae
30—70 cm IM: Inflorescence a simple raceme.
D: Flowers up to 5 cm in diameter. Stem erect. Leaves narrow, almost grass-like.
H: Dry turf, light woodland and edges of woods. Rather calcifugous. Likes a warm situation.

❻ **Branched Lily Spiderwort** *(Anthericum ramosum)*
Liliaceae
30—100 cm IM: Inflorescence branched (a panicle).
D: Flowers up to 3.5 cm in diameter. Stem erect. Leaves narrow, grass-like (2—6 mm wide).
H: Dry turf, light woodland and thickets. Likes a porous, calcareous soil.
AI: M; ♃

❶

30—80 cm

Dropwort *(Filipendula vulgaris; F. hexapetala)*
Rosaceae
IM: Leaves simple pinnate. Leaflets about 2 cm long, in 8—30 pairs.
D: Flowers in branched cymes; some flowers with only 5 petals. Stem without leaves at the top, erect. Leaflets pinnate or serrate.
H: Moist meadows, semi-dry turf, light woodland. Found particularly on soil which is at least occasionally saturated.
AI: P; ♃; (†)
This plant has apparently been used as an ingredient in a drink similar to beer. It contains (particularly in the root) a slightly poisonous glycoside. An old medicinal plant and also a constituent of 'wild' salad. Even the root tubers were eaten.

❷

30—60 cm

Marguerite, Moon Daisy, Ox-eye Daisy *(Leucanthemum vulgare; Chrysanthemum leucanthemum)*
Asteraceae (Compositae)
See p. 56

❸

8—25 cm

Cat's-foot, Mountain Cat's-foot *(Antennaria dioica; Gnaphalium dioicum)*
Asteraceae (Compositae)
See p. 258

❹

20—40 cm

Wood Cudweed *(Gnaphalium silvaticum)*
Asteraceae (Compositae)
IM: Capitula in spikes or racemes. Only disc florets present. Bracts membranous, yellowish or brownish, glabrous. Leaves undivided.
D: Flowers brownish white. Stem erect. Middle leaves shorter than the lower leaves, all with glabrous upper surfaces, but with white down on the lower surface.
H: Light woodland, clearings, woodland paths, heaths and poor meadowland. Likes a sandy, loamy and often stony soil; somewhat calcifugous and indicative of superficial acidity.
AI: G; ♃

❺

30—100 cm

Canadian Fleabane, Erigeron *(Conyza canadensis; Erigeron canadensis)*
Asteraceae (Compositae)
IM: Flowers in small, numerous capitula. The outer parts consist of several rows of inconspicuous ray florets, the centre of yellow disc florets. Stem branched, with leaves. Leaves undivided, alternate, linear-lanceolate, with bristly hairs.
D: Capitula arranged in panicles. Ray florets thread-like, only a little longer than the disc florets. Stem erect with bristly hairs.
H: Weedy places on piles of stones by roadsides, on walls, waste ground and in woodland clearings, more rarely in fields. Will tolerate a variety of soils but likes a warm, nitrogenous soil.
AI: G; ☉; ⊙
This species was introduced into Europe from North America in the middle of the 17th century. By the end of the 18th century it had already spread throughout most of central Europe. A medicinal plant, containing ethereal oils and tannins.

❻

15—30 cm

 Hollow Wort, Hollow Corydalis, Hollow Fumitory *(Corydalis cava)*
Papaveraceae
See p. 224

Woods, Thickets, Hedgerows **White**

❶

15—30 cm

Fingered Fumitory *or* **Corydalis** *(Corydalis solida)*
Papaveraceae
   See p. 260

---

❷

20—50 cm

White *or* **Pale Helleborine** *(Cephalanthera damasonium; C. grandiflora; C. alba)*
Orchidaceae
   See p. 186

---

❸

20—40 cm

Lesser Butterfly Orchid *(Platanthera bifolia)*
Orchidaceae
IM: Corolla spur slender, attenuated. Flowers with a strong scent. Stem bears two
     large oval leaves.
D: Raceme with several flowers. Spur to corolla $1\frac{1}{2}$—2 times as long as the twisted
     ovary.
H: Light deciduous, mixed or coniferous woodland, also on poor pasture and
     heathland. Likes a soil with some superficial acidity, but otherwise calcareous.
     Warm situations.
AI: M; ♃
     This Lesser Butterfly Orchid smells particularly strongly at night. It attracts
     moths by means of its scent, but only those with long probosces can reach the
     nectar at the base of the long corolla spur. In their quest for nectar the moths
     bring about pollination of the flowers.

---

❹

20—60 cm

Greater Butterfly Orchid *(Platanthera chlorantha)*
Orchidaceae
   See p. 100

---

❺

15—60 cm

Mountain Clover *(Trifolium montanum)*
Fabaceae (Leguminosae)
IM: Flowers clearly stalked. Leaflets with hairs on the underside.
D: Flowers pure white to ivory. Stem with woolly hairs erect. Leaflets linear,
     sharply serrate.
H: Dry or semi-dry turf, dry thickets, light, open woodland. Likes a calcareous,
     occasionally moist soil. Root system goes deep, so the plant avoids shallow
     soils.
AI: P; ♃
     Old medicinal plant. Little use as a fodder plant; its tissues are rich in cellulose
     and therefore tough.

---

❻

20—60 cm

Mountain Woundwort *(Stachys recta)*
Lamiaceae (Labiatae)
IM: Sessile flowers in false whorls in the leaf axils, also terminal. Lobes of the lower
     lip broad and blunt. Calyx without any projecting ribs.
D: Flowers 1—2 cm long. Stem erect or decumbent. Leaves ovoid or lanceolate,
     with an entire margin or serrate.
H: Dry or semi-dry turf, dry thickets, light woodland. Likes a calcareous, stony
     but nevertheless deep soil. On karst rocks often occurs in vertical fissures.
     Likes a warm situation. In localities where it occurs it may be abundant.
AI: G; ♃
     It is said that Roman gladiators used to carry this plant as a charm against
     injury.

❶

5—45 cm

Mountain Saxifrage *(Saxifraga aizoon)*
Saxifragaceae
IM: Petals often with red spots. Leaves thick, fleshy, stiff and form basal rosettes. They often have white spots round their borders.
D: Racemes. Petals invert-ovoid, obtuse. Stem stiffly erect. Leaves light green or blue green, sharply toothed. Non-flowering rosettes occur alongside the flowering ones.
H: Rock fragments associated with calcareous rock, more rarely on gravel. Likes a warm situation and thrives in extremely dry habitats.
AI: P; ♃
The name (Latin *saxifraga* = stonebreaker) refers to the stony habitats of many species in the genus. The Mountain Saxifrage excretes chalk from fine apertures on the leaf blade. Because of this the borders of the leaves often have white spots.

❷

30—60 cm

Nottingham Catchfly *(Silene nutans)*
Caryophyllaceae
IM: Petals deeply cleft. Calyx with 10 veins. Flowers drooping.
D: Umbellate panicles. Stem with soft hairs towards the base and sticky, glandular hairs (hence name) at the top. Lower leaves spatulate and petiolate; upper leaves opposite, lanceolate, sessile or almost sessile.
H: Semi-dry turf, heaths, dry woodland and thickets, rocky debris. Likes a warm, porous soil and is indifferent to plant nutrients.
AI: P; ♃
Night flowering. The flowers begin to exhale their scent at dusk and are pollinated by moths.

❸

5—15 cm

White Stonecrop *(Sedum album)*
Crassulaceae
IM: Inflorescence glabrous. Leaves linear, smooth and cylindrical, dark green in colour.
D: Stem prostrate, decumbent, more rarely erect. Leaves 6—12 mm long.
H: Dry and semi-dry turf, rocks, walls, road rubble. Likes a calcareous, stony soil.
AI: P; ♃
The White Stonecrop is the foodplant of the most beautiful of the middle European butterflies, the rare Apollo.

❹

30—60 cm

White Dogbane *(Cynanchum vincetoxicum; Vincetoxicum officinale)*
Asclepiadaceae
See p. 72

❺

5—15 cm

Alpine Butterwort *(Pinguicula alpina)*
Lentibulariaceae
IM: No possibility of confusion with other species.
D: Flowers solitary, white, with yellow spots in the throat of the corolla, spurred. Leaves basal, forming a rosette, linear or elliptical, with entire margins which are somewhat upturned, sticky.
H: Swamps, wet alpine mats, wet rock debris. Likes a wet, calcareous soil. Grows on rock fragments where there is little soil.
AI: G; ♃
An insectivorous plant. See Common Butterwort, p. 350.

❶ **Large Bittercress** *(Cardamine amara)*
Brassicaceae (Cruciferae)

5 — 30 cm   See p. 60

---

❷ **True Watercress** *(Nasturtium officinale ; Rorippa nasturtium-aquaticum)*
Brassicaceae (Cruciferae)

15 — 50 cm
- IM: Stamens yellow. Ovary and fruit more than 3 times as long as broad. Stem hollow and round.
- D: Cymose racemes. The lower parts of the stem frequently with rootlets emerging from the axils. Lower leaves with 3 leaflets, upper leaves unpaired pinnate. Leaflets ovoid; the terminal leaflet mostly with a heart-shaped base.
- H: Springs, ditches, brooks with running, cool water and sand.
- AI: P; ♃
  Contains mustard oil, ethereal oils, a bitter substance and considerable amounts of vitamin C. An old medicinal plant. Can be used to produce a vitamin-rich salad.

---

❸ **Dragonroot, Marsh Calla** *(Calla palustris)*
Araceae

15 — 50 cm
- IM: Bract (spathe) white on the inside, spadix ovoid or round.
- D: Leaves heart-shaped, leathery, shining. Berries coral red.
- H: Alder swamps, reed beds, muddy ditches and ponds. Indicates soil moisture. Somewhat calcifugous.
- AI: M; ♃; †
  The name Dragonroot refers to the creeping rhizome. At one time the plant was regarded as a cure for snake bite. The whole plant is poisonous. Believed to be pollinated by snails.

---

❹ **Procumbent Pearlwort** *(Sagina procumbens)*
Caryophyllaceae

2 — 5 cm   See p. 22

---

❺ **Common Frogbit** *(Hydrocharis morsus-ranae)*
Hydrocharitaceae

15 — 30 cm
- IM: No possibility of confusion with other species.
- D: Male flowers 1 — 3; 12 stamens. Female flowers solitary, 6 styles. Leaves float, leathery.
- H: A floating plant in stagnant, usually shallow water. Somewhat calcifugous. Likes water which is warm and shaded in summer.
- AI: M; ♃

---

❻ **Canadian Pondweed** *(Anacharis canadensis ; Elodea canadensis ; Helodea canadensis)*
Hydrocharitaceae

1 — 3 m
- IM: No possibility of confusion with other species.
- D: Plant recognizable by its form of growth. Leaves mainly 3 in each whorl.
- H: Stagnant or running water; submerged. Likes water rich in nutrients.
- AI: M; ♃
  The Canadian Pondweed was introduced into Europe from North America about the middle of the last century. It spread so rapidly that it became a regular 'pest' and has interfered with fishing and shipping in inland waterways. In the last half century there has been some retreat of the species. Canadian Pondweed is dioecious.

❶

30—130 cm

Arrowhead *(Sagittaria sagittifolia)*
Alismataceae
IM: No possibility of confusion with other species.
D: Verticillate panicles. Flowers unisexual, the upper ones male, the lower ones female; white in colour, with a pinkish or violet tinge at the base of the petals. Stem triangular, erect. Submerged leaves linear.
H: Slow-flowing or stagnant waters, also on land near the banks of rivers or lakes which is occasionally submerged. Likes water rich in dissolved nutrients; an indicator of muddy conditions.
AI: M; ♃

❷

10—100 cm

Common Water Plantain *(Alisma plantago-aquatica)*
Alismataceae
IM: 6 styles, longer than the ovaries.
D: Whorled panicles. Flower pedunculate. Petals markedly deciduous, white or pink, yellowish at the base. Stem erect. Leaves on long petioles, forming a rosette. Submerged leaves narrower. Similar species: *Alisma gramineum.* Submerged leaves ribbon-like. Styles shorter than ovaries. Margins of water.
H: Margins of slow-running or stagnant water, also in reed beds or along river banks which are sometimes submerged.
AI: M; ♃
The juice of this plant has an acrid, burning taste and is poisonous to cattle. By contrast, goats readily eat the plant without ill effects. The active principle of the Common Water Plantain is still not defined, although sometimes termed an 'alkaloid'. However, no true alkaloids or cyanide compounds have been recovered from the plant.

❸

30—130 cm

Cleavers, Goosegrass, Sticky Willie *(Galium aparine)*
Rubiaceae
See p. 26

❹

15—40 cm

Marsh Bedstraw *(Galium palustre)*
Rubiaceae
IM: Leaves in whorls of 4. Each leaf has a single vein. Stem rough with backward-pointing prickles.
D: Diffuse panicles. Stem quadrangular, prostrate or decumbent. Leaves dark green, linear, rounded at the tip.
H: Margins of stagnant or slow-running water, reed beds, ditches, river banks, also in wet meadows and wet alpine mat. Likes a soil rich in humus and saturated with ground water. Prefers a peaty or loamy soil.
AI: G; ♃

❺

20—100 cm

Gypsy Wort *(Lycopus europaeus)*
Lamiaceae (Labiatae)
IM: Flowers with 4—5 corolla lobes, and a weak bilateral symmetry; the inside of the flowers with red spots. Inflorescences form dense whorls in the leaf axils.
D: Flowers small. Stem simple or branched. Leaves opposite and decussate, petiolate; the lower leaves often pinnate, the upper leaves crenate.
H: Margins of stagnant or flowing water, reed beds, ditches, river banks, marshy woodland. Found on a variety of soils, but usually soil which is sometimes flooded.
AI: G; ♃

---

❶   **Buckbean, Bogbean, Marsh Trefoil** *(Menyanthes trifoliata)*
         Gentianaceae
10—30 cm   See p. 272

---

❷   **Hair-leaved Crowfoot** *(Ranunculus trichophyllus)*
         Ranunculaceae
10—50 cm   IM: Flowers 0.5—1.5 cm in diameter. Leaves sessile or with a short stalk.
             D: Flowers with long stalks. Floating leaves divided into 3 segments; submerged leaves in multiple divisions of 3 with narrow points.
             H: Aquatic habitats with stagnant water. Likes water rich in nutrients, rather muddy. Present in large numbers in localities where it occurs.
             AI: P; ♃
                 Name: see Bulbous Crowfoot, p. 124.

---

❸   **Riverine Water Crowfoot** *(Ranunculus fluitans)*
         Ranunculaceae
1—6 m   IM: Flowers 1—2 cm in diameter. Segments of submerged leaves 7—15 cm long, lying parallel to current. Only found in flowing water.
             D: Flowers solitary, with long peduncles. Mostly without floating leaves. Submerged leaves stalked. Aerial leaves brush-like.
             H: Aquatic habitats in flowing water. Likes clear and somewhat acid water. Forms extensive growths in rivers.
             AI: P; ♃
                 Name: see Bulbous Crowfoot, p. 124.

---

❹   **Common Water Crowfoot** *(Ranunculus aquatilis)*
         Ranunculaceae
10—50 cm   IM: Flowers 2—2.5 cm in diameter. Leaves clearly petiolate. Most plants have a few reniform, floating leaves with five blunt lobes.
             D: Flowers solitary with long peduncles. Submerged leaves divided into brush-like segments.
             H: Aquatic habitats associated with stagnant or slow-flowing water. Likes water which is rich in nutrients and slightly acid.
             AI: P; ♃
                 Submerged flowers remain closed and are self-pollinating; otherwise they are pollinated by flies and beetles.

---

❺   **Meadowsweet** *(Filipendula ulmaria)*
         Rosaceae
1—2 m   See p. 50

---

❻   **Grass of Parnassus** *(Parnassia palustris)*
         Saxifragaceae
15—45 cm   IM: No possibility of confusion with other species.
             D: Flowers solitary. Stem angular with only 1 stem leaf. Basal leaves heart-shaped with long stalks.
             H: Wet moorland, also wet flushes in semi-dry turf, somewhat calcicolous. Abundant in habitats where it occurs.
             AI: P; ♃
                 The stamens become ripe one after the other and shed their pollen in the order that they become ripe. The plant contains tannin.

4

6

3

1

2

5

Marshes, Moorland, Shore and Aquatic Vegetation　　　**White**

❶

20—100 cm

Water Stitchwort, Water Chickweed *(Myosoton aquaticum ; Malachium aquaticum ; Stellaria aquatica)*
Caryophyllaceae
IM: Petals cleft right down to the base. 5 styles. Calyx hairy, almost as long as the petals. Leaves sessile or with very short stalks.
D: Inflorescence furcate. Stem flaccid, prostrate, decumbent or climbing; frequently rooting at the nodes. Leaves opposite, heart-shaped to ovoid, pointed at the tip and sessile. Only the lowest leaves have no flower stalks in their axils.
H: Valley woodland, banks of streams or ponds. Likes a soil rich in humus and nutrients. Indicator of soil moisture.
AI: P; ♃

❷

10—30 cm

Bog Stitchwort *(Stellaria alsine)*
Caryophyllaceae
IM: Petals 1—3 mm long, shorter than the sepals. 3 styles.
D: Cymes in the leaf axils. Stem terminates in a flowerless shoot, prostrate. Leaves opposite; lanceolate or narrowly lanceolate.
H: Banks of streams, ditches, springs. Calcifugous but likes a soil rich in nitrogen. Most frequently found on loamy or sandy soils. Occurs in masses.
AI: P; ♃

❸

30—60 cm

Common Soapwort *(Saponaria officinalis)*
Caryophyllaceae
See p. 274

❹

10—20 cm

English Sundew *(Drosera anglica)*
Droseraceae
IM: Inflorescence springing from the middle of the rosette. Stem erect and at least twice as long as the leaves.
D: Spicate cincinnus. Leaf blades elongate, wedge-shaped, 1.5—5 cm long by 5 mm broad, erect. A similar species is the Intermediate Sundew, *Drosera intermedia*, in which the inflorescence springs from under the leaf rosette and bends upwards; it is only a little longer than the leaves. Leaves 7—10 mm long, 3.5 mm broad.
H: Moist, open places in bogs and moorland. Only on peaty soils, which are frequently flooded.
AI: P; ♃
An insectivorous plant. For method of catching the insects see next species.

❺

10—20 cm

Common *or* **Round-leaved Sundew** *(Drosera rotundifolia)*
Droseraceae
IM: No possibility of confusion with other species.
D: Spicate cincinnus, with few flowers. Leaves in a basal rosette, round, petiolate, somewhat hollowed out and with red 'tentacles'.
H: Moorland, bogs. Often occurs on sphagnum hummocks but may also be found on sandy peat. Forms considerable masses where it occurs.
AI: P; ♃
The end of the 'tentacle' exudes a sticky fluid, which contains a proteolytic enzyme. Small insects are held fast and later digested by the secretion. If an insect touches the 'tentacle' and sticks to it, the tentacle gradually bends down towards the leaf blade. The tentacle can be stimulated experimentally with a small fragment of cheese. A medicinal plant. Active substance unknown.

94

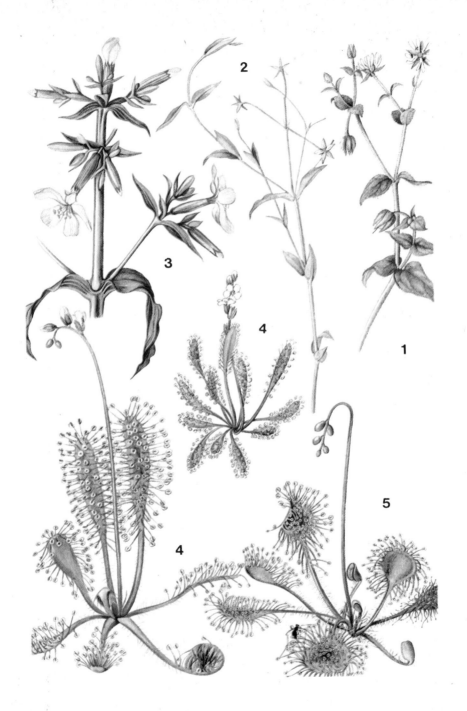

❶ **Pale Polygonum, Pale Persicaria** *(Polygonum lapathifolium)*
Polygonaceae
20—80 cm   See p. 274

❷ **White Convolvulus, Greater Bindweed** *(Calystegia sepium; Convolvulus sepium)*
Convolvulaceae
150—300 cm   See p. 74

❸ **Marsh Pennywort, White Rot** *(Hydrocotyle vulgaris)*
Apiaceae (Umbelliferae)
5—25 cm   IM: Flowers in umbels. Leaves round. Petiole joins the middle of the underside of
the leaf. The leaf has a sharp, burning taste if chewed.
D: Umbels form rounded heads, very small. Stem creeping.
H: Mosses, reed beds, marshes, damp meadows. Likes a saturated, non-calcareous,
clayey soil.
AI: P; ♃; (†)
The common name of the plant refers to the shape of the leaves. The plant
contains a sharp-tasting substance, which is possibly slightly poisonous, but
has not been investigated.

❹ **Bulbous Chervil, Tuberous Cow Parsley** *(Chaerophyllum bulbosum)*
Apiaceae (Umbelliferae)
1—1.8 m   IM: Flowers in umbels with 15—20 glabrous rays. No involucral bracts. Bracteoles
4—6, with non-ciliate edges. Petals cleft almost into halves. Only the basal
part of the stem flecked with red and bearing stiff hairs. Stem round with
bluish bloom. Leaves tri- or quadripinnate.
D: Umbels compound. Leaflets of the upper leaves narrowly linear. Root with
a bulbous swelling.
H: Valley woodland, weedy places on the banks of rivers and in water meadows.
Likes a porous, calcareous soil, saturated with ground water.
AI: P; (†)
The plant contains the poison chaerophyllin in its leaves but not in the
rootstock, which is very rich in starch. In the Middle Ages this plant was
cultivated for its tuberous roots which were used as we now use potatoes.
Their flavour is like that of sweet chestnuts. Those who might be inclined to
eat this plant are advised that it closely resembles the very poisonous umbelli-
ferous plants such as Hemlock and is therefore best avoided.

❺ **Cowbane, Water Hemlock** *(Cicuta virosa)*
Apiaceae (Umbelliferae)
60—130 cm   IM: Flowers in umbels. Umbels with 15—25 rays. Involucral bracts absent or
reduced to 1—2. Bracteoles numerous. Stem erect or decumbent. Leaves
bi- or tripinnate. Pinnules lanceolate, sharply toothed.
D: Umbels compound. Stem and petioles hollow. Leaf sheaths inflated. Rootstock
thick with hollow cells.
H: Margins of stagnant and flowing water, reed beds. Likes a slightly acid and
peaty soil, calcifugous, resists flooding.
AI: P; ♃; †
This plant contains a highly poisonous substance, cicutoxin, in all its parts, but
particularly in the rootstock, which has a pleasant celery-like smell and
a sweet taste.

❶ **Wood Angelica** *(Angelica sylvestris)*
Apiaceae (Umbelliferae)

50—200 cm
IM: Flowers in umbels with 20—40 rays. Bracts absent or reduced to 1—3, bracteoles numerous. Stem round, hollow, with a whitish bloom. Leaves bi- or tripinnate, the lower ones longer than 50 cm.

D: Umbels compound, with rounded secondary umbels. Leaflets 1.5—3 cm wide, serrate. Leaf sheaths inflated.

H: Fen woodlands, damp meadows, thickets and weedy places along paths, in gardens, and on banks of rivers and ponds. Likes a loamy soil saturated with ground water.

AI: P; ♃; (†)
For name and constituents: see p. 76.

❷ **Fine-leaved Water Dropwort** *(Oenanthe aquatica)*
Apiaceae (Umbelliferae)

50—150 cm
IM: Flowers in umbels. Umbel with 8—12 rays. Involucral bracts absent or reduced. Bracteoles of 4 leaflets. Stem not flecked. Leaves bipinnate to 5-fold pinnate. Leaflets of the leaves which are not submerged 4—6 mm long.

D: Umbels compound; umbel rays not hollow. Stem sparingly branched.

H: Margins of stagnant and running water, reed beds. Likes muddy soils subject to flooding.

AI: P; ⊙
Old medicinal plant, containing ethereal oils in the fruits.

❸ **Hog's Fennel, Milk Parsley** *(Peucedanum palustre)*
Apiaceae (Umbelliferae)

50—150 cm
See p. 76

❹ **White Butterbur** *(Petasites albus)*
Asteraceae (Compositae)

15—35 cm
IM: Flowers in capitula forming a racemose head. Plant without leaves at the time of flowering, the only trace of leaves being the leaf-scales on the stem. Stem with cobweb-like covering of hairs.

D: Ray florets and disc florets yellowish white. Leaves first appear at the end of the flowering period; they are very large, round or heart-shaped, with serrate edges and a white felt on the underside.

H: Canyon forest, valley woodlands, mountain forest, mixed woodlands. Likes a stony soil rich in humus.

AI: G; ♃
Name: see Butterbur, p. 276.

❺ **European Trientalis, Chickweed Wintergreen, Seven Star** *(Trientalis europaea)*
Primulaceae

10—20 cm
IM: No possibility of confusion with other species.

D: Flowers solitary, 1.2—1.5 cm in diameter, on long peduncles. Petals yellow at the base. Stem erect, with 5—7 elliptical leaves in a rosette near the top.

H: Moist coniferous woods, more rarely in mixed woodland or heath. Likes a wet, marshy, acid, rather peaty soil.

AI: G; ♃
The plant propagates itself vegetatively by means of runners. The rootstock contains saponin.

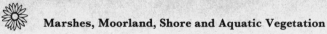

❶ White Waterlily *(Nymphaea alba)*
Nymphaeaceae
at a water
depth of up
to 2.5 m
IM: Stigmas yellow (If red: *Nymphaea candida*)
D: Flowers large; wide open with a faint but pleasant scent. Leaf stalk rope-like. Floating leaf almost circular, but with a deep, heart-shaped indentation, margin entire. Submerged leaves are rolled up, leathery and glossy.
H: Aquatic habitats associated with stagnant or slow-flowing water. Likes warm water, but is also found in cool, moorland lakes poor in nutrients. Occurs in large numbers in those localities where it is present.
AI: P; ♃; (†)
The rootstock, which is rich in tannins, was formerly used in tanning leather. The flowers of the White Waterlily open from about 7 a.m. to 4 p.m. Pollination is by flies and beetles. The plant contains a slightly poisonous alkaloid.

❷ Sneezewort *(Achillea ptarmica)*
Asteraceae (Compositae)
30—70 cm
See p. 56

❸ Alpine Butterwort *(Pinguicula alpina)*

Lentibulariaceae
5—15 cm
See p. 86

❹ Hedge Hyssop *(Gratiola officinalis)*
Scrophulariaceae
15—30 cm
IM: No possibility of confusion with other species.
D: Flowers solitary, in the axils of leaves. Petals whitish or pink, corolla tube yellowish. Stem erect or decumbent. Leaves opposite and decussate, sessile, lanceolate, serrate and glabrous.
H: Margins of stagnant or slow-flowing water, river banks, damp meadows. Likes a muddy, somewhat calcareous, dense soil. Withstands summer drought.
AI: G; ♃; †
Hedge Hyssop contains the poisonous glycosides gratioline and gratiotoxin. An old medicinal plant.

❺ Greater Butterfly Orchid *(Platanthera chlorantha)*
Orchidaceae
20—60 cm
IM: Corolla spurs long and curved, somewhat thicker at the end. Flowers with hardly any scent. Stem bears 2 large oval leaves.
D: Racemes with many flowers. Flowers slightly greenish or yellowish.
H: Deciduous woodland, mosses or wet meadows. Calcicolous.
AI: M; ♃

❻ Marsh Helleborine *(Epipactis palustris)*
Orchidaceae
30—50 cm
IM: Corolla without spurs. Flowers slightly drooping. Petals spreading. Lip with reddish veins.
D: Unilateral racemes. Outer petals rather greenish or brownish, rounded in front. Lip strongly constricted near the base, expanded distally (the distal part often breaks off). Leaves linear-lanceolate.
H: Mosses; grows among rushes and sedges in marshes and fens. Calcicolous.
AI: M; ♃

❶

1 — 3.5 m

Sea Buckthorn *(Hippophaë rhamnoides)*
Eleagnaceae
IM: Branches bearing thorns. Leaves with entire margins, grey-green on the upper
surface, silvery white below.
D: Plant dioecious. Flowers inconspicuous. Leaves linear 5 — 8 cm long.
H: Thickets and scrub in sand dunes, alluvial valleys, the edges of woods. Likes
a moist, and sometimes, saline soil. Forms considerable stands in those localities
where it does occur. Often planted and occasionally escapes into the wild.
AI: P
The berries contain flavones and are rich in vitamin C (about 900 mg/100 g
fresh weight). The flavones activate the vitamin C activity, so that Sea
Buckthorn berries are a particularly good source of the vitamin.

❷

Up to 7 m

Traveller's Joy, Old Man's Beard, Wild Clematis *(Clematis vitalba)*
Ranunculaceae
IM: No possibility of confusion with other species.
D: Flowers in leaf axils and terminal racemes. Flowers consist of 4 — 5 coloured
sepals (not petals). These are white on the inside, but greenish yellow with
a white border on the outside. Leaves opposite, pinnate. Leaflets elongate ovoid
or elongate heart-shaped, pointed. Petiole tendril-like.
H: Valley woodlands, borders of woods, thickets, hedgerows. Likes a deep,
calcareous, porous, loamy soil rich in nitrogen. Warm situations.
AI: P; †
This plant is recognizable in autumn and winter because of its numerous,
white, silky fruits (cf. common name Old Man's Beard). Flowers have
a Hawthorn-like scent. Contains the poison protoanemonine.

❸

1 — 7 m

Common Holly *(Ilex aquifolium)*
Aquifoliaceae
IM: Leaves shiny, leathery, with prickles.
D: Flowers in axillary clusters, small. Wood hard, yellowish to greenish white.
Leaves ovoid to elliptical, with a short petiole.
H: Deciduous woodland, mixed woodland, coniferous forest, marshy woodland.
Likes a moist, rather acid soil. Sensitive to frost.
AI: P; †

❹

3 — 5 m

Dogwood *(Cornus sanguinea)*
Cornaceae
IM: Flowers in flat corymbs. Leaves with pinnately branched venation. Twigs
often with a reddish tinge; in autumn and winter always blood red.
D: Leaves with entire margins, ovoid, green on both sides.
H: Mixed and deciduous woodland, thickets. Likes a rather stony, loamy soil, rich
in nutrients.
AI: P

❺

1.5 — 3 m

Common Privet *(Ligustrum vulgare)*
Oleaceae
IM: No possibility of confusion with other species.
D: Panicles. Flowers small with an unpleasant smell. Twigs rod-shaped. Leaves
glabrous, opposite and decussate, linear-lanceolate.
H: Dry woods and thickets, valley woodlands and edges of woods. Likes a porous,
often rather stony, calcareous soil in warm situations.
AI: G; †

❶ Wild Pear *(Pyrus communis; Pirus communis)*
Rosaceae
6 — 20 m
IM: Stamens red.
D: Umbels with few flowers. Fruit a pear. Twigs often rather spinous. Leaves rounded or ovoid, leathery, glossy on the upper surface, alternate, with fine serrations.
H: Deciduous woodland. Likes a loamy soil rich in nutrients.
AI: P
The most important wild ancestor of the cultivated pear. The seeds taste bitter, as they contain an organic cyanide compound.

❷ Wild Apple, Crab Apple *(Malus sylvestris; M. communis,* ssp. *acerba)*
Rosaceae
Up to 10 m
IM: Stamens yellow; petals reddish or pink.
D: Umbels with few flowers. Fruit an apple. Twigs often rather spinous. Leaves broadly ovoid or elliptical, pointed at the apex, crenate-serrate, the upper surface somewhat wrinkled.
H: Deciduous woodland. Likes a somewhat calcareous soil, rich in nutrients.
AI: P
The most important wild ancestor of the cultivated apple. The seeds taste bitter, as they contain an organic cyanide compound.

❸ Blackthorn, Sloe *(Prunus spinosa)*
Rosaceae
2 — 3 m
IM: Flowers usually solitary. Twigs with thorns.
D: Flowers appear before the leaves. Drupes blue-black, with a bluish bloom. Leaves elliptical, with short petioles; sharply toothed.
H: Thickets, hedgerows, the edges of woods. Likes stony, shallow soils.
AI: P
Occasionally one sees the corpses of insects or mice impaled on the thorns of Blackthorn. The 'culprit' is a bird — the Red-backed Shrike, which likes to nest in Blackthorn hedges. The fruits contain much tannin and have a 'dry' taste. Used to make sloe gin. Flowers are dried and used as 'tea'.

❹ Common Wild Cherry, Gean *(Prunus avium,* ssp. *sylvestris)*
Rosaceae
Up to 18 m
IM: Flowers in umbel-like clusters, without leaves at the base.
D: Flowers 2 — 4. Fruit a cherry. Leaves invert-ovoid, pointed at the apex, up to 15 cm long.
H: Deciduous and mixed woodland, more rarely in copses.
AI: P
Fruit edible, the wild form of the cultivated cherry.

❺ Bird Cherry *(Prunus padus)*
Rosaceae
3 — 15 m
IM: Flowers in many-flowered, pendulous racemes.
D: Racemes hang down from the end of a twig bearing leaves. Flowers have a strong smell. Leaves elliptical, pointed at the apex, alternate, serrate, somewhat wrinkled.
H: Copses, moist deciduous woodland, thickets along watercourses. Likes a deep, loamy soil, rich in nutrients.
AI: P
Fruit edible. The skin contains bitter organic cyanide compounds.

❶   **Common Amelanchier, Rock Pear** *(Amelanchier ovalis; A. vulgaris)*
                Rosaceae

1—3 m   IM: Flowers in racemose clusters. Petals narrow linear 1—2 cm long, 5—8 mm wide, underside hairy.
                D: Fruits the size of peas, bluish black. If the fruit or the receptacle is cut transversely, it is possible to see the characteristic 10 locules. Twigs without thorns or spines. Leaves oval, obtuse, 2—4 cm long, petiolate, crenate, with fine hairs on the underside when young.
                H: Rocky slopes, warm thickets. Likes a stony, shallow soil in warm situations.
                AI: P

❷   **Medlar** *(Mespilus germanica)*
                Rosaceae

2—6 m   IM: Flowers solitary on twigs. Calyx lobes longer than the petals.
                D: Young twigs with felt-like covering of hairs. Leaves linear-lanceolate, with a short point at the apex. Undersides of leaves densely covered with hairs.
                H: Dry thickets and woodland, warm deciduous woods, rocky slopes. Calcicolous. Likes warm situations.
                AI: P
                A tree of which the fruit was eaten in the Middle Ages. It is however only pleasant to eat when thoroughly ripe. Contains pectin and is used in the production of jellies.

❸   **Bearberry** *(Arctostaphylos uva-ursi)*
                Ericaceae

30—100 cm   IM: Leaves elongate-invert-ovoid, leathery, bright green underneath, not rolled up.
                D: 3—12 flowers in a terminal raceme. Fruit red, floury in texture. Shoots often creeping. Leaves with entire margins.
                H: Coniferous woodland, alpine mats and bushes. Likes a porous, superficially acid soil, rich in humus.
                AI: G
                The Bearberry bush can live for about 100 years. A medicinal plant, the leaves of which contain arbutin.

❹   **Cowberry, Red Whortleberry** *(Vaccinium vitis-idaea)*
                Ericaceae

10—30 cm   IM: Leaves evergreen, leathery (test the lowest leaves), rolled up at the edge.
                D: Several flowers in terminal racemes. Flowers pedunculate. Corolla tube finely toothed at the end. Stem erect, round. Leaves with entire margins or slightly crenate, blunt.
                H: Mixed woodland, coniferous woodland, moorland, alpine mats and bushes. Likes a rather moist, acid soil, rich in humus.
                AI: G
                The Cowberry is a valuable wild fruit. It contains, in addition to organic acids and tannins, some provitamin A (carotene) and a considerable amount of vitamin C. The leaves are rich in arbutin and may be used as tea.

❺   **Bog Whortleberry** *(Vaccinium uliginosum)*
                Ericaceae

30—90 cm   See p. 286

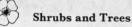
❶

50—100 cm

Dewberry *(Rubus caesius)*
Rosaceae
IM: Sepals thickly covered with grey hairs. Stem unevenly provided with prickles, round, creeping. Leaves with 3—7 teeth. Shoots with a bluish bloom.
D: Umbel-like panicles. Shoots climbing or scrambling on the ground.
H: Valley woodland, marshy woods, weedy places on moist, uncultivated soil, more rarely in fields. Likes a wet, nitrogenous soil, rich in humus.
AI: P

❷

1.2—2 m

Bramble, Blackberry *(Rubus fruticosus)*
Rosaceae
IM: Stem mostly overhanging and very prickly, more rarely creeping or decumbent. Leaves mostly palmately compound, alternate.
D: Racemes. Compound fruit black or reddish black. Flowering shoots erect, non-flowering shoots bending downwards to the ground.
H: Wood margins, fields, gardens, heaths, hedgerows.
AI: P
The fruits taste good and are rich in vitamin C.

❸

50—120 cm

Wild Raspberry *(Rubus idaeus)*
Rosaceae
IM: Stem erect or somewhat bent, provided with fine prickles. Leaves bright green, mostly compound pinnate, the undersides with a thick covering of white hairs, alternate.
D: Drooping panicles with few flowers. Leaves with 3—7 leaflets, which are ovoid, toothed and have their upper surface wrinkled.
H: Damp, light, deciduous, mixed or coniferous woodland, clearings, wood margins. Likes a soil rich in nitrogen and other nutrients.
AI: P; ⊙
The fruits taste good and are rich in vitamin C.

❹

Up to 12 m

Midland *or* **Two-styled Hawthorn** *(Crataegus laevigata; C. oxyacantha)*
Rosaceae
IM: Flowers with 2—3 styles. Peduncle glabrous. Twigs with sharp thorns. Leaves only weakly lobed.
D: Erect umbel-like panicles. Flowers with a strong scent. Leaves ovoid in outline, cuneate at the base, undivided or with 3—5 lobes.
H: Deciduous or mixed woodland, thickets along waysides, on waste ground, in canyon forests. Likes a calcareous soil.
AI: The rather unpleasant smell of the flowers is due to trimethylamine. Leaves contain organic acids which affect the heart. Medicinal plant.

❺

Up to 8 m

Common *or* **One-styled Hawthorn** *(Crataegus monogyna)*
Rosaceae
IM: Flowers with 1 style. Peduncle hairy. Twigs thorny. Leaves deeply lobed.
D: Erect umbel-like panicles. Flowers with a strong scent. Twigs with sharp thorns. Leaves usually with 3—5 lobes, rarely with more. Lobes of leaves serrate at the front and pointed.
H: Deciduous or mixed, dry woodland, thickets along waysides, hedgerows, rocky places. Likes a shallow, somewhat stony soil and withstands drought.
AI: P
See Midland Hawthorn above.

❶

1.5—2.5 m

Alder Buckthorn *(Frangula alnus ; Rhamnus frangula)*
Rhamnaceae
IM: Twigs and leaves alternate.
D: Flowers small, 2—6 in a cymose, axillary inflorescence. Twigs thornless.
     Leaves ovoid-elliptical, with entire margins.
H: Deciduous, mixed and coniferous woodland, thickets in mosses and fens.
     Likes a dense, wet or, at least, moist soil.
AI: P; (†)
     The specific name *Frangula* draws attention to the fragility of the wood
     (Latin *frangere* = to break). The bark has an unpleasant smell and contains
     glycosides, tannins and an alkaloid. Medicinal plant.

❷

1.3—2.5 m

Wayfaring Tree *(Viburnum lantana)*
Caprifoliaceae
IM: Flowers in terminal, umbrella-like cymes. Leaves without lobes.
D: Flowers all the same. Young branches with a greyish felt. Leaves elliptical,
     finely toothed, undersides wrinkled with a greyish felt.
H: Thickets, deciduous and mixed woodland, mountain and valley woodland.
     Likes a porous, rather stony, calcareous soil. Calcicolous.
AI: G; †
     Poisonous substance in berries not known.

❸

2—4 m

Guelder Rose *(Viburnum opulus)*
Caprifoliaceae
IM: Flowers in terminal, umbrella-like or globose cymes.
D: Marginal flowers of the cyme larger than the rest and sterile. Twigs glabrous.
     Leaves with long petioles, 3-lobed. Lobes coarsely serrate.
H: Marshy woodland, canyon forest, mountain forest, deciduous and mixed
     woodland. Likes a wet, loamy soil. Indicator of moisture.
AI: G

❹

3—10 m

Common *or* **Black Elder** *(Sambucus nigra)*
Caprifoliaceae
IM: Flowers in umbrella-like cymes. Leaves with aromatic smell.
D: Cyme usually with 5 main rays, at first erect, later drooping. Twigs bent
     outwards from the main branch and with distinct, white pith. Leaflets 3—7,
     ovoid, serrate.
H: Mixed and deciduous woodland, marshy woodland, thickets, clearings. Likes
     a nitrogenous soil rich in humus. An indicator of moisture.
AI: G
     A medicinal plant. The leaves contain ethereal oil. The berries, which are
     edible, contain vitamin C (10 mg/100 g) and vitamin A.

❺

3—9 m

White Beam *(Sorbus aria)*
Rosaceae
IM: Petals 3—5 mm long. Leaves slightly lobed or doubly serrate.
D: Umbrella-like cymes. Fruit red or yellow, floury. Twigs greyish at first, olive
     brown later. Leaves linear-elliptical, cuneate at the base, with a short petiole.
     Sometimes the leaves are doubly serrate or slightly lobed from the middle
     to the apex; upper side glossy, lower side hairy, white; alternate.
H: Mixed woodland, rocky mountain forest, dry woodland. Likes a shallow,
     stony soil.
AI: P; (†)

110

❶   **Wild Service Tree** *(Sorbus torminalis; Pirus torminalis; Pyrus torminalis)*
          Rosaceae
5—20 m   IM: Petals 3—5 mm long. Leaves 3—7 lobed.
             D: Umbel-like panicles. Leaves in outline broadly ovoid, rather heart-shaped at the base, up to 10 cm long, alternate. Lobes of leaves irregularly serrate and clearly separated, upper sides glossy, dark green, lower sides bright green.
             H: Mixed and deciduous woodland, dry woodland. Likes a calcareous soil, rich in nutrients. Prefers warm situations.
             AI: P; (†)

❷   **Mountain Ash, Rowan Tree** *(Sorbus aucuparia; Pirus aucuparia; Pyrus aucuparia)*
          Rosaceae
Up to 15 m   IM: Petals 4—5 mm long. Leaves compound, unpaired pinnate.
             D: Umbel-like panicle of many flowers. Leaves with 9—15 leaflets, petioles short. Leaflets linear-lanceolate with toothed apices. Leaves smell unpleasant.
             H: Damp, deciduous and mixed woodland, marshy woodland, moorland. Grows on dense, rather acid soils.
             AI: P; (†)
                 Fruits contain vitamin C and provitamin A (carotene).

❸   **Field Rose** *(Rosa arvensis; R. repens)*
          Rosaceae
1.5—2 m   IM: Stem prostrate, creeping, prickly. Leaves compound pinnate.
             D: Flowers solitary, 3—5 cm in diameter. Peduncles very long. 5—7 leaflets.
             H: Dry, deciduous and mixed woodland. Calcicolous.
             AI: P
                 Fruits poor in vitamins (cf. Dog Rose, p. 286).

❹   **False Acacia, Robinia** *(Robinia pseudo-acacia: R. pseudacacia)*
          Fabaceae
Up to 25 m   IM: Flowers in pendulous racemes. The petiole often has 2 thorns situated close together.
             D: Flowers with a pleasant scent. Leaves compound, unpaired pinnate. 9—19 elongate-ovoid leaflets.
             H: Embankments; light, dry woodland, dry thickets. On soils of various kinds in warm situations. Either planted or a garden escape.
             AI: P
                 This tree was introduced into Europe from America in the 16th century. It is called after J. Robin (1550—1629).

❺   **Fly Honeysuckle** *(Lonicera xylosteum)*
          Caprifoliaceae
1.2—2.5 m   IM: Twigs rod-shaped, hollow, not twining. Leaves with downy hairs.
             D: Flowers in pairs on the peduncle, axillary, ivory coloured. Leaves entire, round-elliptical.
             H: Deciduous and mixed woodland; more rarely in coniferous forest. Likes a porous, loamy, often rather stony soil. Calcicolous.
             AI: G; †

❻   **Common Honeysuckle** *(Lonicera periclymenum)*
          Caprifoliaceae
Up to 3 m   See p. 212

❶

8—25 cm

Small Alison *(Alyssum alyssoides; A. calycinum)*
Brassicaceae (Cruciferae)
See p. 144

❷

50—140 cm

Woad *(Isatis tinctoria)*
Brassicaceae (Cruciferae)
IM: Flowers in panicles. Fruits pendulous, broader towards the extremity, ultimately black.
D: Umbel-like panicles. Petals twice as long as sepals. Leaves bluish green, glabrous, with entire margins and with a heart-shaped or sagittate attachment to the stem.
H: Weedy places in vineyards, along waysides, more rarely in semi-dry turf. Likes a porous, chalky soil, rich in nitrogen. Prefers a warm situation. First cultivated over 2,000 years ago. Indigo is obtained from the plant. The pigment indigo is poisonous.
AI: P: ⊙; ♃; (†)

❸

20—100 cm

Flixweed *(Descurainia sophia; Sisymbrium sophia)*
Brassicaceae (Cruciferae)
IM: Ovaries and fruit more than 3 times as long as broad. Fruits possess 3 ribs on each side. Seeds form a single row in each locule. Leaves compound, bi- or tripinnate, subdivided into narrow segments.
D: Racemes. Petals up to 2 mm long.
H: Weedy places on verges, wasteland and embankments. Likes a warm situation and sandy or gravelly soils. An indicator of nitrogen.
AI: P; ⊙
     Flixweed was described in 16th-century herbals as 'sophia chirurgorum' (wisdom of surgeons), as it was alleged to further the healing of wounds. No active principle has so far been discovered in the plant.

❹

30—60 cm

Hedge Mustard *(Sisymbrium officinale)*
Brassicaceae (Cruciferae)
IM: Ovaries and fruit more than 3 times as long as broad. Fruits possess 3 ribs on each side. Seeds form a single row in each locule. Fruits erect, pressed against the stem. Lower leaves coarsely serrate.
D: Racemes. Flowers pale yellow. Petals up to 3 mm long.
H: Weedy places on waysides, wasteland and embankments, also on walls and ruins. Indicator of nitrogen.
AI: P; ⊙
     Old medicinal plant, but so far no active principle has been found in it.

❺

30—60 cm

Treacle Mustard *(Erysimum cheiranthoides)*
Brassicaceae (Cruciferae)
See p. 194

❻

30—60 cm

Gold of Pleasure *(Camelina sativa)*
Brassicaceae (Cruciferae)
IM: Petals 4—5 mm long. Fruits 5—10 mm long, pear-shaped.
D: Racemes. Leaves spreading, linear-lanceolate, with a sagittate base.
H: Weedy places in cornfields, wasteland, more rarely in vegetable fields or along waysides. Likes a porous soil in warm situations.
AI: P; ⊙

114

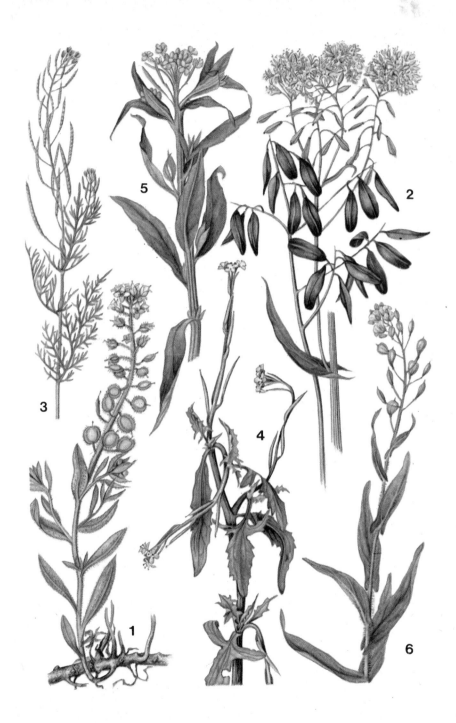

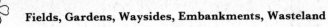

❶

15—50 cm

Paniculate Finchseed *(Neslia paniculata)*
Brassicaceae (Cruciferae)
IM: Flowers 2—6 mm in diameter. Fruit spherical, 1—2 mm in diameter, directed outwards.
D: Cymose panicles with numerous flowers. Flowers golden yellow. Stem simple or branched in the middle, with hairs towards the base. Leaves lanceolate, the upper ones narrower towards the petiole, the lower ones sessile, pointed and hairy.
H: Weedy places particularly in cornfields. Prefers loamy soils and warm situations; occasionally on loess soils.
AI: P; ⊙

❷

30—60 cm

Field Mustard *(Sinapis arvensis)*
Brassicaceae (Cruciferae)
IM: Ovaries and fruit more than 3 times as long as broad. Flowers yellow, 12—15 mm in diameter. Sepals spread out horizontally.
D: Umbel-like racemes. Leaves ovoid, undivided, the lower ones almost lyre-shaped, irregularly crenate or dentate.
H: Weedy places in fields and occasionally in gardens, also on wasteland. Likes a calcareous, loamy soil, rich in nutrients.
AI: P; ⊙
Contains mustard oil in the seeds. Old medicinal plant.

❸

30—60 cm

Wild Radish *(Raphanus raphanistrum)*
Brassicaceae (Cruciferae)
See p. 26

❹

20—60 cm

Wall Rocket, Wall Mustard, Stinkweed *(Diplotaxis muralis)*
Brassicaceae (Cruciferae)
IM: Flowers yellow, 8—15 mm in diameter. Ovary more than 3 times as long as broad and, like the fruit, compressed. Seeds form 2 rows in each locule. Peduncle only slightly longer than the open flower.
D: Stem leaves confined to the base.
H: Weedy places in vegetable fields, along roadsides, in walls, occasionally on stony wasteland and embankments. Likes porous, stony, loamy or sandy ground.
AI: P; ⊙; ⊖

❺

30—100 cm

Perennial Wall Rocket *(Diplotaxis tenuifolia)*
Brassicaceae (Cruciferae)
IM: Ovaries and fruit more than three times as long as wide, compressed. Flowers sulphur yellow or bright yellow, 12—20 mm in diameter. Seeds form 2 rows in each locule. Peduncle 2 or 3 times as long as the fully open flower.
D: Racemes with many flowers on the main stem and lateral branches. Stem woody at the base, mainly glabrous, with a dense concentration of leaves below the inflorescence. Leaves bluish green, mostly deeply pinnate.
H: Weedy places along waysides, on embankments, wasteland and uncultivated land. Likes a porous, calcareous soil.
AI: P; ♃

❶

30—60 cm

Winter Cress, Yellow Rocket *(Barbarea vulgaris)*
Brassicaceae (Cruciferae)
    See p. 194

❷

15—50 cm

Creeping Yellow Cress *(Rorippa sylvestris; Nasturtium sylvestre)*
Brassicaceae (Cruciferae)
IM: Petals clearly longer than the sepals, golden yellow. Ovaries and fruit more than 3 times as long as broad.
D: Cymose racemes. Stem branched, decumbent, hollow. Leaves pinnate.
H: Weedy places in damp meadows and along waysides, also sandy wasteland and banks of streams; more rarely on ruins. Likes a firm soil, rich in nitrogen. Indicator of muddy conditions. Somewhat calcifugous.
AI: P; ♃

❸

30—60 cm

Wild *or* Yellow Mignonette *(Reseda lutea)*
Resedaceae
IM: Leaves pinnate or bipinnate.
D: Dense racemes. Flowers pale yellow. Stem simple or branched.
H: Weedy places along waysides, on embankments, and wasteland; more rarely in vineyards and sunny vegetable fields. Likes a sandy, stony soil, but one which is rich in nutrients.
AI: P; ⊙—♃
Wild Mignonette contains mustard oil and flavone. A medicinal plant.

❹

30—100 cm

Greater Celandine *(Chelidonium majus)*
Papaveraceae
    See p. 168

❺

60—100 cm

Evening Primrose *(Oenothera biennis)*
Onagraceae (Oenotheraceae)
IM: Flowers 3—5 cm in diameter. Petals shorter than the sepals.
D: Flowers in spikes. Petals longer than the stamens. Basal leaves form a compressed rosette on the ground.
H: Weedy places on embankments, wasteland and occasionally on stony slopes. Likes a dry soil.
AI: P; ⊙
The flowers of the Evening Primrose open about 6 p.m. and close again about 24 hours later. Then the pollen appears on the anthers, but the stigma is still not receptive. The stigma becomes receptive towards the evening of the following day when the flower opens once again and is particularly fragrant. Pollination is by moths. The plant contains tannins in the leaves.

❻

40—100 cm

Small-flowered Evening Primrose *(Oenothera parviflora; O. muricata)*
Onagraceae (Oenotheraceae)
IM: Flowers 2—3 cm in diameter. Petals as long as sepals.
D: Flowers in spikes. Stamens as long as the petals. Basal leaves form a rosette on the ground.
H: Weedy places on embankments and wasteland. Likes a porous, sandy soil, rich in nitrogen. Prefers warm situations.
AI: P; ⊙

❶   **Sun Spurge** *(Euphorbia helioscopia)*
Euphorbiaceae
5—30 cm   IM: Cymes with 4—5 rays. Glands on the bracts transversely oval, bright yellow.
      D: Stems mostly erect. Leaves invert-oval, serrate anteriorly, glabrous. Plant
           has white, milky juice.
      H: Weedy places in vegetable fields, gardens and vineyards, also on wasteland.
           Likes a porous soil and indicates nitrogenous conditions.
      AI: P; ☉; †
           The Sun Spurge has its inflorescence drawn towards the sun, a fact known to
           Pliny. Hence its scientific specific name (Greek *helios* = sun; *skopein* = to look
           to). The milky juice contains the poison euphorbone.

❷   **Dwarf Spurge** *(Euphorbia exigua)*
Euphorbiaceae
5—25 cm   IM: Cyme with 3—5 rays, all of which are forked. Glands on the bracts crescent-
           shaped. Leaves 1—4 mm wide.
      D: Stem prostrate, decumbent or erect, usually richly branched. Leaves linear,
           sessile, pointed. Plant has white, milky juice.
      H: Weedy places in vegetable fields and wasteland, also on wayside verges and
           embankments. Likes a dry, calcareous soil.
      AI: P; ☉; †
           The flower of the various spurges is in reality a strongly involute inflorescence.
           Between the petalloid bracts are situated a single female and several male
           flowers. The milky juice of the Dwarf Spurge contains the poison euphorbone.

❸   **Purple Spurge** *(Euphorbia peplus)*
Euphorbiaceae
5—35 cm   IM: Cyme with 3 rays, all of which are forked. Glands on the bracts crescent-shaped.
           Leaves 5—10 mm wide.
      D: Stem erect and usually branched. Leaves alternate, invert-ovoid to round.
           Plant has white, milky juice.
      H: Weedy places in vegetable fields and on wasteland, also on roadside verges.
      AI: P; ☉; †
           For flower construction and poisonous qualities, see Dwarf Spurge above.

❹   **Cypress Spurge** *(Euphorbia cyparissias)*
Euphorbiaceae
15—30 cm   See p. 142

❺   **Crosswort** *(Cruciata laevipes; Galium cruciata; G. cruciatum)*
Rubiaceae
15—70 cm   See p. 168

❻   **Ladies' Bedstraw** *(Galium verum)*
Rubiaceae
15—60 cm   IM: Terminal panicles of many flowers. Leaves needle-shaped in whorls of 8—12.
      D: Flowers lemon yellow, smelling of honey. Stem erect or decumbent, round,
           with 4 prominent lines. Leaves white on the underside.
      H: Dry or semi-dry turf, wayside verges.
      AI: G; ♃
           This plant contains 1 g of rennin, the enzyme which curdles milk, in 100 g of
           the leaf tissue. Because of the presence of rennin in its leaves, this plant was
           formerly used in cheesemaking. An old medicinal plant.

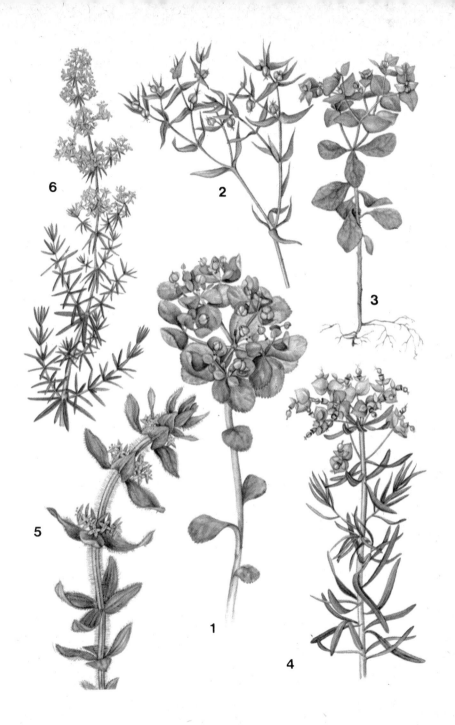

❶ **Spring Cinquefoil** *or* **Potentilla** *(Potentilla tabernaemontani; P. verna)*
Rosaceae
5—15 cm   IM: Panicles. Petals crenate, not overlapping at the edges. Stem sometimes creeping. Leaves with 5—7 leaflets or lobes. Palmate, without a silky gloss at the edge.
D: Stem usually with 3—5 flowers. Petals ovoid, light or dark yellow. Peduncle 1—2 cm long, often bending downwards after flowering has finished. Stem frequently with a reddish tinge, prostrate or decumbent, usually hairy. Stem leaves often decreasing in size towards the top of the stem, the upper leaves sessile and usually undivided. The plants grow in small cushion-like clumps.
H: Dry or semi-dry turf, roadside verges, walls, more rarely on sandy hillsides covered with rock debris or on screes. Likes porous, rather chalky ground and a warm situation.
AI: P; ♃
This species consists of numerous races which are difficult to distinguish. One striking feature of the races is that the more westerly and northerly races are much more hairy than the southern and eastern ones, also that the races associated with moist, shady habitats are less hairy.

❷ **Creeping** *or* **Common Cinquefoil** *(Potentilla reptans)*
Rosaceae
30—60 cm   See p. 146

❸ **Silverweed** *(Potentilla anserina)*
Rosaceae
15—50 cm   See p. 198

❹ **Hoary Potentilla** *(Potentilla argentea)*
Rosaceae
10—40 cm   IM: Panicles. Stem densely covered with hairs. Leaves divided into 5—7 digitate lobes. Leaflets rolled up at the edges with a dense covering of white hairs on the undersides.
D: Leaves rather small, about 1—1.5 cm in diameter. Peduncle erect or spreading after flowering. Stem erect or decumbent, with white hairs.
H: Waysides, banks, uncultivated sandy soils. Likes a shallow, porous, stony or sandy soil. Calcifugous.
AI: P; ♃
Within the species are numerous races which differ in the division of the leaves into leaflets, the growth form of the stem and their hairiness.

❺ **Corn Buttercup** *(Ranunculus arvensis)*
Ranunculaceae
30—60 cm   IM: Flowers only 4—15 mm in diameter, sulphur yellow. Fruits (and carpels of flowers) strikingly prickly.
D: Inflorescence of several flowers. Stem erect or decumbent, richly branched. Lower leaves undivided, cuneate, dentate. Upper leaves divided into narrow segments.
H: Weedy places, particularly in cornfields (hence name). Likes a loamy soil.
AI: P; ☉; †
Contains the poisonous substances protoanemonine and anemonine.

122

❶ **Creeping Buttercup** *(Ranunculus repens)*
Ranunculaceae
15—50 cm
See p. 148

---

❷ **Bulbous Crowfoot** *(Ranunculus bulbosus)*
Ranunculaceae
15—30 cm
IM: Sepals reflexed and pressed against the peduncle.
D: Flowers solitary, terminal. Peduncle grooved. Stem widens to a bulb at ground level (usually just under the soil surface). Lower leaves with long petioles, divided into 3 parts (often doubly divided).
H: Semi-dry turf, dry meadows, roadside verges. Likes a warm, chalky soil.
AI: P; ♃; †
The scientific generic name refers to the shape of the fruits (Latin *ranunculus* = little frog).

---

❸ **Herb Bennet, Wood** *or* **Common Avens** *(Geum urbanum)*
Rosaceae
25—50 cm
See p. 172

---

❹ **Creeping Jenny, Moneywort** *(Lysimachia nummularia)*
Primulaceae
5—30 cm
See p. 176

---

❺ **Trailing St John's Wort** *(Hypericum humifusum)*
Hypericaceae
5—15 cm
IM: Stem prostrate.
D: Panicles. Stamens clustered. Stem round or angular. Leaves opposite, linear-ovoid, the upper leaves with transparent dots.
H: Weedy places in wet vegetable fields, on uncultivated soil, along roadsides, and in damp, open woodland. Likes a moist, sandy or loamy soil. Calcifugous.
AI: P; ⊙—♃
Name and pigmentation: see Common St John's Wort, p. 150.

---

❻ **Yellow Portulaca** *(Portulaca oleracea)*
Portulacaceae
10—30 cm
IM: No possibility of confusion with other species.
D: Flowers small, solitary or 2—3. Petals are shed early. Stem prostrate to decumbent, often with a pinkish tinge. Leaves 1—2 cm long, fleshy, sessile, wedge-shaped to invert-ovoid.
H: Weedy places in vegetable fields, along waysides and on wasteland. Likes a warm situation and a sandy soil, rich in nitrogen.
AI: P; ⊙—⊙
This plant contains much vitamin C and was formerly used as a herb against scurvy. The flowers of the Yellow Portulaca are normally self-fertilized. The seeds are dispersed by ants.

❶

15—30 cm

Common Rockrose *(Helianthemum nummularium ; H. vulgare ; H. chamaecistus)*
Cistaceae
IM: No possibility of confusion with other species.
D: Terminal racemes of few flowers, which are lemon yellow. Stamens not fasciculate. Sepals often with reddish stripes. Stem woody at the base, prostrate or decumbent. Leaves opposite, entire, oval and ciliate.
H: Dry and semi-dry turf, more rarely on roadside verges. Likes a shallow, stony, calcareous soil in warm situations.
AI: P ; ♃
The stamens spread out in the sunshine, whereas in cloudy weather they stay more erect.

❷

30—60 cm

Henbane *(Hyoscyamus niger)*
Solanaceae
IM: Flowers dirty yellow to orange yellow with violet veins.
D: Several axillary, funnel-shaped flowers to the inflorescence. Stem with sticky hairs. Leaves coarsely digitate, the lower ones stalked, the upper ones clasping the stem at their bases.
H: Weedy places on wasteland, walls and waysides, also often on compost heaps in fields. Likes a loamy, nitrogenous soil in warm situations.
AI: G; ⊙; ⊙; †
Contains a very poisonous alkaloid.

❸

80—200 cm

Large-flowered Mullein *(Verbascum thapsiforme)*
Scrophulariaceae
See p. 178

❹

30—150 cm

Great Mullein, Small-flowered Mullein, Aaron's Rod *(Verbascum thapsus)*
Scrophulariaceae
IM: Flowers 1.5—2 cm in diameter.
D: Dense racemes, with glandular hairs. Flowers have attractive scent. Stem erect. Leaves finely crenate; both surfaces have yellow felt-like covering of hairs, decurrent.
H: Weedy places along roadsides, on embankments and wasteland, also on the edges of woodland and in clearings. Likes a shallow, porous, often stony soil, rich in nitrogen. Found in warm situations.
AI: G; ⊙
Contains saponin and mucilage.

❺

30—100 cm

Dark Mullein *(Verbascum nigrum)*
Scrophulariaceae
IM: Anthers violet or reddish.
D: Racemes. Stem angular at the top. Leaves not decurrent, crenate; the upper sides almost smooth, the lower sides hairy.
H: Weedy places on wasteland, along paths, roadside verges, embankments and in clearings. Likes a sandy, loamy soil, deficient in lime but nitrogenous.
AI: G; ⊙
Contains saponin and mucilage.

❻

50—130 cm

White Mullein *(Verbascum lychnitis)*
Scrophulariaceae
See p. 48

---

❶

5—15 cm

Yellow *or* **Biting Stonecrop, Wall Pepper** *(Sedum acre)*
Crassulaceae
See p. 192

---

❷

5—15 cm

Tasteless Sedum, Insipid Stonecrop *(Sedum sexangulare; S. boloniense; S. mite)*
Crassulaceae
See p. 152

---

❸

30—130 cm

Common Agrimony *(Agrimonia eupatoria)*
Rosaceae
IM: Flowers in long multiflorous racemes.
D: Stem erect, with coarse hairs. Leaves discontinuously unpaired pinnate. Leaflets linear-lanceolate, sessile, serrate, the unpaired terminal leaflet stalked.
H: Semi-dry turf, roadside verges, edges of woods, sunny woodland paths. Likes a porous soil in warm situations.
AI: P; ♃
The specific name *eupatoria* is derived from a Greek legend. It is said that King Mithridates Eupator (132—63 B.C.) was the first person to discover the healing powers of Agrimony. The plant contains tannins in all its organs, but particularly in the leaves. An old medicinal plant.

---

❹

30—100 cm

Common Comfrey, Knitbone *(Symphytum officinale)*
Boraginaceae
See p. 178

---

❺

20—100 cm

Falcate Hare's-ear *(Bupleurum falcatum)*
Apiaceae (Umbelliferae)
IM: Flowers in umbels. Leaves entire, the upper ones falcate, narrow-lanceolate, not clasping the stem.
D: Umbels compound. Stem erect or decumbent.
H: Dry woodland and thickets, edges of woods, more rarely on roadside verges and semi-dry turf near woods. Likes a calcareous soil.
AI: P; ♃
One species of the genus has leaves like a hare's ears, hence the name.

---

❻

30—100 cm

Common Parsnip *(Pastinaca sativa)*
Apiaceae (Umbelliferae)
IM: Flowers in umbels, golden-yellow. Umbels with 5—15 rays. Bracts and bracteoles absent or reduced to 1—2 leaflets. Stem hairy. Leaves pinnate or bipinnate.
D: Umbels compound. Stem erect, branched at top. Plant has a carrot-like smell (rub the leaves).
H: Meadows, weedy places on roadsides, wasteland and in cornfields, more rarely on embankments. Likes a deep, loamy soil, rich in nitrogen.
AI: P; ☉
The plant is sometimes cultivated on account of its aromatic root. The root extract has been used as an additive to Schnaps. The leaves are used as a wild vegetable. The root is rich in protein, starch, pectin and contains about 30 mg vitamin C per 100 g fresh weight.

❶   **Field Gagea** *(Gagea villosa; G. arvensis)*

5—15 cm   Liliaceae

IM: Petals pointed. Two basal leaves present.

D: Cymes composed of 2—10 flowers, from among which spring two narrow leaves. Leaves grass green, 1—2 mm wide, longitudinally grooved. 2 bulbs.

H: Weedy places. Likes a non-calcareous soil, rich in nutrients. Frequently found on sandy soil in warm situations.

AI: M; ♃

❷   **Meadow Gagea** *(Gagea pratensis)*

6—20 cm   Liliaceae

IM: Only one basal leaf and that deeply keeled.

D: Cymes composed of 1—5 flowers, from among which spring 2 narrow leaves. Flowers are yellow, with green stripes on the outside. Leaves 3—4 mm wide, somewhat fleshy, longer than the stem. Near to the bulb from which the flower head springs are two more bulbils.

H: Weedy places, particularly in vegetable fields, also on semi-dry turf, along roadsides and on verges. Likes a warm soil rich in nitrogen. Prefers loamy and loess soils.

AI: M; ♃

❸   **Colt's-foot** *(Tussilago farfara)*

10—30 cm   Asteraceae (Compositae)

See p. 202

❹   **Dandelion** *(Taraxacum officinale)*

10—60 cm   Cichoriaceae (Compositae)

IM: Flowers in one large, solitary capitulum. Only ray florets present. Carpels with a pappus. Stem leafless, hollow, with white sap, which leaves brown stains on the skin after handling the plant.

D: Leaves form a basal rosette, jagged.

H: Fields, meadows, gardens, roadsides, wasteland, sparse woods; in fact, almost anywhere. Likes soil rich in nitrogen.

AI: G; ♃

Medicinal plant. Contains an alkaloid which is said to be slightly poisonous. Young leaves often used in a 'wild' salad.

❺   **Mouse-ear Hawkweed** *(Hieracium pilosella)*

8—30 cm   Cichoriaceae (Compositae)

See p. 192

❻   **Smooth Hawk's-beard** *(Crepis capillaris)*

15—50 cm   Cichoriaceae (Compositae)

IM: Flowers in a capitulum, which measures 1—1.5 cm in diameter arranged in a cymose manner. Carpels with a pappus. Hairs white and readily bent (press down with finger on points of hairs. Cf. Mouse-ear Hawkweed, p. 192).

D: Outer ray florets often reddish. Lower part of stem often with reddish leaves. Leaves coarsely serrate, jagged, the upper ones linear, the lower ones sagittate.

H: Weedy places along paths, in parks, on grazing land and meadows. Likes a rich, nitrogenous loamy soil.

AI: G; ☉

The genus contains several more species which are difficult to distinguish.

❶

30—60 cm

Wood *or* **Wall Hawkweed** *(Hieracium sylvaticum; H. murorum)*
Cichoriaceae (Compositae)
IM: Flowers in paniculately arranged capitula. Only ray florets present. Carpels with a pappus. Hairs on pappus greyish white, fragile (to the touch). Stem usually has 1—2 leaves.
D: Leaves with rough hairs, more or less toothed, rosette-like.
H: Deciduous and mixed woodland, coniferous forest, mountain forest, dry woodland, also along paths and on walls. Likes a stony soil, rich in humus.
AI: G; ♃
A species which may be divided into many races and which itself is very difficult to distinguish from similar species.

❷

15—50 cm

Autumnal Hawkbit *(Leontodon autumnalis)*
Cichoriaceae (Compositae)
See p. 156

❸

5—15 cm

Slender Cudweed, Field *or* **Dwarf Filago** *(Filago minima)*
Asteraceae (Compositae)
IM: 3—7 small capitula in clusters; only ray florets present. Bracts with woolly hairs. Leaves undivided.
D: Capitulum about 3 mm long; 3—6 capitula in each cluster at the end of a shoot. Leaves very small. Stem erect or decumbent. Leaves mostly under 1 cm long, entire, covered in a grey felt.
H: Dunes, sandy turf, roadside verges. Likes an open, porous, sandy soil. Somewhat calcifugous.
AI: G; ☉

❹

10—120 cm

Nipplewort *(Lapsana communis)*
Cichoriaceae (Compositae)
IM: Flowers in small capitula arranged in a paniculate manner. Only ray florets present. Carpels without a pappus of hairs. Leaves present on stem.
D: Capitulum with 8—12 pale yellow flowers. Stem richly branched. Lower leaves lyre-shaped, with a very large terminal segment; upper leaves lanceolate. Plant has a milky juice.
H: Weedy places in vegetable fields, in gardens, on wasteland, in thickets, woodland clearings and on the edges of woods. Likes a rather moist, rich and nitrogenous soil.
AI: G; ☉
The flowers open between 6 and 7 a.m. and close between 3 and 4 p.m.

❺

15—40 cm

Rayless Mayweed *(Matricaria discoidea; M. matricarioides; M. suaveolens)*
Asteraceae (Compositae)
IM: Flowers in hemispherical, greenish-yellow capitula. The majority of flowers possess only disc florets, more rarely a few white ray florets may be present. Leaves double pinnate. The plant has an aromatic smell.
D: Stem erect, branched, glabrous, richly provided with leaves.
H: Weedy places along wayside verges, on walls, embankments and sports fields, also in cornfields. Likes a loamy soil rich in nitrogen.
AI: G; ☉
Contains an ethereal oil (smell), which lacks the healing properties of true chamomile oil however.

1　　　　　　　　2　　　3　　　4

❶

60—130 cm

Tansy *(Tanacetum vulgare ; Chrysanthemum vulgare ; C. tanacetum)*
Asteraceae (Compositae)
IM: Flowers in small capitula arranged in a cymose manner. All flowers consist only of disc florets. Carpels without pappus of hairs. Leaves double pinnate.
D: Capitula hemispherical. Marginal florets occasionally with much shorter corollas. Stem angular, hollow. Leaflets serrate.
H: Weedy places along waysides and embankments, on wasteland, and the edges of woods, in thickets and woodland clearings. Likes a loamy soil rich in nitrogen.
AI: G; ♃; †
Tansy contains ethereal oils and an alkaloid. Medicinal plant.

❷

60—130 cm

Prickly Lettuce *(Lactuca serriola ; L. scariola)*
Cichoriaceae (Compositae)
IM: Flowers in capitula arranged in a paniculate manner. Only ligulate flowers. Carpels with pappus of hairs. Leaves on stem set perpendicularly.
D: Stem mostly whitish green. Leaves linear, coarsely digitate and sagittate at the base; sharply dentate. Plant has a milky juice.
H: Weedy places on verges, embankments and wasteland. Likes a rather stony soil, rich in nitrogen.
AI: G; ⊙; ⊖; (†)
The margins of the leaves are always arranged in a north-south direction, in this way they avoid the strong radiation and heat of the sun at noon (a compass plant). Experiments have shown that leaves exposed to the full heat of the midday sun may attain temperatures 3.6—7.6°C above those set like the leaves of this species. Prickly Lettuce contains a mildly poisonous alkaloid in its milky juice.

❸

15—50 cm

Viscous Senecio *or* **Ragwort** *(Senecio viscosus)*
Asteraceae (Compositae)
See p. 182

❹

15—50 cm

Groundsel *(Senecio vulgaris)*
Asteraceae (Compositae)
IM: Flowers in capitula arranged in a paniculate manner. Only disc florets present. Leaves digitate, often with a cobweb-like covering of hairs.
D: Bracts with black specks.
H: Weedy places in fields, gardens, wasteland and compost heaps. Found on a variety of soils although it prefers nitrogenous ones.
AI: G; ⊙; †
Contains a poisonous alkaloid.

❺

30—100 cm

Narrow-leaved Senecio *or* **Ragwort** *(Senecio erucifolius)*
Asteraceae (Compositae)
See p. 182

❻

30—100 cm

Common Ragwort *(Senecio jacobaea)*
Asteraceae (Compositae)
See p. 182

134

❶

30 — 100 cm

Common Sowthistle (*Sonchus oleraceus*)
Cichoriaceae (Compositae)
IM: Flowers in capitula. Only ray florets present. Carpels with pappus of hairs. Stem branched. Leaves with prickly teeth, sagittate at the base, with auricles.
D: Capitula arranged in a cymose manner. Ray florets with brownish-red stripes on the back. Stem erect, branched, hollow. Leaves coarsely toothed. Plant contains a milky juice.
H: Weedy places in vegetable fields, gardens, vineyards and on wasteland, also on roadside verges. Likes a rich, nitrogenous soil.
AI: G; ⊙
The Common Sowthistle was eaten as a vegetable in the Middle Ages.

❷

50 — 150 cm

Corn Sowthistle (*Sonchus arvensis*)
Cichoriaceae (Compositae)
IM: Flowers in capitula arranged in a cymose manner. Only ray florets present. Carpels with a pappus of hairs. Only the inflorescence is branched, the rest of the stem is not. Leaves with prickly teeth. Rootstock creeping.
D: Bracts and inflorescence covered with glandular hairs. Leaves coarsely serrate and pinnate. Stem leaves undivided, with more or less oppressed auricles. Plant possesses a milky juice.
H: Weedy places in vegetable fields, gardens, vineyards and on wasteland, also on roadsides. Likes a rich, nitrogenous soil.
AI: G; ♃
The flowers only open in sunny weather, commencing between 7 and 8 a.m. and closing again between 10 a.m. and 2 p.m. The plant contains an alkaloid.

❸

90 — 150 cm

Mugwort (*Artemisia vulgaris*)
Asteraceae (Compositae)
See p. 184

❹

5 — 30 cm

Bird's-foot Trefoil (*Lotus corniculatus*)
Fabaceae (Leguminosae)
See p. 160

❺

10 — 30 cm

Kidney Vetch, Lady's Fingers (*Anthyllis vulneraria*)
Fabaceae (Leguminosae)
IM: Flowers in heads. Leaves unpaired pinnate. Terminal leaves linear-ovoid, much bigger than the lateral leaves which are often missing.
D: Stem prostrate or decumbent. Lowest leaves often undivided. Stem leaves pinnate, leaflets linear.
H: Dry or semi-dry turf, roadside verges. Likes a porous, sandy, loamy soil or one with stones; somewhat calcicolous, and has a preference for warm situations.
AI: P; ♃
Kidney Vetch was formerly used as a plant to heal wounds. It contains saponin. On occasion the plant is grown on shallow, dry, chalky soils as a fodder plant. It can be cut only once a year.

❶

8—30 cm

Horseshoe Vetch *(Hippocrepis comosa)*
Fabaceae (Leguminosae)
See p. 162

❷

10—50 cm

Golden Clover *or* **Trefoil** *(Trifolium aureum ; T. strepens)*
Fabaceae (Leguminosae)
IM: 20—50 flowers in a 7—10 mm broad head. Petals persist after flowering; light brown in colour. The 3 leaflets have petioles of equal length.
D: Stem erect, glabrous. Leaflets linear-lanceolate.
H: Semi-dry turf, heaths, roadside verges. Rather calcifugous and an indicator of surface acidity.
AI: P; ⊙; ⊖

❸

10—40 cm

Black Medick, Nonsuch *(Medicago lupulina)*
Fabaceae (Leguminosae)
IM: Flowers 2—5 mm long, in spherical or ovoid heads. 10—15 flowers to the head. Petals fall off immediately after flowering. Leaves composed of 3 leaflets.
D: Stem erect or prostrate. Leaflets with hairy undersides.
H: Semi-dry turf, meadows, roadside verges, embankments. Usually on a loamy soil, rich in nutrients, particularly nitrogen.
AI: P; ⊙; ⊖; ♃
The name Black Medick refers to the colour of the seeds which are jet black.

❹

5—30 cm

Hop Trefoil, Yellow Field Clover *(Trifolium campestre ; T. procumbens)*
Fabaceae (Leguminosae)
See p. 164

❺

10—20 cm

Heart's-ease, Field *or* **Wild Pansy** *(Viola tricolor)*
Violaceae
See p. 160

❻

30—100 cm

Birthwort, Erect Aristolochia *(Aristolochia clematitis)*
Aristolochiaceae
IM: No possibility of confusion with other species.
D: Flowers axillary, consisting of long tubes which are expanded spherically at the base. Stem erect or slightly twining. Leaves heart-shaped to ovoid, with long petioles.
H: Weedy places, particularly in vineyards, occasionally on walls or on roadside verges, in thickets and valley woodland. Likes warm situations and a calcareous soil.
AI: G; ♃; †
The flowers of Birthwort are of the 'fly-trap' variety. The inside of the cone-shaped orifice is so smooth, as a result of a waxy secretion, that any fly landing on it slips down into the 'trap' at the base of the tube. Projecting hairs prevent the fly crawling out. If it has brought pollen from another plant of this species the stigmas at the bottom of the corolla tube become dusted with the pollen and fertilization is achieved. By then the guard hairs will have wilted and the fly can escape. Old medicinal plant containing unknown poisonous substance.

138

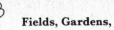

❶ **Common Toadflax** *(Linaria vulgaris)*

30—60 cm
Scrophulariaceae
IM: No possibility of confusion with other species.
D: Racemes. Flowers with a long spur. Lower lip with an orange fleck. Stem usually erect. Leaves linear-lanceolate, rolled back at the edge.
H: Weedy places on embankments, waysides, walls, hedgerows. More rarely in vineyards, cornfields, and woodland clearings. Likes a porous, stony or sandy soil and prefers warm situations.
AI: G; ♃
The flowers of Common Toadflax are pollinated by bumblebees. Seed production is extremely high (up to 32,000 per plant). Old medicinal plant, containing flavone.

❷ **Lesser Balsam** *(Impatiens parviflora)*

20—60 cm
Balsaminaceae
IM: Flowers erect, small, with long spurs. Spurs straight, bright yellow.
D: 4—10 flowers in racemose, axillary inflorescences. Stem somewhat glassy, swollen at the nodes. Leaves ovoid, serrate.
H: Deciduous and mixed woodland, thickets, gardens, wasteland. Likes a porous soil, poor in calcareous material, but moist and containing nitrogen. Shade-loving.
AI: P; ⊙; (†)
Name, poisonous qualities and seed-dispersal mechanism, see Yellow Balsam, p. 204.

❸ **Arrowhead Broom** *(Genistella sagittalis; Genista sagittalis)*

15—25 cm
Fabaceae (Leguminosae)
IM: Stem winged, with few leaves. Leaves ovoid-lanceolate, hairy.
D: Flowers in terminal, dense racemes. Stem decumbent to erect. Leaves alternate, sessile, linear, pointed.
H: Semi-dry turf, sloping meadows, roadside verges, light, dry woodland habitats, heaths, occasionally also on rocks. Somewhat calcifugous, and an indicator of superficial acidity.
AI: P
The winged stem is an adaptation to drought and strong sunlight. The 'wings' are organs of assimilation which conserve water. When growing in moist, shady places, and under certain experimental conditions, this plant may develop a stem covered in leaves and with hardly any 'wings'.

❹ **Sickle Medick** *(Medicago falcata)*

20—50 cm
Fabaceae (Leguminosae)
See p. 162

❺ **Yellow Vetchling** *(Lathyrus aphaca)*

15—50 cm
Fabaceae (Leguminosae)
IM: Long tendrils between 2 large, heart-shaped or ovoid, blue-green leaves (really stipules).
D: Flowers mostly solitary. Stem decumbent or climbing. Whole plant blue green.
H: Weedy places in cornfields. Likes a chalky, loamy soil.
AI: P; ⊙

140

❶ **Common Melilot** *(Melilotus officinalis)*

30—120 cm
Fabaceae (Leguminosae)

IM: Flowers in long, narrow, erect, axillary racemes. Leaves trifoliate. The dried fruit smells like Woodruff.

D: Stem decumbent to erect. Leaflets invert-ovoid, dentate.

H: Wayside verges, embankments. Indicator of nitrogen.

AI: P; ⊙

The smell of Woodruff is due to coumarin, which the plant contains as an organic complex and which is released on drying. Medicinal plant.

❷ **Purple** *or* **Cow Wheat** *(Melampyrum arvense)*

10—30 cm
Scrophulariaceae

See p. 228

❸ **Hairy Yellow Rattle** *(Rhinanthus alectorolophus; Alectorolophus hirsutus)*

10—50 cm
Scrophulariaceae

See p. 166

❹ **Branched Broomrape** *(Orobanche ramosa)*

3—40 cm
Orobanchaceae

IM: Flowers 1—1.5 cm long. Stem branched; plant brownish yellow to pale yellow.

D: Loose spikes with many flowers. Petals pale yellow with blue or violet border.

H: Vegetable fields, where it is a root parasite of tobacco, hemp, potatoes and maize. Numerous in those localities where it occurs.

AI: G; ⊙; (†)

Produces over 100,000 seeds per plant, which because of their lightness are readily carried by the wind. Contains aucubin (cf. Red Rattle, p. 278).

❺ **Lesser Broomrape** *(Orobanche minor; O. barbata)*

10—50 cm
Orobanchaceae

See p. 166

Meadows, Pastures, Grazing Land   **Yellow**

❻ **Cypress Spurge** *(Euphorbia cyparissias)*

15—30 cm
Euphorbiaceae

IM: Cyme with 4 rays. Stem densely covered with leaves, which are narrow and linear, 1—2 mm wide. Plant bluish green. Exudes a milky juice when cut.

D: Stem erect or decumbent. Leaves alternate, glabrous, entire.

H: Dry or semi-dry turf, poor pasture, wayside verges, also on old rubbish dumps and tips. Likes a shallow soil.

AI: P; ♃; †

Flowers: See Dwarf Spurge, p. 120.

The milky juice contains the poisonous substance euphorbone. The plant is not eaten by cattle. It is, however, worth noting that it is the sole foodplant for caterpillars of the Spurge Hawk moth. The Cypress Spurge is also the intermediate host of Pea Rust fungus. Plants affected by the fungus have an unusual appearance: they are likely to be unbranched, with small, ovoid leaves and no flowers. The stem and leaves of the diseased plant are yellowish green and there are pinkish-red pustules on the undersides of the leaves.

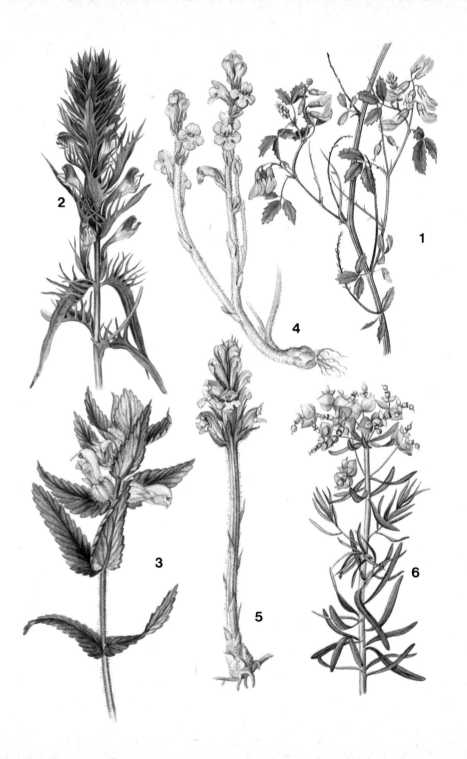

❶ **Mountain Alison** *(Alyssum montanum)*
Brassicaceae (Cruciferae)
5—20 cm   IM: Flowers golden yellow, 3—8 mm in diameter. Carpels and fruits at the most 3 times as long as broad, 5—8 mm long, lens-shaped. Leaves entire, with a greyish downy covering.
     D: Dense racemes. Stem with lower part woody, richly branched. Leaves invert-ovoid to lanceolate; lower leaves petiolate, upper leaves sessile.
     H: Dry turf and strips of turf on rock debris. Likes a porous, calcareous, loamy soil in warm situations. Forms numerous small clusters in those localities where it does occur.
     AI: P; ♃

❷ **Small Alison** *(Alyssum alyssoides; A. calycinum)*
Brassicaceae (Cruciferae)
8—25 cm   IM: Flowers pale yellow to whitish yellow, 1—4 mm in diameter. Carpels and fruits 3 times as long as broad, 2—4 mm long, hairy. Leaves entire, with a greyish downy covering.
     D: Dense racemes. Stem erect or decumbent, branched. Lower leaves invert-ovoid, upper leaves lanceolate.
     H: Dry and semi-dry turf, stony slopes, embankments, walls, roadside verges, occasionally in weedy places in vineyards and meadows and on south-facing slopes. Likes a calcareous, nitrogenous soil.
     AI: P; ☉

❸ **Smooth Biscutella** *(Biscutella laevigata)*
Brassicaceae (Cruciferae)
15—30 cm   See p. 168

❹ **Common Meadow Rue** *(Thalictrum flavum)*
Ranunculaceae
50—120 cm   IM: Flowers in clusters in a panicle. Leaflets ovoid to linear-lanceolate.
     D: Flowers erect, with a pleasant smell and 4 pointed petals, which fall off soon after opening. Stamens yellow. Stem erect, glabrous, grooved, usually un-branched. Lower leaves petiolate, upper leaves sessile, bi- or tripinnate.
     H: Moist meadows, mosses and fens. Likes a wet, loamy soil which dries out in summer.
     AI: P; ♃

❺ **Crosswort** *(Cruciata laevipes; Galium cruciata; G. cruciatum)*
Rubiaceae
15—70 cm   See p. 168

❻ **Ladies' Bedstraw** *(Galium verum)*
Rubiaceae
15—60 cm   See p. 120

❶ **Common Tormentil** *(Potentilla erecta; P. tormentilla; Tormentilla erecta)*
Rosaceae
15—30 cm   See p. 196

---

❷ **Spring Cinquefoil** *or* **Potentilla** *(Potentilla tabernaemontani; P. verna)*
Rosaceae
5—15 cm   See p. 122

---

❸ **Creeping** *or* **Common Cinquefoil** *(Potentilla reptans)*
Rosaceae
30—60 cm   IM: Flowers solitary in the leaf axils, 1.5—2.5 cm in diameter. 5 petals. Leaves
mostly palmately divided into 5 leaflets (sometimes only 3).
D: Stem creeping to decumbent. Leaflets invert-ovoid, hairy underneath.
H: Damp meadows, roadside verges, wasteland, also in fields and vineyards.
Likes a deep, somewhat dense soil, more rarely on sand or gravel. An indicator
of nitrogenous conditions.
AI: P; ♃
The rootstock and leaves contain tannins.

---

❹ **Oxlip** *(Primula elatior)*
Primulaceae
15—30 cm   See p. 170

---

❺ **Cowslip** *(Primula veris; P. officinalis)*
Primulaceae
15—30 cm   IM: Flowers golden yellow with orange flecks. Corolla campanulate.
D: Onesided umbels. Leaves form a basal rosette, linear-ovoid, crenate, wrinkled.
H: Dry, deciduous and mixed woodland, more rarely in open coniferous forest,
thickets and alpine meadows. Likes a calcareous, porous soil in warm situations.
AI: G; ♃
The scientific name *Primula* is derived from the Latin *primus* (first) and
refers to the early flowering time. The plant contains saponin, particularly in
the root. An old medicinal plant. The leaves are also rich in vitamin C, but
because of their saponin content cannot be used as human food.

---

❻ **Meadow Silaus** *(Silaum silaus; Silaus pratensis)*
Apiaceae (Umbelliferae)
30—100 cm   IM: Flowers pale yellow, in umbels, with 5—10 rays. Bracts absent or reduced to
1—2. Bracteoles of 4 leaves. Leaves tri- or quadripinnate. Leaf segments linear
with spiny serrations.
D: Umbels compound. Stem with medulla. Leaves at the top of the stem only
simply pinnate.
H: Meadows, semi-dry turf. Likes a moist, loamy soil, which must dry out
during the summer months.
AI: P; ♃
The Meadow Silaus is one of the foodplants of the caterpillars of the Swallowtail
butterfly. They can be occasionally found on the plant in August.

❶   **Marsh Marigold, Kingcup** *(Caltha palustris)*
Ranunculaceae
15—50 cm   See p. 170

---

❷   **Mountain Buttercup** *(Ranunculus montanus)*
Ranunculaceae
8—40 cm

IM: Plant small. Stem with a single flower, or, more rarely, a few flowers; not hollow. Basal leaves partly evergreen.

D: Peduncle round, not grooved. Stem erect, with 1—2 sessile leaves, divided into lobes. Basal leaves divided into digitate segments. Leaflets may, or may not, be deeply indented or crenate.

H: Semi-dry meadows and shady valleys where the snow is late to melt ('snow-valleys') in the mountains, screes. Likes a stony, calcareous soil.

AI: P; ♃; †
Contains the poisonous substances protoanemonine and anemonine.

---

❸   **Acrid Crowfoot, Acrid Buttercup** *(Ranunculus acris; R. acer)*
Ranunculaceae
30—100 cm

IM: Flowers golden yellow. Peduncle round, not grooved. Basal leaves deeply divided, tripinnate to 5-fold pinnate. Plant glabrous or covered with closely set hairs.

D: Flowers in loose panicles. Sepals yellow, with adpressed hairs. Lower leaves with long petioles, palmate with 5—7 lobes or segments, upper leaves sessile. Petioles become progressively shorter towards the top of the plant. Leaflets cleft.

H: Meadows. Likes a rather moist, nitrogenous loamy soil. This is the species which gives a golden hue to meadows in the middle of May.

AI: P; ♃; †
Acrid Buttercup is not grazed by cattle and therefore the groups of plants form ungrazed 'islands' in meadows and pastures where cattle are kept. Because of the acrid taste of the poisonous anemonine the fresh plant is not eaten by any grazing animals. On drying the plant loses its poisonous qualities.

---

❹   **Bulbous Buttercup** *(Ranunculus bulbosus)*
Ranunculaceae
15—30 cm   See p. 124

---

❺   **Creeping Buttercup** *(Ranunculus repens)*
Ranunculaceae
15—50 cm

IM: Stem with aerial, creeping runners which often root at the leaf attachments. Basal leaves divided into 3 segments, each of which is dissected. Middle segment with a distinct stalk.

D: Flowers solitary in the leaf axils, about 2—3 cm in diameter, golden yellow, glossy. Leaves with 3—5 segments. Leaflets lobed or crenate.

H: Banks of rivers or ponds, weedy places in gardens, wet fields and meadows, wet verges, valley woodland. Likes a damp, loamy soil and is an indicator of nitrogen.

AI: P; ♃; (†)
Contains protoanemonine and is therefore slightly poisonous.

❶ **Creeping Jenny, Moneywort** *(Lysimachia nummularia)*
Primulaceae
5—30 cm   See p. 176

---

❷ **Common Rockrose** *(Helianthemum nummularium; H. vulgare; H. chamaecistus)*
Cistaceae
15—30 cm IM: No possibility of confusion with other species.
       D: Terminal racemes of few flowers which are lemon yellow. Stamens are fasciculate. Sepals often with reddish stripes. Stem woody at the base, prostrate or decumbent. Leaves opposite, entire, oval and ciliate.
       H: Dry and semi-dry turf, more rarely on roadside verges. Likes a shallow, stony, calcareous soil in warm situations.
      AI: P; ♃
          The stamens spread out in the sunshine, whereas in cloudy weather they stay more erect.

---

❸ **Imperforate St John's Wort** *(Hypericum maculatum)*
Hypericaceae
15—40 cm IM: Plant glabrous. Stem erect, round, with 4 raised ridges.
       D: Cymose racemes. Stamens fasciculate. Stem erect or decumbent. Leaves opposite, sessile, broadly ovoid with faint spotting.
       H: Moist to wet meadows, mountain pastures. Likes a rather acid soil which is at least moist to wet part of the time.
      AI: P; ♃
          For generic name see Perforate St John's Wort below.

---

❹ **Common** *or* **Perforate St John's Wort** *(Hypericum perforatum)*
Hypericaceae
30—60 cm IM: Plant glabrous. Stem erect, round, with 2 raised ridges.
       D: Umbel-like panicles. Stamens fasciculate. Leaves opposite, linear-oval, transparently punctate (oil glands).
       H: Mixed and deciduous woodland, coniferous forest, particularly in open places, clearings in woods and the edge of woodland, on sparse meadows, heathland and semi-dry turf. On various kinds of soil.
      AI: P; ♃
          The name St John's Wort is derived from the time of flowering of these plants (24 June is St John's Day). The St John's Wort plays an important role in folk superstition as its crushed flowers are coloured red (the symbol of blood). The red pigment hypericine exists as crystals in the flowers and is responsible for illness in animals which have eaten the plant. Only if animals which have eaten hypericine remain in sunlight do they suffer poisoning which can be fatal. The leaves of the plant contain ethereal oil. An old medicinal plant.

---

❺ **Common Agrimony** *(Agrimonia eupatoria)*
Rosaceae
30—130 cm   See p. 128

---

❻ **Common Parsnip** *(Pastinaca sativa)*
Apiaceae (Umbelliferae)
30—100 cm   See p. 128

1

2

3

5   4   6

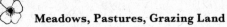

❶

5 — 15 cm

Tasteless Sedum, Insipid Stonecrop *(Sedum sexangulare; S. boloniense; S. mite)*
Crassulaceae
IM: Plant does not have a strong taste (chew a piece). Petals 3 — 5 mm long. Leaves
   rolled up, with a spur at the base.
D: Cymes with few flowers. Stem creeping, erect or decumbent.
H: Dry and semi-dry turf, rock clefts, more rarely on walls or embankments. Likes
   warm situations and chalky soils.
AI: P; ♃

❷

20 — 50 cm

Orpine, Livelong *(Sedum telephium; S. maximum)*
Crassulaceae
See p. 176

❸

5 — 15 cm

Yellow *or* **Biting Stonecrop, Wall Pepper** *(Sedum acre)*
Crassulaceae
See p. 192

❹

40 — 140 cm

Yellow Gentian *(Gentiana lutea)*
Gentianaceae
IM: No possibility of confusion with other species (when in flower).
D: 3 — 10 flowered cymes in the axils of the shell-like upper stem leaves. Flowers
   deeply divided into 5 — 6 lobes. Stem erect. Leaves opposite (cf. White False
   Hellebore, p. 54), elliptical, up to 30 cm long and 15 cm wide.
H: Semi-dry turf, mountain pastures, alpine mat, light mountain forest. Likes
   a porous, calcareous soil, which is moist at least part of the time. Numerous
   where it does occur.
AI: G; ♃
   The seeds of the Yellow Gentian weigh only about 0.001 g and are spread by
   the wind. Each plant produces about 10,000 seeds. Yellow Gentian does not
   flower until it is 10 years old or more. It contains an alkaloid and tannins in
   all its organs, but particularly in the root, which is often used to flavour
   Schnaps. An old medicinal plant.

❺

50 — 130 cm

White Mullein *(Verbascum lychnitis)*
Scrophulariaceae
See p. 48

❻

30 — 100 cm

Common Comfrey, Knitbone *(Symphytum officinale)*
Boraginaceae
See p. 178

❼

6 — 20 cm

Meadow Gagea *(Gagea pratensis)*
Liliaceae
See p. 130

❽

5 — 15 cm

Lesser Celandine *(Ficaria verna; Ranunculus ficaria)*
Ranunculaceae
See p. 180

Meadows, Pastures, Grazing Land **Yellow**

❶   **Spring Adonis** *(Adonis vernalis)*
              Ranunculaceae
15—25 cm   IM: No possibility of confusion with other species.
              D: Flowers solitary, terminal, 4—8 cm in diameter, with 10—25 petals. Stem with leaves at the top. Leaves pinnate, with many pinnules.
              H: Dry and semi-dry turf and in open pine woods. Likes a very porous, sandy, calcareous soil.
              AI: P; ♃; †
                 The plant contains the poisonous digitalis glycoside.

❷   **European Globe-Flower** *(Trollius europaeus)*
              Ranunculaceae
30—50 cm   IM: Flower a closed, yellow sphere.
              D: Flowers up to 3 cm in diameter, 6—15 petals. Stem erect, the basal part branched. Leaves palmate with 3—5 segments.
              H: Moist meadows and mountain pastures. Likes a soil rich in humus. Occurs in large stands in some localities.
              AI: P; ♃;(†)
                 The Globe-Flower contains protoanemonine and is therefore slightly poisonous.

❸   **Dandelion** *(Taraxacum officinale)*
              Cichoriaceae (Compositae)
10—60 cm   See p. 130

❹   **Mouse-ear Hawkweed** *(Hieracium pilosella)*
              Cichoriaceae (Compositae)
8—30 cm   See p. 192

❺   **Goatsbeard** *(Tragopogon pratensis)*
              Cichoriaceae (Compositae)
30—60 cm   IM: Capitula 4—6 cm in diameter. Only ray florets present. Carpels with pappus of hairs. Only one row of involucral bracts, 3—7 cm long. Stem with leaves.
              D: Stem inflated at the top. Leaves sessile, narrowly linear, clasping the stem at the base.
              H: Meadows. Likes a loamy soil rich in nutrients.
              AI: G; ☉ — ♃;(†)
                 The name Goatsbeard corresponds with the scientific generic name (Greek *tragos* = goat; *pogon* = beard) and denotes the appearance of the pappus hairs sticking out from the involucral bracts after flowering has finished. The capitula open about 8 a.m. and close between 11 a.m. and 2 p.m. (with differences according to the species concerned).

❻   **Mountain Arnica** *(Arnica montana)*
              Asteraceae (Compositae)
30—60 cm   IM: Flowers in one capitulum, consisting of both ray florets and disc florets. Carpels with a pappus of hairs. Most of the leaves contribute to a basal rosette.
              D: Ray florets bright yellow to orange. Stem usually unbranched, hairy. Basal leaves form a rosette, invert-ovoid, almost entire, stout, hairy. 1—2 pairs of opposite stem leaves present. Plant has an aromatic smell.
              H: Meadows and poor pastures. Likes a sandy, acid soil, with humus or peat. Numerous in those localities where it does occur.
              AI: G; ♃
                 A medicinal plant containing ethereal oils and alkaloids.

❶
30—60 cm
Willow-leaved Inula *(Inula salicina)*
Asteraceae (Compositae)
See p. 202

❷
60—120 cm
Rough Hawksbeard *(Crepis biennis)*
Cichoriaceae (Compositae)
IM: Capitula arranged in umbel-like panicles. Capitula 3—4.5 cm in diameter. Only ray florets present. Carpels with pappus of hairs, which are white and bendable (press with finger). Lower leaves lobed or pinnate, upper leaves undivided.
D: Stem bearing leaves, often reddish at the base.
H: Meadows. Likes a loamy soil, rich in nutrients.
AI: G; ⊙
The fruits of this plant are sometimes used as canary food.

❸
30—120 cm
Marsh Hawksbeard *(Crepis paludosa)*
Cichoriaceae (Compositae)
IM: Capitula arranged in umbel-like panicles. Only ray florets present. Carpels with pappus of hairs, which are yellowish white and fragile (press with finger). Lower leaves crenate, clasping the stem; upper leaves lanceolate, all of them glabrous.
D: Stem bearing leaves, and usually brownish green. Leaves often with brown spots.
H: Mountain pastures, alpine mats, wet meadows, moorland. Likes a soil rich in nutrients and saturated with ground water, one which is peaty or loamy.
AI: G; ♃

❹
30—130 cm
Savoy Hawkweed *(Hieracium sabaudum)*
Cichoriaceae (Compositae)
See p. 182

❺
5—30 cm
Common Hawkbit *(Leontodon hispidus)*
Cichoriaceae (Compositae)
IM: Flowers in large capitula. Only ray florets present. Carpels with a pappus of hairs. Upper part of stem bears 1—2 scale leaves, otherwise leafless. Basal leaves broad, clearly petiolate, entire or pinnately lobed.
D: Stem thickened below the capitulum and bearing rough hairs. Plant exudes a milky sap when bruised.
H: Semi-dry turf, meadows. Likes a moist soil rich in nutrients.
AI: G; ♃
The flowers open at about 5 a.m. and shut at about 3 p.m.

❻
15—50 cm
Autumnal Hawkbit *(Leontodon autumnalis)*
Cichoriaceae (Compositae)
IM: Flowers in large capitula. Only ray florets present. Carpels with a pappus of hairs. These hairs are feathery (magnifying glass required!). Stem branched. Leaves mostly pinnate, more rarely only coarsely serrate.
D: Stem leafless, grooved, not hollow. Leaves form basal rosette. Plant exudes a milky sap when bruised.
H: Meadows, roadside verges. Likes a nitrogenous, sandy loam.
AI: G; ♃
The scientific name of the genus (Latin *leo* = lion; *dens* = tooth) refers to the toothed leaves.

156

❶
5—15 cm

Slender Cudweed, Field *or* **Dwarf Filago** *(Filago minima)*
Asteraceae (Compositae)
    See p. 132

❷
30—150 cm

Hawkweed Bitterwort *(Picris hieracioides)*
Cichoriaceae (Compositae)
IM: Flowers in large capitula. Only ray florets present. Carpels with pappus of hairs. Stem bears leaves and, like the leaves, is covered in rough hairs.
D: Capitula arranged in a cymose manner. Flowers sulphur yellow to gold, tinged on the outside with red. Stem branched at the top. Leaves crenately lobed.
H: Semi-dry turf, roadside verges, meadows. Likes a calcareous, rather stony, loamy soil.
AI: G: ☉ — ♃

❸
30—100 cm

Narrow-leaved Senecio *or* **Ragwort** *(Senecio erucifolius)*
Asteraceae (Compositae)
IM: Flowers in capitula which are arranged in a cymose manner. Both ray florets and disc florets present. Carpels with pappus of hairs. Leaves pinnate, with a web of hairs on the underside. Rootstock creeping.
D: Stem usually with a reddish-brown tinge, angular.
H: Semi-dry turf, roadside verges, edges of woods, thickets. Likes a calcareous, often rather stony, loamy soil, rich in nitrogen.
AI: G; ☉ — ♃
The scientific name of the genus *Senecio* (Latin *senex* = old man) refers to the white hairs which occur on the fruit.

❹
30—100 cm

Common Ragwort *(Senecio jacobaea)*
Asteraceae (Compositae)
IM: Flowers in capitula which are arranged in a cymose manner. Both ray florets and disc florets present. Carpels with a pappus of hairs. Leaves pinnate with a web of hairs. Rootstock goes straight down into the ground.
D: Stem erect, with angular furrows, usually with a brownish-red tinge.
H: Semi-dry turf, roadside verges, edges of woods. Likes a rather stony soil which is moist at least part of the time.
AI: G; ☉ — ♃; †
Name: see Narrow-leaved Senecio above. Contains a poisonous alkaloid.

❺
50—150 cm

Cabbage Thistle *(Cirsium oleraceum)*
Asteraceae (Compositae)
IM: No possibility of confusion with other species.
D: Capitulum terminal, surrounded by pale, soft-spined leaves. Only yellowish-white disc florets present. Leaves not decurrent, glabrous, somewhat prickly; those at the top of the stem usually undivided and clasping the stem, lower leaves pinnate with serrated segments.
H: Wet meadows, ditches, banks of streams, valley woodland. Likes a wet, loamy soil, rich in nutrients. In meadows is an indicator of wetness.
AI: G; ♃

❶ **Heart's-ease, Field** *or* **Wild Pansy** *(Viola tricolor)*
10—20 cm
Violaceae
IM: Leaves longer than they are broad.
D: Flowers solitary, on long peduncles, whitish yellow, violet or tricoloured. Stem usually branched, erect or decumbent. Lower leaves heart-shaped or ovoid, crenate. Bracts pinnate.
H: Weedy places in fields, gardens and more rarely in vineyards, occasionally in mountain pastures. Likes an acid soil.
AI: P; ☉
The plant contains saponin in the root. An old medicinal plant.

❷ **Yellow Mountain Violet** *(Viola biflora)*
8—12 cm
Violaceae
See p. 186

❸ **Yellow Asparagus Pea** *(Tetragonolobus maritimus ; Lotus siliquosus)*
15—40 cm
Fabaceae (Leguminosae)
IM: Flowers solitary, 2—3 cm long, bright yellow. Leaves bluish green.
D: Stem prostrate to decumbent, bluish green. Lower leaves usually with 5 leaflets, fleshy, petiolate, upper leaves sessile or with very short petioles.
H: Semi-dry turf, wet meadows, mountain pastures with springs, moorland. Likes a soil saturated with ground water, but which dries out in summer.
AI: P; ♃
The common name refers to the large pods of the fruit.

❹ **Bird's-foot Trefoil** *(Lotus corniculatus)*
5—30 cm
Fabaceae (Leguminosae)
IM: 3—6 flowers in an umbellate head. Flowers 8—15 mm long. Standard often tinged red. Stem narrow, tubular. Leaves with 5 segments (2 are bracts which resemble the other 3 true leaflets quite closely).
D: Stem decumbent to erect. Leaflets linear-ovoid.
H: Semi-dry turf, meadows, wayside verges. Likes a calcareous soil and prefers porous loams.
AI: P; ♃
The common name refers to the shape of the leaves. In very dry localities the Bird's-foot Trefoil develops a very deep and extensive root system (up to 1 m long).

❺ **Marsh** *or* **Large Bird's-foot Trefoil** *(Lotus uliginosus ; L. pedunculatus)*
10—60 cm
Fabaceae (Leguminosae)
IM: 8—12 flowers in umbellate heads. Flowers 8—15 mm long. Stem broadly tubular.
D: Stem erect or decumbent; leaflets linear-ovoid.
H: Moist meadows, moorland; likes wet soil but can withstand summer drought.
AI: P; ♃
In moist meadows this species is a valuable fodder plant and at one time was cultivated as such.

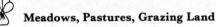

❶   **Horseshoe Vetch** *(Hippocrepis comosa)*
               Fabaceae (Leguminosae)
8—30 cm   IM: 4—8 flowers in an umbel. Leaves compound pinnate with 9—15 leaflets.
               D: Stem prostrate to decumbent. Leaves with long petioles.
               H: Dry and semi-dry turf, quarries, less often on the limestone gravel of embank-
                      ments and verges. Likes a porous, calcareous soil. Calcicolous.
               AI: P; ♃
                      The name Horseshoe Vetch refers to the form of the fruit (legume).

❷   **Kidney Vetch, Lady's Fingers** *(Anthyllis vulneraria)*
               Fabaceae (Leguminosae)
10—30 cm   See p. 136

❸   **Meadow Pea** *(Lathyrus pratensis)*
               Fabaceae (Leguminosae)
30—100 cm   IM: Stamens fused together in a tube which has a straight border. Stem not winged.
                      Leaves pinnate, consisting usually of only 2 leaflets and a tendril.
               D: Axillary racemes with long peduncles. Stipules (at base of petioles) sagittate.
               H: Damp meadows. Likes a loamy soil rich in nitrogen and humus.
               AI: P; ♃
                      The Meadow Pea contains an alkaloid and is therefore not eaten by cattle
                      (although it would otherwise be a useful fodder plant because of its high
                      protein content).

❹   **Sickle Medick** *(Medicago falcata)*
               Fabaceae (Leguminosae)
20—50 cm   IM: Flowers 8—11 mm long in ovoid heads. Petals fall off after flowering. Leaves
                      with 3 leaflets.
               D: Stem decumbent to erect. Usually richly branched. Leaflets dentate at the tips.
               H: Dry and semi-dry turf, roadside verges. Likes a porous calcareous soil.
               AI: P; ♃
                      Sickle Medick is closely related to Lucern *(Medicago sativa)*. Hybrids between
                      the two plants are often formed and these have flowers which are yellow when
                      they first appear, then become greenish and finally purple at the end of the
                      flowering period. The true Violet-flowered Lucerne produces a valuable fodder
                      which is rich in protein.

❺   **Golden Clover** *or* **Trefoil** *(Trifolium aureum; T. strepens)*
               Fabaceae (Leguminosae)
10—50 cm   IM: 20—50 flowers in a 7—10 mm broad head. Petals persist after flowering;
                      light brown in colour. The 3 leaflets have petioles of equal length.
               D: Stem erect, glabrous. Leaflets linear-lanceolate.
               H: Semi-dry turf, heaths, roadside verges. Rather calcifugous and an indicator
                      of surface acidity.
               AI: P; ☉; ⊙

❶ **Hop Trefoil, Yellow Field Clover** *(Trifolium campestre ; T. procumbens)*
Fabaceae (Leguminosae)
5 — 30 cm IM: 20 — 50 flowers in a 7 — 10 mm broad head. Petals persist after flowering;
light brown. Leaves with 3 leaflets, of which the middle one has a distinctly
longer stalk than the 2 laterals.
D: Stem prostrate to decumbent, or erect, hairy. Leaflets invert-ovoid.
H: Semi-dry turf, dry meadows, embankments, verges. Likes a porous, calcareous
soil, rich in nutrients.
AI: P; ⊙
The dried corolla, which persists around the fruit, may possibly help in
distribution of the latter by air currents.

❷ **Black Medick, Nonsuch** *(Medicago lupulina)*
Fabaceae (Leguminosae)
10 — 40 cm See p. 138

❸ **Arrowhead Broom** *(Genistella sagittalis ; Genista sagittalis)*
Fabaceae (Leguminosae)
15 — 25 cm IM: Stem winged, with few leaves. Leaves ovoid-lanceolate, hairy.
D: Flowers in terminal, dense racemes. Stem decumbent to erect. Leaves
alternate, sessile, linear, pointed.
H: Semi-dry turf, sloping meadows, roadside verges, light, dry woodland habitats,
heaths, occasionally also on rocks. Somewhat calcifugous, and an indicator
of superficial acidity.
AI: P
The winged stem is an adaptation to drought and strong sunlight. The
'wings' are organs of assimilation which conserve water. When growing in
moist, shady places, and under certain experimental conditions, this plant
may develop a stem covered in leaves and with hardly any 'wings'.

❹ **Large-flowered Foxglove, Pale Foxglove** *(Digitalis grandiflora ; D. ambigua)*
Scrophulariaceae
50 — 130 cm IM: Flowers 3 — 4.5 cm long.
D: Unilaterally directed racemes. Flowers sulphur yellow, inflated, campanulate,
with brown veins on the inside of the corolla tube. Stem erect, hairy. Leaves
elongate, ciliate, serrate.
H: Mountain forest, mixed and deciduous woodland, particularly in clearings,
thickets, more rarely in mountain pastures and alpine mat. Likes a porous,
stony soil, damp with seepage water. Forms small clumps.
AI: G; ♃; †
Contains a poisonous digitalis glycoside.

❺ **Lesser Yellow Rattle** *(Rhinanthus minor ; Alectorolophus minor)*
Scrophulariaceae
15 — 40 cm IM: Corolla tube straight.
D: Flowers solitary in the leaf axils. Teeth to the upper lip usually white. Leaves
narrowly lanceolate, glabrous.
H: Meadows, semi-dry turf. Likes a chalk-deficient or non-calcareous soil which
is damp.
AI: G; ⊙; (†)
Hemiparasite. Contains the poisonous substance aucubin (cf. Red Rattle,
p. 278).

5

1

4

3

2

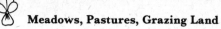

❶   **Hairy Yellow Rattle** *(Rhinanthus alectorolophus; Alectorolophus hirsutus)*

           Scrophulariaceae

10—50 cm   IM: Calyx hairy.

           D: Flowers in leaf axils. Corolla tube bent upwards. Leaves linear-lanceolate.

           H: Semi-dry turf, meadows, weedy places in cornfields, also on roadside verges. Likes a porous, rather calcareous, loamy soil, rich in nutrients.

           AI: G; ⊙; (†)

           Hemiparasite. Contains the poisonous substance aucubin (cf. Red Rattle, p. 278).

❷   **Greater Yellow Rattle** *(Rhinanthus serotinus; R. glaber; Alectorolophus major)*

           Scrophulariaceae

30—60 cm   IM: Calyx glabrous.

           D: Flowers solitary in leaf axils. Corolla tube curved. Teeth on the upper lip violet. Stem quadrangular. Leaves linear-lanceolate.

           H: Meadows. Likes a loamy, rather damp soil, rich in nutrients.

           AI: G; ⊙; (†)

           Hemiparasite. Contains the poisonous substance aucubin (cf. Red Rattle, p. 278).

❸   **Common Cow Wheat, Meadow Cow Wheat** *(Melampyrum pratense)*

           Scrophulariaceae

15—30 cm   See p. 190

❹   **Wood Cow Wheat, Small-flowered Cow Wheat** *(Melampyrum sylvaticum)*

           Scrophulariaceae

15—25 cm   IM: Flowers 0.8—1 cm long.

           D: Unilaterally directed spikes. Stem erect or decumbent. Leaves below the inflorescence lanceolate, entire, almost sessile.

           H: Mixed and deciduous woodland, coniferous forest, heaths. Likes a mossy, loamy soil with surface acidity.

           AI: G; ⊙; (†)

           Hemiparasite. The flowers are commonly visited by short-tongued bees, which bite through the base of the corolla to get to the nectar, without bringing about pollination. The seeds contain the poisonous substance aucubin in large amounts.

❺   **Lesser Broomrape** *(Orobanche minor; O. barbata)*

           Orobanchaceae

10—50 cm   IM: Flowers 1—1.8 cm long. Lobe of upper lip with straight stripes; does not appear to have dark spots in transmitted light. Stem not branched.

           D: Inflorescence a spike. Flowers pale yellow. Upper lip with reddish or purplish stripes. Stem reddish yellow. Plant without green leaves, only yellowish scales. Many similar, rarer species, which are difficult to distinguish, parasitizing various plants.

           H: Clover fields, semi-dry turf, edges of woods, thickets. Parasitizes many plants, but particularly Clover.

           AI: G; ⊙; (†)

           Contains aucubin (cf. Red Rattle, p. 278).

❶ **Alternate-leaved Golden Saxifrage** *(Chrysosplenium alternifolium)*
Saxifragaceae
8—15 cm   See p. 194

---

❷ **Crosswort** *(Cruciata laevipes; Galium cruciata; G. cruciatum)*
Rubiaceae
15—70 cm   IM: Flowers in leaf axils. Leaves in whorls of 4.
           D: Flowers 2—2.5 mm in diameter. Stem square. Leaves with 3 veins.
           H: Edges of woods, thickets, weedy places along paths, also on wasteland; more
               rarely in meadows near woods. Likes a porous, humus soil.
           AI: G; ♃

---

❸ **Greater Celandine** *(Chelidonium majus)*
Papaveraceae
30—100 cm IM: Plant contains an orange-yellow, milky juice (pluck off a leaf).
           D: Flowers in umbels, also solitary in leaf axils. Stem branched, with slender
               hairs or glabrous. Leaves pinnate, broadly crenate or toothed, with fine hairs
               or glabrous, undersides blue-green.
           H: Weedy places on waste ground, on walls and along the edges of woods; also
               along paths and on the outskirts of villages (gardens) and in damp, open
               woodland and thickets. An indicator of nitrogenous conditions.
           AI: P; ♃; †
               The Greater Celandine contains, particularly in its milky juice, several
               poisonous alkaloids. Medicinal plant. The juice is an old folk remedy against
               warts.

---

❹ **Smooth Biscutella** *(Biscutella laevigata)*
Brassicaceae (Cruciferae)
15—30 cm   IM: Branched racemes. Flowers bright yellow. Carpels and fruits consist of two
               circular structures resembling spectacles. Fruit stays erect.
           D: Basal leaves elongate, with orbicular bases, entire or coarsely toothed. Stem
               leaves linear, sessile and partly encircling stem.
           H: Stony, dry and semi-dry turf, strips of turf on rocky debris, alpine screes and
               dry pinewoods. Calcicolous.
           AI: P; ♃

---

❺ **Greater Watercress, Great Yellow Cress** *(Rorippa amphibia)*
Brassicaceae (Cruciferae)
20—100 cm IM: Petals distinctly longer than calyx, golden yellow. Carpels about 2—3 times
               as long as broad. Stem hollow.
           D: Cymose racemes. Flowers 8—10 mm long on erect peduncles. Stem decumbent,
               thick, mostly hollow, grooved. Lower leaves with short petioles, pinnate or
               deeply lobed. Upper leaves sessile, lanceolate, entire or irregularly crenate.
           H: Margins of stagnant or flowing water, reedy places, more rarely in the wettest
               part of marshy woodland. Indicator of muddy conditions. Likes a nitrogenous
               soil.
           AI: P; ♃

---

❻ **Winter Cress, Yellow Rocket** *(Barbarea vulgaris)*
Brassicaceae (Cruciferae)
30—60 cm   See p. 194

❶ **Common Tormentil** *(Potentilla erecta; P. tormentilla; Tormentilla erecta)*
Rosaceae
15—30 cm   See p. 196

❷ **Yellow Bird's Nest** *(Monotropa hypopitys)*
Pyrolaceae
10—30 cm   IM: Entire plant pale yellow. Only scale leaves present.
D: Raceme initially drooping, but becomes erect before the fruits are fully formed.
Flowers campanulate; terminal flower with 5 corolla lobes. Petals 12—16 mm
long. Stem waxy yellow to brown, more rarely reddish or flesh colour. Leaves
scale-like, yellowish or brownish. Root richly branched, looking like a bird's
nest.
H: Mixed woodland and pine forest. Likes an acid, loamy or sandy soil.
AI: G; ♃
The root system of this plant is similar to a bird's nest, hence the common name.
The plant contains glycosides. An old medicinal plant for animal ailments.

❸ **Oxlip** *(Primula elatior)*
Primulaceae
15—30 cm   IM: Flowers sulphur yellow. Margin of the corolla saucer-like.
D: Umbels with long peduncles. Basal leaves form a rosette, linear-lanceolate,
crenate, wrinkled.
H: Mixed and deciduous woodland, more rarely in coniferous forest, canyon
forest, marshy woodland, mountain forest or wet meadows. Likes a porous,
damp and rather loamy soil.
AI: G; ♃
The scientific name *Primula* comes from the Latin *primus* (first) and refers to the
early time of flowering. The plant contains saponin in its roots. Old medicinal
plant.

❹ **Cowslip** *(Primula veris; P. officinalis)*
Primulaceae
15—30 cm   See p. 146

❺ **Marsh Marigold**, **Kingcup** *(Caltha palustris)*
Ranunculaceae
15—50 cm   IM: Leaves kidney-shaped, glossy. Flowers also very distinctly glossy.
D: Flowers consist of 5 large, orange-yellow sepals. Diameter up to 4 cm. Stem
hollow, prostrate to decumbent. Leaves finely crenate, with long petioles,
the upper leaves sessile with distinctly cabbage-like laminae. Petiole grooved.
H: Wet meadows, ditches, edges of ponds and lakes, reed beds, marshy woodland.
Likes a soil saturated with ground water and rich in nutrients. Withstands
occasional flooding.
AI: P; ♃; (†)
Marsh Marigolds have seeds which float on the surface of the water and are
spread in this way. The flowers are particularly rich in nectar. Because of its
protoanemonine content the plant has a distinctly burning taste. It is slightly
poisonous, and for this reason, the common practice of using its leaves in wild
salads and the collection of its unopened flower buds as a substitute for capers
is not recommended. There are several subspecies, which are difficult to
distinguish.

1

2

3

4

5

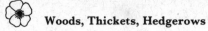

❶

15—30 cm

Yellow Wood Anemone *(Anemone ranunculoides)*
Ranunculaceae
IM: 1 or 2 flowers emerging from a whorl of stem leaves.
D: Usually 2, more rarely a single flower above the whorl of stem leaves. Except for this whorl the stem is leafless. Occasionally there are palmate compound leaves (3 leaflets) on the rootstock.
H: Valley woodland, canyon forest, moist deciduous woodland and thickets. Likes a rich, porous, calcareous, loamy soil, saturated with ground water. Occurs in considerable numbers in some localities.
AI: P; ♃; †
    Contains the poisonous substances protoanemonine and saponin.

❷

15—50 cm

Goldilocks *(Ranunculus auricomus)*
Ranunculaceae
IM: Petals fall off very readily. Basal leaves small, only slightly divided, with a kidney-shaped outline. Leaves limited to 2—6.
D: Flowers usually few, golden yellow in colour, and 1—2 cm in diameter. Peduncles hairy, round. Stem erect, branched, with few hairs. The stem leaves extend to the base, are 5—7 in number, sessile and divided into linear segments.
H: Mixed and deciduous woodland, fens. Likes calcareous, loamy soils, rich in nutrients and saturated with ground water.
AI: P; ♃; (†)
    Probably contains the poisonous substance protoanemonine.

❸

15—50 cm

Creeping Buttercup *(Ranunculus repens)*
Ranunculaceae
    See p. 148

❹

30—100 cm

Woolly Buttercup *(Ranunculus lanuginosus)*
Ranunculaceae
IM: Flowers deep yellow. Stem and leaves densely covered with hairs.
D: Flowers numerous, 2.5—4 cm in diameter. Peduncle round. Stem erect, usually richly branched, hollow below and thickly covered with yellowish hairs. Basal leaves petiolate, with 5 segments. Stem leaves like the basal leaves, but sessile or with a very short petiole.
H: Mixed and deciduous woodland. Likes a chalky, loamy soil, saturated with ground water.
AI: P; ♃; (†)
    Probably contains the poisonous substance protoanemonine.

❺

25—50 cm

Herb Bennet, **Wood** *or* **Common Avens** *(Geum urbanum)*
Rosaceae
IM: Flowers golden yellow in loose panicles. Fruits with hooked awns. Leaves irregular, simply pinnate. Terminal leaflet larger than the others.
D: Stem richly branched. Upper leaves palmate, sessile.
H: Mixed and deciduous woodland, edges of woods and along woodland paths, on wasteland and in thickets. Likes a moist, nitrogenous soil.
AI: P; ♃; (†)
    The rootstock contains a slightly poisonous oil (eugenol) and tannins. Old medicinal plant. The dried rootstock was formerly used as a substitute for cloves.

❶ **Common Agrimony** *(Agrimonia eupatoria)*
Rosaceae
30—130 cm   IM: Flowers in long multiflorous racemes.
     D: Stem erect, with coarse hairs. Leaves discontinuously unpaired pinnate. Leaflets linear-lanceolate, sessile, serrate, the unpaired terminal leaflet stalked.
     H: Semi-dry turf, roadside verges, edges of woods, sunny woodland paths. Likes a porous soil in warm situations.
     AI: P; ♃
     The specific name *eupatoria* is derived from a Greek legend. It is said that King Mithridates Eupator (132—63 B.C.) was the first person to discover the healing powers of Agrimony. The plant contains tannins in all its organs, but particularly in the leaves. An old medicinal plant.

❷ **Mountain St John's Wort** *(Hypericum montanum)*
Hypericaceae
30—60 cm   IM: Flowers bright yellow, without any black dots at the edge. Plant glabrous. Stem erect, rounded.
     D: Cymes. Stamens clustered. Leaves opposite, sessile, with a heart-shaped base and with black spots on the edge of the leaves; only the upper spots are transparent.
     H: Dry thickets and woodland, which may be mixed, deciduous or coniferous, usually at high altitudes. Likes a loamy, calcareous soil.
     AI: P; ♃
     Name: see Common St John's Wort, p. 150.

❸ **Hairy St John's Wort** *(Hypericum hirsutum)*
Hypericaceae
30—120 cm   IM: Plant hairy.
     D: Loose, pyramidal panicles. Stamens clustered. Stem decumbent to erect, round. Leaves opposite, with short petioles, and with transparent spots.
     H: Light, rather moist woodland, particularly in clearings and on the edges of woods. Likes a loamy, somewhat calcareous soil, which is at least damp part of the time.
     AI: P; ♃
     Name: see Common St John's Wort, p. 150.

❹ **Slender St John's Wort** *(Hypericum pulchrum)*
Hypericaceae
15—50 cm   IM: Flowers golden yellow. Petals with dark red spots at the edge. Plant glabrous. Stem erect, rounded.
     D: Loose panicles. Stamens clustered. Stem erect or decumbent. Leaves opposite, sessile, heart-shaped at the base, with transparent spots.
     H: Deciduous, mixed or coniferous woodland, mostly in clearings or on the edges of woods. Likes an acid, sandy or loamy soil. Calcifugous. An indicator that the soil has been leached of calcium salts.
     AI: P; ♃
     Name: see Common St John's Wort, p. 150.

❺ **Common** *or* **Perforate St John's Wort** *(Hypericum perforatum)*
Hypericaceae
30—60 cm   See p. 150

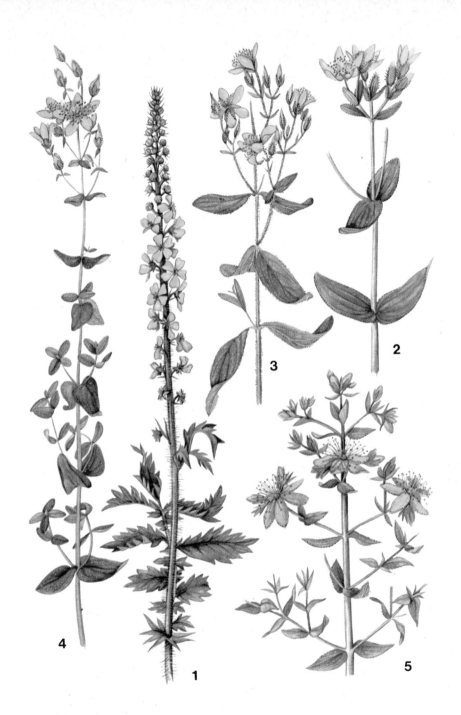

4   1   5

❶

5 — 30 cm

Creeping Jenny, Moneywort *(Lysimachia nummularia)*
Primulaceae
IM: Petals 1 — 1.5 cm long. Stem prostrate or decumbent. Leaves round or ellip-
tical.
D: Flowers solitary or 2 in a leaf axil. Petals lemon yellow, often with red dots on
the inside. Leaves opposite.
H: Meadows, also woodland, ditches, river banks, wet fields and the edges of
paths. Likes a dense, moist, loamy soil, rich in nitrogen.
AI: G; ♃
The plant contains saponin and tannins in the leaves. An old medicinal plant.

❷

20 — 50 cm

Orpine, Livelong *(Sedum telephium; S. maximum)*
Crassulaceae
IM: Stem erect. Leaves ovoid-linear, fleshy.
D: Flowers in panicles, greenish yellow, pink or dark red (subspecies *purpureum*) in
colour. Leaves blunt, unevenly serrate, alternate, opposite or in whorls,
sessile.
H: Rocky screes, hillsides covered with rock debris, poor turf, light mountain
forest. Likes a stony soil but one rich in nutrients.
AI: P; ♃
An old medicinal plant, used by the Romans. The active principle is still
unknown.

❸

5 — 15 cm

Trailing St John's Wort *(Hypericum humifusum)*
Hypericaceae
IM: Stem prostrate.
D: Panicles. Stamens clustered. Stem rounded or angular. Leaves opposite,
linear-ovoid, the upper leaves with transparent dots.
H: Weedy places in wet vegetable fields, on uncultivated soil, along roadsides
and in damp, open woodland. Likes a moist, sandy or loamy soil. Calcifugous.
AI: P; ☉ — ♃
Name and pigmentation: see Common St John's Wort, p. 150.

❹

60 — 130 cm

Common Loosestrife *(Lysimachia vulgaris)*
Primulaceae
IM: Flowers in terminal panicles involving the leaves. Flowers 1 — 1.5 cm long.
D: Panicles with few to many flowers. Stem erect, slightly angular. Leaves
opposite or in whorls of 3 — 4, large, linear-ovoid.
H: Ditches, river banks, moorland, more rarely fens. Likes a moist, peaty soil.
AI: G; ♃

❺

20 — 100 cm

Falcate Hare's-ear *(Bupleurum falcatum)*
Apiaceae (Umbelliferae)
IM: Flowers in umbels. Leaves entire, the upper ones falcate, narrow-lanceolate,
not clasping the stem.
D: Umbels compound. Stem erect or decumbent.
H: Dry woodland and thickets, edges of woods, more rarely on roadside verges
and semi-dry turf near woods. Likes a calcareous soil.
AI: P; ♃
One species of the genus has leaves like a hare's ears, hence the name.

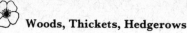

❶

40—140 cm

Yellow Gentian *(Gentiana lutea)*
Gentianaceae
IM: No possibility of confusion with other species (when in flower).
D: 3—10 flowered cymes in the axils of the shell-like upper stem leaves. Flowers deeply divided into 5—6 lobes. Stem erect. Leaves opposite (cf. White False Hellebore, p. 54), elliptical, up to 30 cm long and 15 cm wide.
H: Semi-dry turf, mountain pastures, alpine mat, light mountain forest. Likes a porous, calcareous soil, which is moist at least part of the time. Numerous where it does occur.
AI: G; ♃
The seeds of the Yellow Gentian weigh only about 0.001 g and are spread by the wind. Each plant produces about 10,000 seeds. Yellow Gentian does not flower until it is 10 years old or more. It contains an alkaloid and tannins in all its organs, but particularly in the root, which is often used to flavour Schnaps. An old medicinal plant.

❷

80—200 cm

Large-flowered Mullein *(Verbascum thapsiforme)*
Scrophulariaceae
IM: Flowers about 3.5—4 cm in diameter.
D: Dense racemes with glandular hairs. Flowers with a pleasant scent. Leaves crenate, both sides covered with a mat of yellowish hairs, decurrent.
H: Weedy places on roadside verges, embankments, wasteland and on the edges of woods and in clearings. Likes a porous, shallow, often stony soil, rich in nitrogen. Prefers warm situations.
AI: G; ⊙
A medicinal plant. Contains mucilage, and also saponin in its seeds, flowers and leaves.

❸

30—150 cm

Great Mullein, Small-flowered Mullein, Aaron's Rod *(Verbascum thapsus)*
Scrophulariaceae
See p. 126

❹

50—130 cm

White Mullein *(Verbascum lychnitis)*
Scrophulariaceae
See p. 48

❺

30—100 cm

Common Comfrey, Knitbone *(Symphytum officinale)*
Boraginaceae
IM: Leaves distinctly decurrent. Plant with rough hairs.
D: Inflorescence drooping, cymose. Flowers a dirty purple, pinkish violet or yellowish white. Stem richly branched at the base. Stem leaves furrowed.
H: River banks, ditches, fen woodland, wet meadows, also on damp wasteland and waysides. Likes a moist, nitrogenous soil.
AI: G; ♃; (†)
In the Middle Ages this plant was used as a remedy for broken bones, hence the folk name Knitbone. The rootstock is black. The plant contains alkaloids and tannins. It is not eaten by cattle.

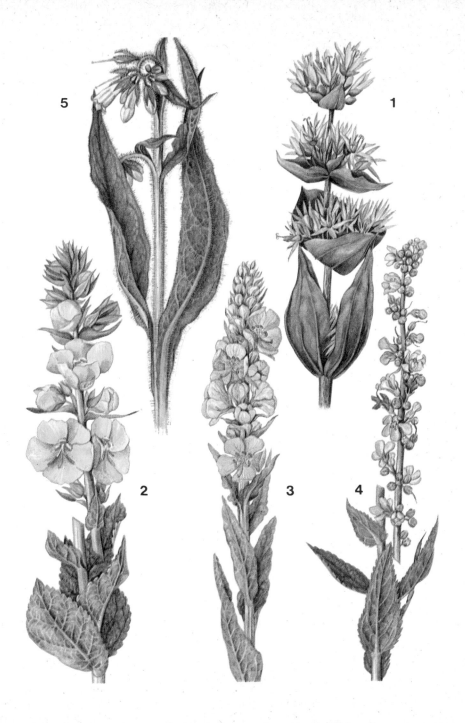

❶   **Spring Adonis** *(Adonis vernalis)*

15 — 25 cm   Ranunculaceae
           See p. 154

---

❷   **Lesser Celandine** *(Ficaria verna; Ranunculus ficaria)*

5 — 15 cm   Ranunculaceae

IM: 8 — 12 petals. Leaves heart-shaped, undivided. Stem prostrate or decumbent.

D: Flowers solitary, with long peduncles. Stem hollow. Leaves heart-shaped to kidney-shaped, crenate, the upper leaves palmately angular, glossy. Reproductive nodules often occur in the leaf axils.

H: Moist deciduous woodland and thickets, also other types of woodland and meadows. Likes a deep, nitrogenous soil saturated with ground water.

AI: P; ♃ ; (†)
        The plant was formerly used as a medicinal plant against scurvy, the vitamin C deficiency disease. The leaves, even from their first appearance, are relatively rich in vitamin C, so that the use of the plant against scurvy was well-founded. The leaves were picked before the flowering period, which once again was justified, for the older leaves contain the poisonous substance protoanemonine which has a burning taste. The rhizomes of Lesser Celandine were at one time used as a cure for warts.

---

❸   **Yellow Gagea** *(Gagea lutea; G. silvatica)*

15 — 30 cm   Liliaceae

IM: Only a single basal leaf present. This leaf is 7 — 8 mm wide, flat or slightly keeled.

D: False umbels of 1 — 10 flowers, between which arise two narrow bracts. Flowers yellow with greenish stripes outside.

H: Fen woodland and moist mixed woodland. Likes a porous, moist, calcareous, loam soil, rich in humus and saturated with ground water.

AI: M; ♃

---

❹   **Dandelion** *(Taraxacum officinale)*

10 — 60 cm   Cichoriaceae (Compositae)
           See p. 130

---

❺   **Mouse-ear Hawkweed** *(Hieracium pilosella)*

8 — 30 cm   Cichoriaceae (Compositae)
           See p. 192

---

❻   **Yellow Ox-eye Daisy** *(Buphthalmum salicifolium)*

15 — 50 cm   Asteraceae (Compositae)

IM: Flowers in capitula, 3 — 6 cm in diameter. Both ray florets and disc florets present. Carpels without a pappus of hairs. Leaves alternate, entire or slightly toothed and covered with soft hairs.

D: Capitula solitary, terminal. Ray florets deep yellow. Leaves lanceolate, the upper ones sessile, the lower ones with a short petiole.

H: Dry woodland, dry thickets, edges of woods, semi-dry turf. Likes a calcareous, rather stony soil.

AI: G; ♃

1

2

3

4

5

6

❶
30—130 cm

Savoy Hawkweed *(Hieracium sabaudum)*
Cichoriaceae (Compositae)
IM: Flowers in capitula arranged in umbels. Only ray florets present. Carpels with a pappus of hairs. Hairs greyish white, brittle (press with finger). Outer involucral bracts not bent back. Basal leaves have shrivelled by the time the flowers appear.
D: Stem stiff, densely covered with leaves. Middle and upper leaves sessile, lower leaves with short stalk, linear-lanceolate, dentate or serrate.
H: Oakwoods, oak thickets, edges of woodland, clearings. Likes a sandy, porous, loamy soil without lime.
AI: G; ♃
A species which consists of many different forms, which are difficult to distinguish from each other and from certain other species of the genus.

❷
30—60 cm

Wood *or* **Wall Hawkweed** *(Hieracium sylvaticum; H. murorum)*
Cichoriaceae (Compositae)
See p. 132

❸
15—50 cm

Viscous Senecio *or* **Ragwort** *(Senecio viscosus)*
Asteraceae (Compositae)
IM: Flowers in capitula arranged in a paniculate manner. Both ray florets and disc florets present. Carpels only slightly hairy. Stem sticky as a result of glandular hairs. Leaves pinnate.
D: Ray florets usually rolled back. Inner bracts black at the tips. Leaflets lanceolate, coarsely serrate.
H: Weedy places on waysides, slopes, wasteland and in clearings. Likes a porous, nitrogenous, loamy soil.
AI: G; ⊙
Name: see Narrow-leaved Senecio, below.

❹
30—100 cm

Narrow-leaved Senecio *or* **Ragwort** *(Senecio erucifolius)*
Asteraceae (Compositae)
IM: Flowers in capitula which are arranged in a cymose manner. Both ray florets and disc florets present. Carpels with a pappus of hairs. Leaves pinnate, with a web of hairs on the underside. Rootstock creeping.
D: Stem usually with a reddish-brown tinge, angular.
H: Semi-dry turf, roadside verges, edges of woods, thickets. Likes a calcareous, often rather stony, loamy soil, rich in nitrogen.
AI: G; ⊙—♃
The scientific name of the genus *Senecio* (Latin *senex* = old man) refers to the white hairs which occur on the fruit.

❺
30—100 cm

Common Ragwort *(Senecio jacobaea)*
Asteraceae (Compositae)
IM: Flowers in capitula which are arranged in a cymose manner. Both ray florets and disc florets present. Carpels with a pappus of hairs. Leaves pinnate, with a web of hairs. Rootstock goes straight down into the ground.
D: Stem erect, with angular furrows, usually with a brownish-red tinge.
H: Semi-dry turf, roadside verges, edges of woods. Likes a rather stony soil, which is moist at least part of the time.
AI: G; ⊙—♃; †
Name: see Narrow-leaved Senecio, above.
Contains a poisonous alkaloid.

❶

15—50 cm

Wood Senecio *(Senecio sylvaticus; S. silvaticus)*
Asteraceae (Compositae)
IM: Flowers in small capitula arranged in panicles. Both ray florets and disc florets present. Carpels slightly hairy. Leaves pinnate.
D: Ray florets mostly rolled back. Leaflets dentate.
H: Edges of woods, clearings, light deciduous and mixed woodland. Likes a non-calcareous, nitrogenous soil, rich in humus.
AI: G; ⊙; †
Name: see Narrow-leaved Senecio, p. 182.
Contains a poisonous alkaloid.

❷

60—100 cm

Common Goldenrod *(Solidago virgaurea)*
Asteraceae (Compositae)
IM: Numerous small capitula (7—8 mm long) in racemes or panicles. There are 5—12 ray florets surrounding the disc florets.
D: Flowers golden yellow. Stem erect, branches rod-like. Lower leaves elliptical, serrate; middle leaves ovoid-lanceolate with winged petioles.
H: Mixed and deciduous woodland, coniferous forest, mountain forest, particularly in clearings and on the edge of the forest. Likes a deep, porous, calcareous soil.
AI: G; ♃

❸

30—200 cm

Wall Lettuce *(Mycelis muralis)*
Cichoriaceae (Compositae)
IM: Capitula arranged in panicles. Usually only 5 ray florets in each small capitulum. Carpels with pappus of hairs.
D: Flowers mainly pale yellow. Stem erect, branched at the top. Leaves often with a reddish tinge; the lower leaves petiolate, the upper ones sessile. All leaves lyre-shaped with a large terminal segment. Plant has a milky juice.
H: Mixed and deciduous woodland, coniferous forest, mountain forest. Likes a porous, sometimes rather stony soil, rich in nutrients.
AI: G; ♃

❹

10—120 cm

Nipplewort *(Lapsana communis)*
Cichoriaceae (Compositae)
See p. 132

❺

50—150 cm

Cabbage Thistle *(Cirsium oleraceum)*
Asteraceae (Compositae)
See p. 158

❻

90—150 cm

Mugwort *(Artemisia vulgaris)*
Asteraceae (Compositae)
IM: Flowers in small capitula (2—6 mm long) arranged in racemose spikes. Carpels without pappus of hairs. Leaves pinnate, green on the upper side, covered with a white down on the underside, with an aromatic smell.
D: Capitula erect, hairy on the outside. Flowers brownish yellow. Stem erect, branched, often tinged with red.
H: Weedy places along paths, on embankments and wasteland, also on the edges of woods, in thickets, and on river banks. Occurs on various soils, providing they contain nitrogen.
AI: G; ♃ ; (†)

❶

15 — 30 cm

Pale Orchid *(Orchis pallens)*
Orchidaceae
IM: Labellum with a cylindrical and backwardly directed spur.
D: Flowers spiral on a spike. Outer petals spreading. Labellum only slightly trilobed. Leaves ovoid to linear, up to 4 cm wide.
H: Beechwood, mixed deciduous woodland, dry woodland. Likes a porous, calcareous, rather moist soil, rich in humus. Grows in warm situations.
AI: M; ♃

❷

10 — 60 cm

Bird's-nest Orchid *(Neottia nidus-avis)*
Orchidaceae
IM: Whole plant yellowish brown. Labellum without a spur.
D: Spikes of many flowers. Labellum bilobed. Stem has no leaves, only scale leaves. Root system like a bird's nest.
H: Deciduous and mixed woodland. Coniferous forest.
AI: M; ♃
The Bird's-nest Orchid owes its name to its tightly interwoven roots which resemble a bird's nest. It is not a true parasite, but absorbs organic material from humus in a saprophytic manner. To do this it requires the help of a fungus.

❸

15 — 80 cm

Lady's Slipper *(Cypripedium calceolus)*
Orchidaceae
See p. 262

❹

20 — 50 cm

White *or* **Pale Helleborine** *(Cephalanthera damasonium ; C. grandiflora ; C. alba)*
Orchidaceae
IM: Flowers erect, without spurs. Leaves ovoid.
D: Flowers in a spike, 15 — 20 mm long. The apparent 'peduncle' is really the compressed ovary. Flowers mainly ivory white, more rarely yellowish or yellow.
H: Beechwood, mixed deciduous woodland, coniferous woodland (especially pine), dry woodland, thickets. Likes a porous, calcareous soil.
AI: M; ♃

❺

15 — 50 cm

Yellow Deadnettle, Yellow Archangel *(Lamium galeobdolon ; Galeobdolon luteum)*
Lamiaceae (Labiatae)
IM: Plant nettle-like, without stinging hairs. Lower lip of flower with brown spots.
D: Mostly 6 flowers in an axillary whorl. Stem erect or decumbent. Leaves opposite and decussate, ovoid to heart-shaped, crenate.
H: Deciduous and mixed woodland, fen woodland, more rarely in coniferous forest. Likes a loamy, rather damp soil rich in nutrients.
AI: G; ♃

❻

8 — 12 cm

Yellow Mountain Violet *(Viola biflora)*
Violaceae
IM: Leaves broader than they are long.
D: Usually 2 flowers in a leaf axil. Flowers lemon yellow, often with brown stripes. Stem erect or decumbent. Leaves alternate, heart-shaped or kidney-shaped, crenate.
H: Deciduous and mixed woodland, coniferous forest, alpine meadows and mats. A calcicolous species.
AI: P; ♃

❶

60—130 cm

Milkvetch *(Astragalus glycyphyllos)*
Fabaceae (Leguminosae)
IM: Flowers in racemes. Stem creeping or decumbent. Leaves unpaired pinnate, with 8—15 leaflets.
D: Flowers pale yellow to ivory. Stem only slightly hairy.
H: Light, dry, deciduous and mixed woodland, clearings, woodland paths, dry thickets. Likes a calcareous, loamy soil.
AI: P; ♃
The Milkvetch contains sugars and other sweet-tasting compounds in its roots and leaves. An old medicinal plant.

❷

15—25 cm

Arrowhead Broom *(Genistella sagittalis; Genista sagittalis)*
Fabaceae (Leguminosae)
See p. 140

❸

30—100 cm

Birthwort, Erect Aristolochia *(Aristolochia clematitis)*
Aristolochiaceae
See p. 138

❹

20—60 cm

Lesser Balsam *(Impatiens parviflora)*
Balsaminaceae
See p. 140

❺

30—60 cm

Yellow Balsam, Touch-me-not *(Impatiens noli-tangere)*
Balsaminaceae
IM: Flowers hanging down, large, with long spurs, golden yellow, with red spots on the inside of the corolla. Spurs curved.
D: 2—4 flowers in axillary racemes. Stem glassy, swollen at the nodes. Leaves alternate, ovoid, coarsely serrate.
H: Fen woodland, canyon forest, damp mixed and deciduous woodland, more rarely in coniferous forest. Likes a loamy soil, but also occurs on gravel. Prefers shady places.
AI: P; ⊙; (†)
The fruit ejects its seeds violently on contact, hence the scientific and common names. A central column of tissue in the fruit is under tension. If the ripe fruit is touched or shaken, the carpels separate, roll back and the seeds are ejected. They can be thrown several metres. The plant contains a slightly poisonous alkaloid, the identity of which is still not known.

❻

50—150 cm

Yellow Monkshood, Wolfsbane *(Aconitum vulparia; A. lycoctonum)*
Ranunculaceae
IM: No possibility of confusion with other species.
D: Flowers in simple or branched racemes, pale yellow. Stem erect, densely hairy at the top, less so below. Leaves pinnate, compound (5—7 segments), the lower leaves with long petioles.
H: Canyon forest, valley and fen woodland, damp deciduous woodland. Likes a damp soil, rich in nutrients and humus.
AI: P; ♃; †
The flowers of Yellow Monkshood are pollinated by bumblebees. The plant has a high alkaloid content, particularly in the rootstock, and is very poisonous. In the Middle Ages, this plant was used as a source of poison for arrows. In addition an extract of the plant was used to poison bait for carnivores, particularly foxes and wolves (hence common name).

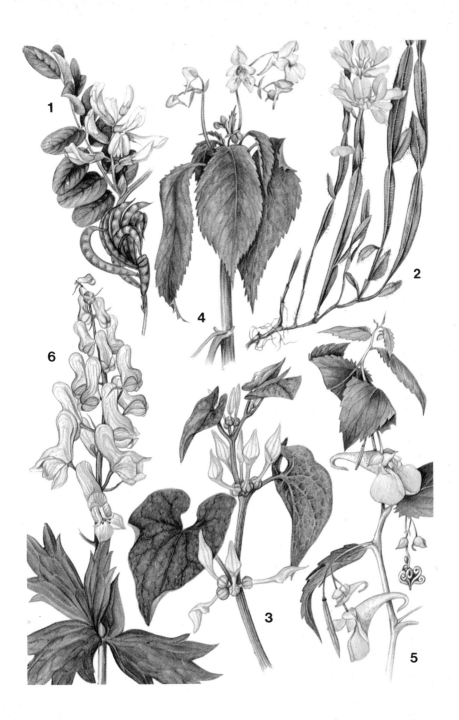

❶
50—100 cm

Yellow Foxglove *(Digitalis lutea)*
Scrophulariaceae
IM: Flowers 2—2.5 cm long.
D: Unilaterally directed racemes. Flowers without a brown network of veins on the inside of the corolla tube. Stem erect, glabrous. Leaves linear, ciliated.
H: Dry mixed and deciduous woodland, light thickets, mountain forest, clearings and felled areas in woods. Likes a porous, stony, somewhat moist soil.
AI: G; ♃; †
This plant contains a poisonous digitalis glycoside.

---

❷
50—130 cm

Large-flowered Foxglove, Pale Foxglove *(Digitalis grandiflora ; D. ambigua)*
Scrophulariaceae
IM: Flowers 3—4.5 cm long.
D: Unilaterally directed racemes. Flowers sulphur yellow, inflated, campanulate, with brown veins on the inside of the corolla tube. Stem erect, hairy. Leaves elongate, ciliate, serrate.
H: Mountain forest, mixed and deciduous woodland, particularly in clearings, thickets, more rarely in mountain pastures and alpine mat. Likes a porous, stony soil, damp with seepage water. Forms small clumps.
AI: G; ♃; †
Contains a poisonous digitalis glycoside.

---

❸
15—30 cm

Common Cow Wheat, Meadow Cow Wheat *(Melampyrum pratense)*
Scrophulariaceae
IM: Flowers 1.2—1.8 cm long.
D: Unilaterally directed, loose spikes. Stem usually erect. Leaves linear-lanceolate, rough. Several other, very similar, but rare species.
H: Heaths, deciduous and mixed woodland, coniferous forest. Likes an acid, porous, sandy, loamy soil, rich in humus.
AI: G; ⊙; (†)
Hemiparasite. For nectar-robbing habits of visiting bees see next species.

---

❹
15—25 cm

Wood Cow Wheat, Small-flowered Cow Wheat *(Melampyrum sylvaticum)*
Scrophulariaceae
IM: Flowers 0.8—1 cm long.
D: Unilaterally directed spikes. Stem erect or decumbent. Leaves below the inflorescence lanceolate, entire, almost sessile.
H: Mixed and deciduous woodland, coniferous forest, heaths. Likes a mossy, loamy soil with surface acidity.
AI: G; ⊙; (†)
Hemiparasite. The flowers are commonly visited by short-tongued bees, which bite through the base of the corolla to get to the nectar, without bringing about pollination. The seeds contain the poisonous substance aucubin in large amounts.

---

❺
30—60 cm

Common Toadflax *(Linaria vulgaris)*
Scrophulariaceae
See p. 140

---

❻
10—50 cm

Lesser Broomrape *(Orobanche minor ; O. barbata)*
Orobanchaceae
See p. 166

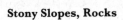

❶

Yellow Whitlow Grass *(Draba aizoides)*
Brassicaceae (Cruciferae)

5—15 cm

IM: Ovaries at the most 3 times as long as broad. Stem leafless. Leaves in a circular rosette.

D: Cymose racemes. Flowers only 2—3 mm long, on erect peduncles, golden yellow. Stem unbranched. Rosette leaves fleshy, linear, pointed at the tip.

H: Scree associated with limestone in warm situations. Where it does occur there are many plants together.

AI: P; 2↳
The flowers remain half-closed in rainy weather and can be self-fertilized. The fruiting body lasts over the winter and the seeds are not released until early spring.

❷

Yellow *or* **Biting Stonecrop, Wall Pepper** *(Sedum acre)*
Crassulaceae

5—15 cm

IM: Plant has a burning taste (chew a little, but do not swallow!). Petals 6—9 mm long. Leaves ovoid, without spurs.

D: Cymes of few flowers. Stem creeping or decumbent. Leaves small, thick and fleshy, sessile.

H: Walls, embankments, rocky screes, road rubble, sand dunes, sandy turf. Likes a dry, shallow, mainly calcareous and often stony soil.

AI: P; 2↳; †
The name Wall Pepper draws attention to both its habitat and burning taste. The plant contains a poisonous alkaloid, therefore take care when testing the taste! It is not advisable to sample more than one leaf. An old medicinal plant.

❸

Tasteless Sedum, Insipid Stonecrop *(Sedum sexangulare; S. boloniense; S. mite)*
Crassulaceae

5—15 cm

See p. 152

❹

Orpine, Livelong *(Sedum telephium; S. maximum)*
Crassulaceae

20—50 cm

See p. 176

❺

Mouse-ear Hawkweed *(Hieracium pilosella)*
Cichoriaceae (Compositae)

8—30 cm

IM: Flowers in solitary capitula. Only ray florets present. Carpels with pappus of hairs, which are greyish white and brittle (press with finger). Stem leafless. Leaves with long hairs, undersides with grey or white felt. Plant with long runners.

D: Flowers often reddish underneath. Leaves invert-ovoid, rather bluish green.

H: Dry and semi-dry turf, heaths, wayside verges, also in light woodland and on rocky screes. Avoids deeply shaded localities. On various soils.

AI: G; 2↳
A species which exists in various forms and is difficult to distinguish from many similar species.

❻

Yellow Foxglove *(Digitalis lutea)*
Scrophulariaceae

50—100 cm

See p. 190

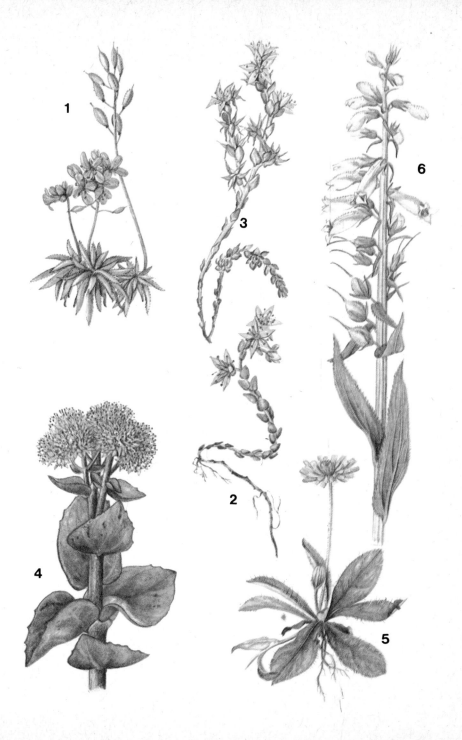

❶

8—15 cm

Alternate-leaved Golden Saxifrage *(Chrysosplenium alternifolium)*
Saxifragaceae
IM: Stem leaves alternate.
D: Cymes. Stem angular, brittle. Leaves with long petioles, rounded kidney-shaped, deeply crenate, with a golden tinge on the upper surface.
H: Deciduous woodland, canyon forest, shady clear brooks, wet mountain meadows, around springs, dripping wells.
AI: P; ♃
An old medicinal plant, although so far no active principle has been found in it.

❷

50—120 cm

Common Meadow Rue *(Thalictrum flavum)*
Ranunculaceae
See p. 144

❸

30—60 cm

Winter Cress, Yellow Rocket *(Barbarea vulgaris)*
Brassicaceae (Cruciferae)
IM: Petals twice as long as the sepals, golden yellow. Carpels more than 3 times as long as broad. Fruits quadrangular, spreading. Terminal lobes of basal leaves small, rounded.
D: Racemes. Lower leaves lyre-shaped, upper leaves pinnate to undivided, invert-ovoid, dentate.
H: Weedy places on roadsides, embankments, on wet, stony wasteland, muddy banks and sometimes in clearings. Likes a pebbly soil with large mineral particles and a high nitrogen content.
AI: P; ♃
This plant probably received its Latin generic name in the 15th century. It remains green well into winter, so that the leaves can be collected on St Barbara's day (4 December) for a winter salad.

❹

30—60 cm

Treacle Mustard *(Erysimum cheiranthoides)*
Brassicaceae (Cruciferae)
IM: Flowers 4—8 mm in diameter. Carpels more than 3 times as long as broad. Peduncle 2—3 times as long as the calyx. Leaves undivided, coarsely serrate, with tridentate hairs (use a magnifying glass).
D: Racemes. Middle leaves linear-lanceolate.
H: Weedy places in fields, on river banks and sandy or gravel banks of streams. Likes a porous, rather moist soil. Somewhat calcicolous.
AI: P; ☉

❺

10—100 cm

Marsh Watercress *(Rorippa islandica; R. palustris)*
Brassicaceae (Cruciferae)
IM: Petals as long as, or shorter than, the calyx; bright yellow. Flowers 2—4 mm in diameter. Carpels and fruit more than 3 times as long as broad.
D: Loose cymes. Stem prostrate, decumbent or erect, angular, hollow. Lower leaves petiolate, lyre-shaped, pinnate. Terminal leaflet broader. Upper leaves with short petioles or sessile, pinnate.
H: Banks of rivers, sandbanks or gravel banks. Likes a nitrogenous soil and withstands occasional flooding. Indicator of muddy conditions.
AI: P; ☉ — ⊙

3

4

2

1

5

❶

30—60 cm

Branched Bur Reed *(Sparganium erectum; S. ramosum)*
Sparganiaceae
IM: Stem branched. The upper flower heads on the branches are male, the lower ones female. The fruits are prickly, resembling a bur (hence the name).
D: Male and female flowers in round heads, with the male flowers at the top of the stem and the female flowers below. Leaves mostly erect, stiff, 3—15 mm wide, triangular on the underside.
H: Banks of slow-flowing and stagnant waters. Likes a soil rich in nutrients.
AI: M; ♃
Similar, Simple Bur Reed *(Sparganium simplex)* with an unbranched stem, upright stiff leaves 3—6 mm wide, with triangular undersides. Narrow-leaved Bur Reed *(S. angustifolium)* with an unbranched stem. Leaves floating in water, 3—8 mm wide. Reed bed and floating-plant communities in oligotrophic lakes at high altitudes. May form large stands where it occurs.

---

❷

20—100 cm

Great Watercress, Great Yellow Cress *(Rorippa amphibia)*
Brassicaceae (Cruciferae)
See p. 168

---

❸

90—130 cm

Marsh Spurge *(Euphorbia palustris)*
Euphorbiaceae
IM: Cymose inflorescences with many rays. Glands on bracts transverse-oval, bright yellow, turning brownish later. Stem with non-flowering branches, hollow.
D: Stem thick with a bluish bloom. Leaves alternate, lanceolate, sessile, almost entire, glabrous. Plant contains a white milky juice.
H: Margins of flowing or stagnant waters, reed beds, wet meadows, river banks. Likes a calcareous, silty soil.
AI: P; ♃; †
Flowers: see Dwarf Spurge, p. 120.
The milky juice contains the poisonous euphorbone. An old medicinal plant.

---

❹

15—30 cm

Common Tormentil *(Potentilla erecta; P. tormentilla; Tormentilla erecta)*
Rosaceae
IM: Flowers solitary in leaf axils, about 1 cm in diameter. Only 4 petals. Basal leaves tridentate, stem leaves with 5 lobes arranged in a palmate manner.
D: Stem prostrate to erect. Leaves sessile.
H: Light mixed and deciduous woodland, coniferous forests, heaths, dry meadows, fens and swamps. Likes a soil which is at least wet part of the time. Calcifugous and indicates surface acidity.
AI: P; ♃
The plant contains the pigment tormentil red, and also tannins, particularly in the rootstock. These are the reasons for its blood-coagulating properties. The root extract is sometimes added to Schnaps to give a stomachic. An old medicinal plant.

---

❺

15—50 cm

Creeping Yellow Cress *(Rorippa sylvestris; Nasturtium sylvestre)*
Brassicaceae (Cruciferae)
See p. 118

1

5

3

2

4

❶

15—50 cm

Marsh Marigold, Kingcup *(Caltha palustris)*
Ranunculaceae
    See p. 170

---

❷

15—50 cm

Creeping Buttercup *(Ranunculus repens)*
Ranunculaceae
    See p. 148

---

❸

40—150 cm

Great Spearwort *(Ranunculus lingua)*
Ranunculaceae
IM: Flowers 2.5—4 cm in diameter, golden yellow, with a distinct gloss. Leaves undivided. Stem erect.
D: Inflorescence usually with many flowers, more rarely with few. Stem erect, vigorous, richly branched at the top. Leaves linear-lanceolate, pointed, entire or slightly dentate.
H: Margins of stagnant or slow-flowing waters, reed beds. Likes a soil which is sometimes submerged but is rich in nutrients.
AI: P; ♃; (†)
     Contains some protoanemonine and is therefore slightly poisonous. The common name refers to the shape of the leaves.

---

❹

15—50 cm

Lesser Spearwort *(Ranunculus flammula)*
Ranunculaceae
IM: Flowers 0.6—2 cm in diameter, golden yellow, with a distinct gloss. Leaves undivided. Stem thick, decumbent.
D: Flowers usually numerous with long peduncles. Stem prostrate, decumbent or erect. Leaves undivided, with long petioles, spoon-shaped, elliptic or linear-lanceolate, grass green.
H: Ditches, banks of streams, ponds and lakes, moorland, reed beds. Likes a wet, occasionally flooded soil.
AI: P; ♃; †

---

❺

10—110 cm

Celery-leaved Crowfoot *(Ranunculus sceleratus)*
Ranunculaceae
IM: Flowers 6—12 mm in diameter, bright yellow. Petals only about as long as the sepals.
D: Loose panicles. Sepals yellowish green, falling away early. Stem decumbent or erect, hollow, glabrous or slightly hairy, richly branched. Leaves fleshy, the lower ones with 3 lobes, invert-ovoid, dissected. Upper leaves 3-lobed, with linear-cuneate segments.
H: Banks of slow-flowing streams, also edges of ponds, ditches and meres.
AI: P; ⊙; †

---

❻

15—50 cm

Silverweed *(Potentilla anserina)*
Rosaceae
IM: Flowers solitary with long peduncles. Flowers up to 2 cm in diameter. Leaves compound, pinnate with hairy undersides.
D: Flowers golden yellow. Stem creeping to decumbent. Leaves with many leaflets, which are linear and deeply serrate.
H: Waysides, embankments, wasteland, river banks, pond margins, uncultivated soil. Likes a compact, loamy soil. Indicator of nitrogen.
AI: P; ♃

❶

At water
depths of
up to
2.5 m

Yellow Water Lily, Brandy Bottle *(Nuphar luteum)*
Nymphaeaceae
IM: Flowers 4—6 cm in diameter. Leaf 12—30 cm long, petiole 4—8 mm thick.
D: Flowers solitary, with a strong scent. Petioles rope-like. Leaves ovoid or
        heart-shaped, entire, leathery, floating.
H: Floating-plant communities in still or slow-running waters; likes cool water,
        rich in nutrients, but may occur in the acid waters of moorland. Abundant
        in those localities where it does occur.
Al: P; ♃; (†)
        The fruits of this species are able to float due to air bladders in the tissue
        of the fruit. These only remain intact for a limited time, after which the fruit
        sinks to the bottom. The fruits can also be carried short distances by water
        birds.
        The plant contains alkaloids.

❷

At water
depths of
up to
2.5 m

Dwarf Water Lily *(Nuphar pumila)*
Nymphaeaceae
IM: Flowers 1—3 cm in diameter. Leaf 4—'12 cm long, petiole 1—2 mm thick.
D: Flowers solitary with hardly any smell. Leaves ovoid, heart-shaped, entire,
        leathery, floating.
H: Floating-plant communities of stagnant waters. Likes cool waters, relatively
        poor in nutrients, over peaty soils.
AI: P; ♃

❸

5—30 cm

Creeping Jenny, Moneywort *(Lysimachia nummularia)*
Primulaceae
        See p. 176

❹

5—15 cm

Trailing St John's Wort *(Hypericum humifusum)*
Hypericaceae
IM: Stem prostrate.
D: Panicles. Stamens clustered. Stem round or angular. Leaves opposite, linear-
        ovoid, the upper leaves with transparent dots.
H: Weedy places in wet vegetable fields, on uncultivated soil, along roadsides,
        in damp, open woodland. Likes a moist, sandy or loamy soil. Calcifugous.
AI: P; ☉—♃
        Name and pigmentation: see Common St John's Wort, p. 150.

❺

60—130 cm

Common Loosestrife *(Lysimachia vulgaris)*
Primulaceae
        See p. 176

❻

30—70 cm

Tufted Loosestrife *(Lysimachia thyrsiflora)*
Primulaceae
IM: Leaves in axillary racemes. Flowers 3—5 mm long.
D: Racemes with many flowers. Leaves opposite, decussate, lanceolate to linear-
        lanceolate.
H: Banks of stagnant or slow-running waters, reed beds. Likes a muddy, often
        submerged and rather acid soil.
AI: G; ♃

200

❶

30—60 cm

Winged St John's Wort *(Hypericum tetrapterum)*
Hypericaceae
IM: Plant glabrous. Stem erect, with 4 rounded angles bearing broad wings.
D: Umbel-like panicles. Stamens clustered. Leaves opposite, ovoid or broadly elliptical with small, transparent spots and a few black glands.
H: Banks of stagnant or running waters, reed beds, springs. Likes a wet, loamy, rather chalky soil.
AI: P; ♃

❷

30—100 cm

Common Comfrey, Knitbone *(Symphytum officinale)*
Boraginaceae
See p. 178

❸

10—30 cm

Colt's-foot *(Tussilago farfara)*
Asteraceae (Compositae)
IM: Flowers in a capitulum. Plant without leaves at flowering time, only leaf scales present on the stem which has a cobweb-like covering of hairs.
D: Capitula solitary. Leaves appear at the end of the flowering period. They have long petioles, are circular to heart-shaped with the undersides covered with a white felt, toothed.
H: Weedy places on uncultivated soil, roadsides, dykes, among ruins.
AI: G; ♃
After flowering the heads droop. A medicinal plant, containing mucilages and tannins, particularly in the leaves.

❹

60—100 cm

Yellow Iris, Yellow Flag *(Iris pseudacorus)*
Iridaceae
IM: Outer petals without a comb of hairs, inner petals smaller, erect. Stigmas large and petalloid. Leaves up to 3 cm wide, about as long as the stem.
D: Outer petals with dark flecks on the inside, inner petals smaller.
H: Margins of stagnant or flowing waters, reed beds. Likes a soil which is occasionally submerged.
AI: M; ♃; †

❺

30—60 cm

Willow-leaved Inula *(Inula salicina)*
Asteraceae (Compositae)
IM: Capitulum about 2.5—3 cm in diameter. Both ray florets and disc florets present. Carpels with a pappus of hairs. Involucral bracts imbricate. Stem and leaves usually glabrous. Upper leaves clasp the stem.
D: 1—5 capitula to plant. Ray florets much longer than disc florets. Stem erect. Leaves entire.
H: Semi-dry turf, damp meadows. Likes a loamy soil.
AI: G; ♃

❻

10—100 cm

Tripartite Bur Marigold *(Bidens tripartitus)*
Asteraceae (Compositae)
IM: Flowers in capitula arranged in a cymose manner. Both ray florets and disc florets present, the latter being a brownish yellow. Fruit with 2 (more rarely 3 or 4) barbed awns. Leaves opposite.
D: Flowers inconspicuous. Stem erect, often with a reddish-brown tinge. Leaves dark green, mostly tripinnate, sometimes with 5 leaflets.
H: Ditches, river banks. Likes a muddy soil.
AI: G; ☉

❶

Cabbage Thistle *(Cirsium oleraceum)*
Asteraceae (Compositae)
50—150 cm   See p. 158

❷

Mugwort *(Artemisia vulgaris)*
Asteraceae (Compositae)
90—150 cm   See p. 184

❸

Marsh *or* **Large Bird's-foot Trefoil** *(Lotus uliginosus; L. pedunculatus)*
Fabaceae (Leguminosae)
10—60 cm   See p. 160

❹

Yellow Asparagus Pea *(Tetragonolobus maritimus; Lotus siliquosus)*
Fabaceae (Leguminosae)
15—40 cm   See p. 160

❺

Greater Bladderwort *(Utricularia vulgaris)*
Lentibulariaceae
15—30 cm

IM: Plant free-floating, green. Leaf segments slightly ciliate.
D: Loose racemes. Flowers 1.3—2 cm long, golden yellow. Leaves long, pinnate or bipinnate, bearing 1.5 mm long bladders to trap insects (cf. name of plant). There are several similar, but much rarer species all very difficult to distinguish.
H: Aquatic communities of stagnant water. Likes waters which are non-calcareous but rich in nutrients and in warm situations. Occurs in large numbers in certain localities.
AI: G; ♃
     An insectivorous plant. The bladders of *Utricularia* are among the most remarkable adaptations in the plant kingdom. The inside of the bladder is at a negative pressure. When an aquatic insect or water flea makes contact with the hairs of the 'trap-door' of the bladder, the 'trap-door' opens and the prey is sucked inside. The door closes again as a result of the counter current set up. The insect is digested inside the bladder as a result of the action of proteolytic enzymes.

❻

Yellow Balsam, Touch-me-not *(Impatiens noli-tangere)*
Balsaminaceae
30—60 cm

IM: Flowers hanging down, large, with long spurs, golden yellow, with red spots on the inside of the corolla. Spurs curved.
D: 2—4 flowers in axillary racemes. Stem glassy, swollen at the nodes. Leaves alternate, ovoid, coarsely serrate.
H: Fen woodland, canyon forest, damp mixed and deciduous woodland, more rarely in coniferous forest. Likes a loamy soil, but also occurs on gravel. Prefers shady places.
AI: P; ⊙; (†)
     The fruit ejects its seeds violently on contact, hence the scientific and common names. A central column of tissue in the fruit is under tension. If the ripe fruit is touched or shaken, the carpels separate, roll back and the seeds are ejected. They can be thrown several metres. The plant contains a slightly poisonous alkaloid, the identity of which is still not known.

❶   **Cornelian Cherry** *(Cornus mas)*
Cornaceae

2.5—6 m   IM: Flowers in small, clustered umbels on leafless twigs.
D: Umbels simple, lateral. Berries red. Twigs round, green, glabrous. Leaves opposite, entire, ovoid or elliptical, with curved veins.
H: Dry woodland and thickets, banks of rivers. Likes a porous, calcareous soil in warm situations. Often planted and escapes into the wild.
AI: P
Berries edible.

❷   **Mistletoe** *(Viscum album)*
Loranthaceae

20—50 cm   IM: Plant yellowish green. Leaves leathery, evergreen. The plant is a parasite on trees.
D: Dioecious. Flowers in clusters, inconspicuous but not very small. Fruit a white berry. Stem forked. Leaves opposite.
H: Dry woodland and thickets, banks of rivers. Likes a porous, calcareous soil in warm situations. Often planted and escapes into the wild.
Mistletoe contains the poisonous viscotoxin. Despite their poisonous content the berries are eaten by thrushes. They pass through the alimentary canal of the bird undigested and are dispersed in the droppings. The mistletoe plays a major role in ancient legends and stories. Among Celtic peoples it is revered as a plant which wards off demons. The custom of kissing under the mistletoe at Christmas goes back to these ancient beliefs.

❸   **Common** *or* **Purging Buckthorn** *(Rhamnus cathartica)*
Rhamnaceae

1—3 m   See p. 374

❹   **Red-berried Elder** *(Sambucus racemosa)*
Caprifoliaceae

2—4 m   IM: Flowers in erect, ovoid panicles, strongly scented.
D: Berries round, red. Pith of branches yellowish brown. Leaves unpaired pinnate, usually with 5 leaflets, almost sessile, ovoid, serrate.
H: Deciduous and mixed woodland, more rarely coniferous forest, clearings in woods, thickets. Likes a rather stony, non-calcareous, loamy soil.
AI: G
The flesh part of the berry contains 25—65 mg of vitamin C per 100 g of fresh weight, also some provitamin A, or carotene. The berries can be eaten in jam, for although they contain a slightly poisonous substance this is destroyed on prolonged heating. An old medicinal plant.

❺   **Norway Maple** *(Acer platanoides)*
Aceraceae

20—25 m   IM: Leaves with 5 lobes, which are toothed. Leaves 8—20 cm long.
D: Umbellate racemes of many flowers. Flowers greenish yellow, appearing before the leaves. Crown of tree broadly rounded.
H: Mountain and canyon forest, also in fen woodland. Likes a moist, porous or gravelly soil. Quite common as a planted tree in parks.
AI: P
In the spring this tree contains a sugary sap in its trunk and branches. Injury to the twigs causes this sap to exude in drops.

Shrubs and Trees   **Yellow**

❶   **Field Maple** *(Acer campestre)*
              Aceraceae
3—20 m   IM: Leaves with 5 lobes, which in turn are bluntly lobed. Leaves 4—7 cm long.
              D: Flowers in erect, umbellate racemes, greenish yellow. Young twigs brown, older twigs greyish brown, with reticulate fissures.
              H: Dry deciduous and mixed woodland, thickets. Likes a chalky, porous soil.
              AI: P

❷   **Sycamore** *(Acer pseudo-platanus)*
              Aceraceae
20—25 m   IM: Leaves with 5 lobes, which are unevenly serrate at the edge.
              D: Racemes at the end of the twigs, pendulous. Twigs with leaves at flowering time. Crown of tree quite round.
              H: Canyon forest, mixed woodland. Likes a porous, somewhat stony, moist soil.
              AI: P

❸   **Large-leaved Lime** *(Tilia platyphyllos)*
              Tiliaceae
Up to 30 m   IM: Underside of leaves with short hairs. A whitish-yellow cluster of hairs in the angle between the veins.
              D: Pendulous cymes of 2—5 flowers. Leaves almost heart-shaped.
              H: Mountain forest, canyon forest.
              AI: P
              Flowers used to make an aromatic tea.

❹   **Small-leaved Lime** *(Tilia cordata; T. ulmifolia)*
              Tiliaceae
Up to 25 m   IM: Leaves glabrous on the underside, rust-coloured hairs confined to angles of veins.
              D: Pendulous cymes of 5—7 flowers. Leaves almost heart-shaped or sometimes triangular, unevenly serrate.
              H: Deciduous woodland. Likes a stony or sandy soil.
              AI: P
              This species of tree can attain an age of more than 1,000 years when its trunk diameter will attain 15 m. The flowers are used to make an aromatic tea.

❺   **Common Barberry** *(Berberis vulgaris)*
              Berberidaceae
1—2.5 m   IM: No possibility of confusion with other species.
              D: Flowers in lateral racemes. Berries elongate and cylindrical, scarlet red in colour. Branches rod-like, with a reddish tinge. Bark bright grey, with bitter taste. Wood yellow, hard. Leaves on the shorter shoots in clusters, with short petioles, ovoid. Leaves on longer shoots with trifid spines at the base.

              H: Light deciduous and mixed woodland. Likes a chalky soil in warm situations.
              AI: P; (†)
              The stamens of Barberry are sensitive and on being stimulated by a pollinating insect undergo shaking movements. In many localities the Barberry has been exterminated because it is the intermediate host of the serious rust disease of wheat. Infection of the Barberry by the rust fungus is indicated by red spots on the leaves. The wood is occasionally used for making toothpicks. The yellow pigment of the wood can also be used to dye leather and wool. Contains an alkaloid and is slightly poisonous. An old medicinal plant.

❶

3 — 10 m

Laburnum *(Laburnum anagyroides; L. vulgare; Cytisus laburnum)*
Fabaceae (Leguminosae)
IM: No possibility of confusion with other species.
D: Pendulous racemes. Leaves compound with 3 leaflets. Twigs with smooth bark. Leaves often clustered, with long petioles. Leaflets pointed, elliptical, entire; upper side dark green, underside grey green, covered with silky hairs.
H: Dry woodland, thickets. Likes a porous, rather moist, calcareous soil, in warm situations. Most examples in woodland result from seeds derived from planted trees.
AI: P; †
Contains a poisonous alkaloid, particularly in the bark and seeds.

❷

15 — 25 cm

Arrowhead Broom *(Genistella sagittalis; Genista sagittalis)*
Fabaceae (Leguminosae)
See p. 164

❸

10 — 25 cm

Hairy Greenweed *(Genista pilosa)*
Fabaceae (Leguminosae)
IM: Keel of flower as long as standard. Stem and twigs without thorns. Leaves solitary or in pairs, hairy.
D: Stem prostrate. Leaves linear-lanceolate, blunt. Twigs and undersides of leaves with silky hairs.
H: Heaths, edges of woodland, clearings, roadside verges, semi-dry turf. On a wide variety of soils in warm situations. Susceptible to frost.
AI: P

❹

30 — 60 cm

Dyer's Greenweed *(Genista tinctoria)*
Fabaceae (Leguminosae)
IM: Flowers in terminal racemes, glabrous. Keel as long as the standard. Stem and twigs without spines.
D: Stem prostrate or decumbent, strongly branched at the top. Twigs forked, without wings. Leaves elongate or elliptical, almost sessile, with soft hairs on the margins.
H: Verges, dry turf, heath, light woodland. Likes a loamy soil, which is not too dry. Not calcicolous.
AI: P; †

❺

30 — 60 cm

German Broom *(Genista germanica)*
Fabaceae (Leguminosae)
IM: Keel of flower longer than standard. Stem with spiny branches at the bottom of the shrub. Leaves simple, with rough hairs.
D: Flowers in terminal racemes. Stem decumbent or erect, branched at the top. Leaves elongate-elliptical, 1 — 2 cm long. The leafy branches at the top of the shrub are without spines.
H: Heaths, light, dry woodland, roadside verges; calcifugous; likes warm situations.
AI: P; †
The seeds contain an alkaloid and are poisonous.

Shrubs and Trees **Yellow**

❶

60—200 cm

Common Broom *(Cytisus scoparius ; Sarothamnus scoparius)*
Fabaceae (Leguminosae)
IM: Leaves solitary or in pairs. Leaves with 3 leaflets, except for the upper leaves which are undivided.
D: Flowers 2—2.5 cm long, golden yellow, in the axils of leaves. Stem erect, and like the branches, with angular ridges. Leaves with soft hairs.
H: Roadside verges, clearings, edges of woods, mountain pastures; calcifugous. It enriches the soil with nitrogen.
AI: P; (†)
Twigs used for making brooms (hence name). Contains an alkaloid. A medicinal plant.

❷

1—1.5 m

Common Gorse, Furze, Whin *(Ulex europaeus)*
Fabaceae (Leguminosae)
IM: Leaves needle-like, prickly.
D: Flowers 1—3 in the axils of the upper leaves. Stem erect. Twigs green, grooved. Leaves mostly replaced by needle-like spines, simple or trifid, upper spines very prickly and pointed.
H: Verges, light, dry woodland and thickets, heaths. Calcifugous. Likes warm situations and cannot withstand hard frosts in winter.
AI: P; †
Gorse is often planted for animal fodder. The seeds contain a poisonous alkaloid.

❸

Up to 3 m

Common Honeysuckle *(Lonicera periclymenum)*
Caprifoliaceae
IM: Stem twining. Upper leaves not concrescent.
D: Flowers in terminal clusters, ivory to pale yellow, often with a reddish tinge. Stem dextrally twining. Leaves oval or invert-ovoid, with short petioles, the upper ones sessile.
H: Mixed and deciduous woodland, mountain woodland and fens. Likes a stony or sandy, loamy soil. Rather calcifugous.
AI: G; (†)
The berries contain a poisonous alkaloid.

❹

5—15 cm

Alpine Milkwort *(Polygala chamaebuxus ; Chamaebuxus alpestris)*
Polygalaceae
IM: Flowers yellowish brown to reddish. Leaves leathery, evergreen.
D: Racemes of few flowers. Stem decumbent. Leaves lanceolate or elliptical, the lower ones smaller than the upper, invert-ovoid.
H: Dry woodland and thickets, edges of woods, semi-dry turf. Likes a crumbly, porous, calcareous soil.
AI: P

❺

50—150 cm

Black Broom *(Lembotropis nigricans ; Cytisus nigricans)*
Fabaceae (Leguminosae)
IM: Racemes erect. Leaves composed of 3 leaflets.
D: 20—100 flowers, each 1 cm long, in elongate racemes. Flowers golden yellow, with a pleasant smell. Shoots on drying become black (hence name). Leaves with long petioles. Leaflets up to 2 cm long and 1 cm wide.
H: Roadside verges, thickets, edges of woods. Likes a stony or sandy, shallow soil, in warm situations.
AI: P

1   2   3   4   5

❶ Red Poppy *(Papaver rhoeas)*

30—80 cm Papaveraceae

IM: Flower stalks with spreading hairs. Ovary and capsule glabrous. Plant contains a milky sap. Flower has an unpleasant smell.

D: Flowers solitary on long peduncles. Petals scarlet, flecked with black at the base. Stem with little branching, hairy. Leaves deeply pinnate, serrate, sessile. Similar species: *Papaver strigosum* with the peduncle covered in stiff hairs; *P. dubium* in which the leaves are double pinnate and the capsule is club-shaped. Both species inhabit similar habitats to *P. rhoeas* and have similar soil preferences.

H: Weedy places in fields, on wasteland and compost heaps. Likes a loamy soil, rich in nutrients, but also occurs on shallow, chalky soils in warm situations.

AI: P; ⊙—⊝; (†)

Known as a weed since Neolithic times. Origin unknown. Contains a slightly poisonous alkaloid, particularly in its milky sap.

❷ Sand Poppy *(Papaver argemone)*

10—30 cm Papaveraceae

IM: Ovary and capsule with stiff bristles. Ovary and fruit club-shaped and covered with bristle-like hairs.

D: Flowers solitary, with long peduncles. Petals dark red, black at the base, easily dropping off. Stem slightly branched, with stiff hairs. Leaves deeply pinnate, toothed; the lower leaves with distinct petioles, the upper leaves sessile. Petioles, when present, with stiff hairs. Similar species: Hybrid Poppy *(Papaver hybridum)*: Ovary and capsule ovoid, up to twice as long as broad; 20—40 cm, cornfields on loamy soil.

H: Weedy places in cornfields, on wasteland or along waysides. Calcifugous.

AI· P; ⊙; ⊝

Known as a weed in cornfields since Neolithic times. Origin unknown.

❸ Sheep Sorrel *(Rumex acetosella)*

8—30 cm Polygonaceae

See p. 230

❹ Great Willowherb, Hairy Willowherb, Codlins-and-Cream
(Epilobium hirsutum)

90—140 cm Onagraceae (Oenotheraceae)

IM: Petals 1—2 cm long, reddish purple. Stem markedly hairy, at least towards the base.

D: Loose racemes. Lower leaves opposite and decussate, linear-lanceolate, clasping the stem.

H: Ditches, banks of flowing water, more rarely on ponds. Weedy places in wet meadows, less frequently on moist wasteland. Likes a loamy, rather calcareous soil.

AI: P; ♃

The seeds of all Willowherbs have long seed hairs, which have not yet been spun, as have the seed hairs of cotton. Occasionally, they have, however, been used to make wicks.

 ❺ Common Comfrey, Knitbone *(Symphytum officinale)*

30—100 cm Boraginaceae

See p. 178

❶

15 — 50 cm

Common Stork's-bill *(Erodium cicutarium)*
Geraniaceae
IM: Leaves unpaired pinnate. Leaflets deeply dissected.
D: Flowers purplish pink, often somewhat spotted. Fruit with awns. Stem prostrate or decumbent, with rough hairs, often tinged with red.
H: Weedy places in vegetable fields and along paths, also on semi-dry turf. Likes uncultivated soil rich in nitrogen.
AI P; ☉ — ☉
The common name refers to the beak-like form of the fruit. The seeds are ejected from the fruit in a similar manner to those of Crane's-bill (cf. Marsh Crane's-bill, p. 272). With their hairy awns they can become attached to the coats of animals and are dispersed in this way. With the aid of their spirally coiled awns the seeds can also penetrate into the ground with atmospheric humidity changes.

❷

8 — 30 cm

Dove's-foot Crane's-bill *(Geranium molle)*
Geraniaceae
See p. 232

❸

10 — 50 cm

Cut-leaved Crane's-bill *(Geranium dissectum)*
Geraniaceae
IM: Flowers mostly in twos, 8 — 10 mm in diameter, bright purplish pink. Stalk of inflorescence shorter than the bract. All leaves petiolate.
D: Stem branched, decumbent to erect. Leaves, including the basal ones, divided into 5 — 7 segments. Leaflets lobed.
H: Weedy places particularly in vegetable fields, wasteland and along roadside verges. Likes a stony, dry soil, rich in nutrients.
AI: P; ☉ — ☉
Name: see Meadow Crane's-bill, p. 300.

❹

25 — 50 cm

Herb Robert *(Geranium robertianum)*
Geraniaceae
See p. 254

❺

30 — 50 cm

Wayside Mallow *(Malva neglecta ; M. vulgaris)*
Malvaceae
IM: Flowers pale rose. Petals 8 — 15 mm long. Stalk of fruit bent upwards. Upper leaves not dissected over more than $\frac{2}{3}$ their radius.
D: Flowers in clusters in the leaf axils. Stem usually prostrate.
H: Weedy places along paths, on embankments, wasteland, compost heaps and walls. An indicator of a nitrogenous soil.
AI: P; ☉ — ♃
Old medicinal plant. Contains mucilage.

❻

50 — 130 cm

Rose Mallow *(Malva alcea)*
Malvaceae
IM: Flowers rose pink. Petals 1.4 — 2.3 cm long. Upper leaves digitately divided into 5 — 7 segments. Hairs on stem branched (magnifying glass needed).
D: Flowers solitary in leaf axils. Stem erect. Leaf segments trifid.
H: Weedy places on roadside verges and wasteland. Likes a sandy but rather chalky soil in warm situations.
AI: P; ♃

❶

20—120 cm

Common Mallow *(Malva sylvestris)*
Malvaceae
IM: Flowers pinkish violet. Petals about 2 cm long. Stalk of fruit not bent upwards. Upper leaves not dissected over more than $\frac{2}{3}$ their radius.
D: A few flowers in clusters in the leaf axils. Stem erect or decumbent. Leaf segments crenate.
H: Weedy places along waysides, on wasteland and old compost heaps. Likes a porous soil, rich in nutrients. Indicator of nitrogen.
AI: P; ♃
A medicinal plant. Contains mucilage.

❷

30—100 cm

Lesser *or* **Field Bindweed** *(Convolvulus arvensis)*
Convolvulaceae
IM: Flowers with rose-pink stripes or completely pink, about 1.5—2.5 cm long.
D: 1—3 flowers in leaf axils. Flowers funnel-shaped, scented. Stem glabrous, prostrate or twining. Leaves alternate, petiolate, sagittate at the base.
H: Weedy places in fields, gardens, vineyards, also on wasteland and along roadsides. Likes a porous, loamy soil. Indicator of nitrogen.
AI: G; ♃
The flowers of Lesser Bindweed open between 7 and 8 a. m. and close on the same day between 1 and 2 p. m. when flowering is over. The tip of the stem undergoes considerable growth movements and in about $1\frac{1}{2}$ hours completes a full anti-clockwise rotation, which is several centimetres in diameter. Contains a cardiac glycoside and tannins in the leaves. An old medicinal plant.

❸

10—60 cm

Common *or* **Lesser Dodder** *(Cuscuta epithymum)*
Cuscutaceae
See p. 236

❹

50—100 cm

Greater Burnet Saxifrage *(Pimpinella major ; P. magna)*
Apiaceae (Umbelliferae)
See p. 34

❺

30—100 cm

Corn Cockle *(Agrostemma githago)*
Caryophyllaceae
IM: Sepals longer than petals. Flowers solitary.
D: Leaves opposite, linear-lanceolate, with rough hairs.
H: Weedy places in cornfields; likes a loamy soil rich in nutrients.
AI: P; ⊙ — ♃; †
At one time the Corn Cockle was a common weed in cornfields and feared because of its poisonous seeds. As a result of careful seed control, this species has been severely reduced. It has been known as a weed of cornfields since Neolithic times. Contains a poisonous saponin.

❻

30—60 cm

Common Soapwort *(Saponaria officinalis)*
Caryophyllaceae
See p. 274

1   4   5

6   2   3

❶ **Wall Gypsy Weed** *(Gypsophila muralis)*
5—15 cm   Caryophyllaceae
IM: Calyx with membranous stripes. Flowers only 6—15 mm long.
D: Panicles. Stem stiffly erect, with forked branches. Leaves opposite, linear, barely 1 mm wide.
H: Weedy places in fields, along woodland paths and on muddy river banks. Rather calcifugous. Indicator of wetness.
AI: P; ☉
Name: see p. 274.

❷ **Scarlet Pimpernel** *(Anagallis arvensis)*
8—15 cm   Primulaceae
IM: No possibility of confusion with other species.
D: Flowers axillary, mainly brick red. Stem usually prostrate. Leaves opposite or in whorls of 3, sessile, ovoid, spotted black on the underside.
H: Weedy places in vegetable fields, more rarely in cornfields, gardens or on wasteland. Likes a loamy soil rich in nutrients.
AI: G; ☉
The plant contains saponin, but is no longer used as a folk remedy.

❸ **Knotweed, Knotgrass** *(Polygonum aviculare)*
10—15 cm   Polygonaceae
See p. 30

❹ **Persicaria** *(Polygonum persicaria)*
10—80 cm   Polygonaceae
IM: Leaf sheaths with a fringe of hairs.
D: Inflorescences in the form of spikes on main and lateral shoots. Stem only slightly branched and with its nodes showing little thickening. Leaves lanceolate, glossy, often with dark flecks on the upper side.
H: Weedy places in fields, wasteland and muddy banks of streams and rivers. Likes a nitrogenous soil.
AI: P; ☉; (†)
The plant contains an ethereal oil and has a burning taste.

❺ **Pale Polygonum, Pale Persicaria, Pale Knotgrass** *(Polygonum lapathifolium)*
10—50 cm   Polygonaceae
See p. 274

❻ **Wood Angelica** *(Angelica sylvestris)*
50—200 cm   Apiaceae (Umbelliferae)
IM: Flowers in umbels with 20—40 rays. Bracts absent or reduced to 1—3, bracteoles numerous. Stem round, hollow, with a whitish bloom. Leaves bi- or tripinnate, the lower ones longer than 50 cm.
D: Umbels compound, with rounded secondary umbels. Leaflets 1.5—3 cm wide, serrate. Leaf sheaths inflated.
H: Fen woodland, damp meadows, thickets and weedy places along paths in gardens and on banks of rivers and ponds. Likes a loamy soil saturated with ground water.
AI: P; ♃; (†)
Name and constituent materials: see p. 76.

❶ **Pheasant's Eye** *(Adonis aestivalis)*
Ranunculaceae
30—50 cm   IM: Flowers scarlet or vermilion, diffuse. Sepals glabrous.
D: Flowers solitary on long peduncles. Petals with a black fleck at the base. Leaves bi- or tripinnate.
H: Weedy places in cornfields. Likes a dry, chalky soil. In the last few years has almost disappeared from many of its former localities.
AI: P; ⊙; (†)
The scientific generic name *(Adonis)* goes back to a Greek legend. When the beautiful Adonis was killed by a wild boar whilst hunting, this plant sprang up from the ground where the drops of his blood had fallen. The plant contains digitalis glycoside in small quantities and is therefore slightly poisonous.

❷ **Crow Garlic** *(Allium vineale)*
Liliaceae
30—60 cm   IM: Bluish-green leaves, like those of chives. Only one bract to the inflorescence and this does not extend beyond the limits of the inflorescence.
D: Cymes, often with bulbils in place of flowers. Flowers with long peduncles. Stem with leaves emerging over half its length. Leaves circular in diameter, except for a narrow, barely discernible furrow on one side.
H: Weedy places in vegetable fields, vineyards, edges of meadows and fen woodland. Likes a soil rich in nutrients but is somewhat calcifugous. Prefers warm situations.
AI: M; 2⊦
There are many similar species which are difficult to distinguish.

❸ **Common, Bitter** *or* **Blue Fleabane** *(Erigeron acer)*
Asteraceae (Compositae)
15—30 cm   See p. 238

❹ **Yarrow, Milfoil** *(Achillea millefolium)*
Asteraceae (Compositae)
15—50 cm   See p. 238

❺ **Spear Thistle** *(Cirsium vulgare; C. lanceolatum)*
Asteraceae (Compositae)
60—130 cm   IM: Flowers in 2—4 cm wide capitula, arranged in a racemose manner. Only disc florets present. Carpels with pinnate hairs (use a magnifying glass). Leaves decurrent.
D: Bracts often covered with a web of hairs. Leaves deeply pinnate with grey felt-like undersides.
H: Weedy places along waysides and on wasteland. Likes a calcareous soil, rich in nitrogen.
AI: G; ⊙

❻ **Musk Thistle** *(Carduus nutans)*
Asteraceae (Compositae)
30—100 cm   IM: Flowers in large, solitary capitula, 3.5—7 cm in diameter, drooping. Only disc florets present. Hairs on carpels not pinnate (magnifying glass needed!).
D: Bracts curved back, pointed. Leaves pinnate.
H: Weedy places along waysides, on scarps and stony wasteland. Likes a stony or sandy, calcareous soil.
AI: G; ⊙

222

1

2

3

4

5

6

❶

50—150 cm

Downy *or* **Felted Burdock** *(Arctium tomentosum)*
Asteraceae (Compositae)
See p. 278

❷

30—180 cm

Greater Burdock *(Arctium lappa; Lappa major)*
Asteraceae (Compositae)
IM: Flowers in spherical or globose capitula arranged in cymose panicles. Flowers 3—3.5 cm in diameter. Only disc florets present. Bracts around flowers with hooks (burs).
D: Stem hairy. Leaves very large, petiolate, rounded or heart-shaped at the base.
H: Weedy places along waysides and on waste ground. Likes a loamy soil, rich in nitrogen.
AI: G; ⊙; ♃
For hybrids and constituents see Lesser Burdock below.

❸

50—130 cm

Lesser Burdock *(Arctium minus)*
Asteraceae (Compositae)
IM: Flowers in spherical or globose capitula. Flowers 1—2 cm in diameter. Only disc florets present. Bracts around flowers with hooks (burs). Branches erect, spreading.
D: Stem leafy. Leaves very large, petiolate, rounded or slightly heart-shaped at the base.
H: Weedy places along waysides, on walls and waste ground. Likes a loamy, nitrogenous soil.
AI: G; ⊙
Hybrids are commonly found near the pure species: these are very difficult to identify. The Lesser Burdock contains in its root ethereal oils, tannins and mucilage. Old medicinal plant.

❹

30—60 cm

Butterbur *(Petasites hybridus; P. officinalis)*
Asteraceae (Compositae)
See p. 276

❺

30—100 cm

Brown-rayed *or* **Meadow Knapweed** *(Centaurea jacea)*
Asteraceae (Compositae)
See p. 240

❻

15—30 cm

Hollow Wort, Hollow Corydalis, Hollow Fumitory *(Corydalis cava)*
Papaveraceae
IM: 10—20 flowers to the inflorescence. Top stem leaves entire. Tuber hollow.
D: Terminal racemes. Flowers mostly dull red, more rarely purple or white, with a faint scent. Stem with 2 leaves, unbranched. Leaves triple pinnate, dissected, fragile, glabrous.
Similar species: Intermediate Corydalis *(Corydalis fabacea)* with only 1—5, often drooping, bright-red flowers and a stem which is usually branched. Top leaves entire. Tuber not hollow. Mixed and deciduous woodland. Likes a porous, loamy soil, rich in nutrients.
H: Fen and deciduous woodland, warm thickets, weedy places in vineyards. Likes a moist, loamy soil in warm situations.
AI: P; ♃; †
The seeds of Corydalis are dispersed by ants. The plant contains an alkaloid, particularly in the tuber, and is therefore poisonous. Old medicinal plant.

❶ Fumitory *(Fumaria officinalis)*
Papaveraceae
15—30 cm
- IM: Flowers at least 8 mm long. Sepals 2—5 mm long.
- D: Racemes. Flowers pale purple, blackish red at the tips. Stem erect or decumbent. Leaves grey green, double pinnate. Leaf segments lanceolate.
- H: Weedy places in vegetable fields and gardens, more rarely in cornfields. Likes a loamy soil.
- AI: P; ⊙; (†)

❷ Henbit *(Lamium amplexicaule)*
Lamiaceae (Labiatae)
15—30 cm
- IM: Plant nettle-like, but without stinging hairs. Upper leaves embracing the stem.
- D: 6—10 flowers in axillary, false whorls. Stem usually branched. Lower leaves with long petioles, opposite and decussate.
- H: In vegetable fields, gardens and vineyards. Likes a loamy soil, rich in nutrients. Prefers a warm situation. Calcifugous.
- AI: G; ⊙

❸ Red Deadnettle *(Lamium purpureum)*
Lamiaceae (Labiatae)
10—25 cm
- IM: Plant nettle-like, but without stinging hairs. Lower lip of corolla with a large, median lobe, divided into two, and 2 small lateral lobes. Flowers 1—2 cm long.
- D: 3—5 flowers in axillary, false whorls. Tip of stem and upper leaves tinged with red. All leaves petiolate, opposite and decussate, ovoid or heart-shaped, wrinkled, crenate or serrate. Plant has an unpleasant smell.
- H: Weedy places in vegetable fields, more rarely in cornfields, along waysides and on waste ground. Likes a loamy soil rich in nutrients.
- AI: G; ⊙

❹ Pink Sicklewort, Pink Coronilla *(Coronilla varia)*
Fabaceae (Leguminosae)
30—130 cm
See p. 266

❺ Earth-nut Pea, Tuberous Pea *(Lathyrus tuberosus)*
Fabaceae (Leguminosae)
30—120 cm
- IM: Flowers red. Stem angular, not winged. Leaves consist of a pair of leaflets and tendrils.
- D: Subterranean stem with tubers.
- H: Weedy places in vegetable fields, more rarely on waste ground. Likes a calcareous soil, rich in nutrients.
- AI: P; ♃

❻ Black Horehound *(Ballota nigra)*
Lamiaceae (Labiatae)
60—130 cm
- IM: Pedunculate flowers in false axillary whorls. Lobes of lower lip broad and blunt. Leaves opposite and decussate. Calyx funnel-shaped with 10 ribs.
- D: Stem angular, branched. Leaves heart-shaped or ovoid, crenate, with soft hairs; they often turn black after flowering is over. Plant has an unpleasant smell.
- H: Weedy places on wasteland, along waysides and on walls. Likes a loose, rather moist, nitrogenous soil.
- AI: G; ♃

1

4

2

3

5

6

❶

10—60 cm

Marsh Woundwort *(Stachys palustris)*
Lamiaceae (Labiatae)
   See p. 280

❷

10—80 cm

Common Hempnettle *(Galeopsis tetrahit)*
Lamiaceae (Labiatae)
IM: Upper lip helmet-shaped. Lower lip with a hollow tooth on each side. Stem swollen below the nodes.
D: Inflorescence consists of several round multiflorous false whorls. Stem simple or branched, hairy at the nodes. Leaves with long petioles, ovoid-lanceolate. There are several similar species which are difficult to distinguish.
H: Weedy places in fields, along waysides, on wasteland and embankments, also on the edges of woods and in clearings. Likes a rather stony soil, rich in nutrients, particularly nitrogen.
AI: P; ⊙—⊙
The Common Hempnettle is derived from two other species of the same genus as a result of hybridization followed by doubling of the chromosomes. This was demonstrated by the Swedish botanist A. Müntzing, who produced the 'synthetic' individuals of *Galeopsis tetrahit* by appropriate experimental crosses.

❸

10—30 cm

Purple *or* **Common Cow Wheat** *(Melampyrum arvense)*
Scrophulariaceae
IM: Flowers and terminal leaves purple. Flowers in dense multilateral spikes.
D: Flowers purple, with a yellow or white splash; total length 2—2.5 cm. Stem erect, branched. Leaves lanceolate, pointed, entire or dentate.
H: Weedy places in cornfields. Likes a chalky soil.
AI: G: ⊙: (†)
Hemiparasite. The seeds of this plant contain the poisonous substance aucubin in large amounts.

❹

30—120 cm

Viper's Bugloss *(Echium vulgare)*
Boraginaceae
IM: No possibility of confusion with other species.
D: Inflorescence loose and mixed with leaves. Flowers first reddish, then blue, funnel-shaped. Stem with stiff hairs which arise from little white or brown tubercles. Leaves with stiff hairs.
H: Weedy places on roadside verges, embankments and wasteland, more rarely on semi-dry turf. Likes a porous, stony soil.
AI: G; ⊙
For note about the colour change in flowers see Mountain Pea, p. 304. Viper's Bugloss contains an alkaloid which is not poisonous to warm-blooded animals, also tannins. An old medicinal plant.

❺

5—30 cm

Common Thyme *(Thymus serpyllum)*
Lamiaceae (Labiatae)
   See p. 248

❻

30—60 cm

Wild Marjoram *(Origanum vulgare)*
Lamiaceae (Labiatae)
   See p. 248

❶

30 — 80 cm

Sorrel, Sorrel Dock *(Rumex acetosa)*
Polygonaceae
IM: Plant more than 30 cm high. Leaves have acid taste. Upper leaves sessile.
D: Inflorescence slender. Plant dioecious. Leaves thickish, compact, sagittate at the base.
H: Meadows. Likes a moist, loamy soil, rich in all nutrients, but particularly nitrogen.
AI: P; ♃ ; (†)
    Because of its high vitamin C content, Sorrel is occasionally used as a wild vegetable, either cooked or in salads. However, it contains organic acid salts (potassium hydrogen oxalate and oxalic acid), which are injurious to health if eaten in any amount, and the plant is therefore best avoided. Cases are known of cattle being poisoned when kept in pastures where the plant is abundant. Like all wind-pollinated plants, sorrel produces a lot of pollen. Indeed, as it produces about 400 million pollen grains per plant it is one of the most prolific producers of pollen in our flora.

❷

8 — 30 cm

Sheep Sorrel *(Rumex acetosella)*
Polygonaceae
IM: Plant less than 30 cm high. Leaves have a bitter taste. All leaves petiolate, the upper ones with an indistinctly visible petiole.
D: Inflorescence slender. Plant dioecious. Leaves spear-shaped, lanceolate or linear.
H: Dry meadows, on sandy soil with little other vegetation, less commonly in weedy places in sandy fields. Indicator of a sandy soil and some soil acidity.
AI: P; ♃ ; (†)
    This plant contains the same acids and acid salts as does Sorrel, above.

❸

60 — 150 cm

Great Burnet *(Sanguisorba officinalis)*
Rosaceae
See p. 380

❹

15 — 100 cm

Pale Willowherb *(Epilobium roseum)*
Onagraceae (Oenotheraceae)
See p. 270

❺

30 — 70 cm

Ragged Robin *(Lychnis flos-cuculi)*
Caryophyllaceae
IM: Petals deeply cleft into 4 segments.
D: Loose cymes. Stem not sticky. Lower leaves spatulate, upper leaves lanceolate.
H: Damp meadows. Likes a deep, loamy soil, rich in humus. Indicates a high ground-water level and only grows in the wettest parts of meadows.
AI: P; ♃
    This is a plant on which clumps of saliva-like froth are commonly found. These are commonly known as 'cuckoo spit' and are produced by the larvae of leaf hoppers. The plant contains saponin.

1

3

5

2

4

❶   **Red Campion** *(Silene dioica; Melandrium rubrum; M. diurnum)*
30—100 cm   Caryophyllaceae
See p. 252

❷   **Viscid Campion** *(Lychnis viscaria; Viscaria vulgaris)*
15—50 cm   Caryophyllaceae
See p. 252

❸   **Cheddar Pink** *(Dianthus gratianopolitanus; D. caesius)*
Caryophyllaceae
10—25 cm   IM: Petals only slightly toothed. The base of the calyx has scale-like bracts (a quarter as long as the calyx itself). Calyx without membranous stripes.
     D: Flowers solitary, on long peduncles, with hairs on the inside of the petals; pink or red. Stem erect or decumbent, richly branched (the plant often forms a small cushion). Leaves rather bluish green, linear, opposite.
     H: Stony dry turf, cliff ledges. Likes warm situations.
     AI: P; ♃

❹   **Common Comfrey, Knitbone** *(Symphytum officinale)*
Boraginaceae
30—100 cm   See p. 274

❺   **Dove's-foot Crane's-bill** *(Geranium molle)*
Geraniaceae
8—30 cm   IM: Flowers mostly in twos, bright purple, 8—12 mm in diameter, drooping after flowering. Stem densely hairy at the bottom. Upper leaves sessile.
     D: Stem richly branched, decumbent. Leaves kidney-shaped in outline, with 5—9 segments. Lower leaves elongate, indented at the front.
       Similar species: Small-flowered Crane's-bill *(Geranium pusillum)*: Flowers 5—7 mm in diameter, violet red. Stem only slightly hairy at the base. Upper leaves sessile. 10—50 cm; ⊙; ☉. Wasteland, roadside verges, likes a nitrogenous soil. Mountain Crane's-bill *(G. pyrenaicum)*: Flowers 1.4—2 cm in diameter, violet red. The whole of the stem densely hairy. Upper leaves sessile. 20—50 cm. Wasteland, roadside verges, walls, gardens. Likes a nitrogenous soil in warm situations.
     H: Weedy places in fields (particularly vegetable fields), in gardens and vineyards, but also on wayside verges, wasteland and on semi-dry turf. Likes a porous, and often a sandy soil.
     AI: P; ⊙
       Name: see Meadow Crane's-bill, p. 300. Dispersal mechanism of fruit: see Marsh Crane's-bill, p. 272.

❻   **Bistort, Snakeweed** *(Polygonum bistorta)*
Polygonaceae
30—120 cm   IM: Thickly packed, pink flower spikes.
     D: Stem erect. Leaves linear-ovoid, greyish green on the undersides. Root thick, twisted like a snake.
     H: Damp meadows, alpine mats, fen woodland and moist places in deciduous and mixed woodland. Likes a soil rich in nutrients. An indicator of moist conditions.
     AI: P; ♃

❶

20—40 cm

Sea Pink, Common Thrift *(Armeria maritima ; A. vulgaris)*
Plumbaginaceae
  See p. 330

❷

30—100 cm

Splendid Pink *(Dianthus superbus)*
Caryophyllaceae
IM: Petals irregularly fimbriate distally and over half their length. Calyx with scale-like bracts at the base, but without membranous stripes.
D: Flowers sweetly scented, mainly terminal. Stem erect, glabrous, cylindrical. Leaves linear-lanceolate, often bluish green.
H: Mixed and deciduous woodland, damp meadows. Likes dense, moist and fairly chalk-free soils.
AI: P; ♃

❸

15—30 cm

Maiden Pink *(Dianthus deltoides)*
Caryophyllaceae
IM: Flowers 1—1.5 cm wide. Petals toothed. Calyx with scale-like bracts at the base, but without membranous stripes. Stem with downy hairs.
D: Flowers on long peduncles, mainly solitary. Petals with paler dots. Stem branched (each branch with one flower). Leaves linear-lanceolate, rough at the edges.
H: Poor turf and heathland. Likes a porous and rather sandy soil. Calcifugous.
AI: P; ♃

❹

20—50 cm

Wood Pink *(Dianthus seguieri ; D. silvaticus)*
Caryophyllaceae
IM: Petals with long fringes. Calyx with scale-like bracts at the base, but without membranous stripes. Upper leaves grass-like, the topmost ones with a membranous edge.
D: Flowers mostly solitary, more rarely a few on one stem. Calyx scales shorter than half the length of the calyx itself. Stem erect, sometimes branched.
H: Poor meadows and mountain pastures. Likes a variably wet soil, but one which is dry in summer. Occurs also on sandy soils and indicates surface acidity.
AI: P; ♃

❺

15—50 cm

Carthusian Pink *(Dianthus carthusianorum)*
Caryophyllaceae
IM: Petals toothed. Calyx with scale-like bracts at the base, but without membranous stripes.
D: Flowers tightly packed together, terminal, more rarely only one flower present. Calyx and upper leaves leathery, brown. Stem glabrous. Leaves narrow, solid, rough at the edges and drawn out into a tube at the base, opposite.
H: Dry and semi-dry turf in warm situations.
AI: P; ♃
The name reminds us that this was a Pink commonly planted by Carthusian monks in their gardens. The plant contains saponin and is usually pollinated by butterflies

❻

50—100 cm

Greater Burnet Saxifrage *(Pimpinella major ; P. magna)*
Apiaceae (Umbelliferae)
  See p. 34

234

❶   **Common Valerian, All-Heal** (*Valeriana officinalis*)
30—170 cm   Valerianaceae
     See p. 256

❷   **Marsh Valerian** (*Valeriana dioica*)
   Valerianaceae
10—30 cm   IM: Lower leaves undivided, upper leaves pinnate.
     D: Cymes. Plants often dioecious. Flowers rose coloured or flesh pink. Stem single, erect, grooved, glabrous.
     H: Moorland, wet meadows, ditches, river banks, marshes, wet deciduous, mixed and coniferous woodland, fen woodland. Likes a rich soil saturated with ground water.
     AI: G; ⒉

❸   **Musk Mallow** (*Malva moschata*)
   Malvaceae
20—60 cm   IM: Flowers bright pink, rose coloured or white. Petals 2—2.5 cm long. Upper leaves divided in a digitate manner to the base, with 5—7 segments. Hairs on stem unbranched (magnifying glass needed).
     D: Flowers 1—3 in the leaf axils, smelling of musk. Leaves with simple or double pinnate segments.
     H: Semi-dry turf, dry meadows and pastures. Rather calcifugous. Likes warm situations.
     AI: P; ⒉
     Old medicinal plant. Contains mucilage.

❹   **Lesser** *or* **Common Centaury** (*Centaurium minus*; *C. umbellatum*; *Erythraea centaurium*)
   Gentianaceae
8—50 cm   IM: Inflorescence cymose. Basal leaves form a rosette.
     D: Cymes flat. Stem branches to form inflorescence, quadrangular. Basal leaves form a rosette; stem leaves linear-oval, with 5 veins, glabrous.
     H: Clearings in woods, light woodland and margins of woods, semi-dry turf. Likes a dry, sandy soil in warm situations.
     AI: G; ☉
     The name Centaury and the scientific name *Centaurium* stem from a Greek legend. The famous centaur Chiron was believed to have been healed by this plant. It is an old medicinal plant containing alkaloids.

❺   **Common** *or* **Lesser Dodder** (*Cuscuta epithymum*)
   Cuscutaceae
10—60 cm   IM: No possibility of confusion with other genera.
     D: Flowers in sessile heads; individual flowers not conspicuous. Stem filamentous, leafless, greenish yellow, twining. Several similar, but less common species, which have different host plants.
     H: Heaths, dry meadows, light woodland, roadside verges. Parasitizes Arrowhead Broom, Thyme, Heather, Gorse and Common Broom.
     AI: G; ☉
     Dodder extracts nutrient material from the host plant by means of haustoria.

❻   **Orpine, Livelong** (*Sedum telephium*; *S. maximum*)
20—50 cm   Crassulaceae
     See p. 176

❶

8—25 cm

Mountain Cat's-foot *(Antennaria dioica ; Gnaphalium dioicum)*
Asteraceae (Compositae)
     See p. 258

---

❷

30—60 cm

Crow Garlic *(Allium vineale)*
Liliaceae
     See p. 222

---

❸

15—30 cm

Common, Bitter *or* **Blue Fleabane** *(Erigeron acer)*
Asteraceae (Compositae)
IM: Flowers in capitula. Ray florets in several rows, pinkish mauve, disc florets yellow. Stem leafy, branched. Leaves undivided, alternate.

D: Capitula arranged in racemes, each flower 5—7 mm long. 1—3 flowers to a branch. Ray florets filamentous, hardly longer than the disc florets, erect. Stem usually reddish, with rough hairs. Leaves entire, lanceolate, also with rough hairs.

H: Dry and semi-dry turf, roadside verges, more rarely in vegetable fields and on uncultivated land. Likes a porous, rather sandy, shallow, calcareous soil, preferably rich in nitrogen.

AI: G; ⊙

The scientific generic name is derived from the Greek *(eri =* early; *geron =* old man) and refers to the appearance of the white hairs of the fruit soon after flowering. The common name suggests the former belief that the plant was repellent to fleas.

---

❹

15—50 cm

Yarrow, Milfoil *(Achillea millefolium)*
Asteraceae (Compositae)
IM: Flowers in capitula, arranged in loose cymes. The outer ray florets are white or reddish, the inner disc florets are yellowish white. Leaves double pinnate, with an aromatic smell.

D: Usually only 4—5 disc florets. Stem erect. Leaflets cleft into 2—5 parts.

H: Semi-dry turf, meadows, wayside verges and paths. Occurs on a variety of soils but prefers those which are nitrogenous.

AI: G; ♃

The scientific generic name *Achillea* is derived from the Greek legendary hero Achilles. Milfoil is an old medicinal plant containing ethereal oils and small quantities of furocoumarin. The juice of this plant can cause inflammation of the skin, if the skin is exposed to sunlight following contact with the juice.

---

❺

5—20 cm

Stemless Thistle *(Cirsium acaulon)*
Asteraceae (Compositae)
IM: Flowers in 3—6 cm broad capitula. Only disc florets present. Hairs on carpels pinnate (magnifying glass needed!). Stem no more than 20 cm high. Leaves form a rosette, very prickly.

D: Leaves sinuous, pinnate. Segments ovoid, cleft into three.

H: Semi-dry turf, meadows. Likes a chalky, loamy soil in warm situations.

AI: G; ♃

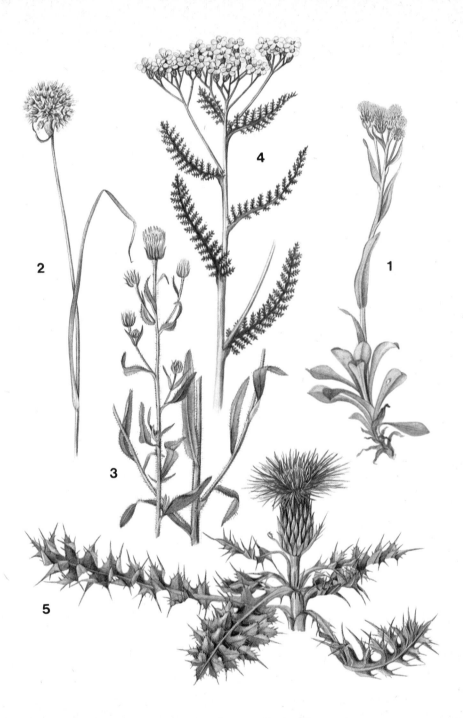

2

1

4

3

5

❶

30 — 100 cm

Brown-rayed *or* **Meadow Knapweed** *(Centaurea jacea)*
Asteraceae (Compositae)
IM: Flowers in large capitula. Only disc florets present. Marginal florets larger than the inner ones. Stem decumbent or prostrate. Middle and upper leaves usually undivided, alternate. Lower leaves sinuous, pinnate.
D: Stem angular, only branched at the top.
H: Semi-dry turf, meadows, roadside verges. Likes a loamy soil.
AI: G; ⚄
Anther filaments sensitive. Contains tannins.

❷

60 — 130 cm

Greater Knapweed *(Centaurea scabiosa)*
Asteraceae (Compositae)
IM: Flowers in large capitula (at least 2 cm long). Only disc florets present. Involucral bracts with a dark border and membranous tips. Leaves pinnate.
D: Capitulum spherical, marginal florets larger than more central ones. Stem erect.
H: Dry and semi-dry turf, meadows. Likes a porous soil.
AI: G; ⚄
The plant contains flavones.

❸

60 — 160 cm

Red Hare's Lettuce *(Prenanthes purpurea)*
Cichoriaceae (Compositae)
See p. 334

❹

50 — 160 cm

Purple Loosestrife *(Lythrum salicaria)*
Lythraceae
IM: No possibility of confusion with other species.
D: Dense, whorl-like racemes. Stem erect, quadrangular. Leaves opposite and decussate, lanceolate, pointed at the tips, rounded or heart-shaped at the base.
H: Banks of stagnant or flowing water, ditches, wet meadows, moorland, reed beds, fens. Likes a firm, wet soil, rich in nitrogen.
AI: P; ⚄
Self-pollination in this species is impossible as the plant has developed two different types of flower which can be distinguished by the lengths of their styles and stamens and also by the size and colour of their pollen grains. The long-styled flowers predominate. Purple Loosestrife contains tannins and was once used as a medicinal plant to stop bleeding.

❺

5 — 20 cm

Autumn Crocus *(Colchicum autumnale)*
Liliaceae
IM: Flowers on a white 'stalk' which is actually the base of the corolla tube. No leaves present at flowering time.
D: Flowers solitary. 6 stamens, 3 styles. Leaves appear first the following spring. They are fleshy, like those of a tulip, and enclose the large capsular fruit.
H: Damp meadows and fen woodland. Likes a deep clay and loamy soil, rich in nutrients, particularly nitrogen.
AI: M; ⚄; †
The ovary of the Autumn Crocus occurs at the bottom of the corolla tube and therefore below the soil surface. It remains there until the following spring. The Autumn Crocus contains the poison colchicine, particularly in the leaves. Colchicine is cytotoxic and effects the division of the cell nuclei so that the chromosomes do not separate. It is used in research to produce plants with multiples of the normal number of chromosomes.

240

❶

8 — 40 cm

Green-winged Orchid *(Orchis morio)*
Orchidaceae
　　　See p. 336

---

❷

25 — 50 cm

Military Orchid *(Orchis militaris)*
Orchidaceae
IM:　Labellum with a blunt, upwardly directed spur. All the other petals contribute
　　　towards a helmet-shaped hood. Labellum longer than it is broad.
D:　　Loose spikes with many flowers. Flowers purple or rose pink, with fine red
　　　spots. Leaves linear.
H:　　Semi-dry turf, light dry woodland, also in localities of variable dampness;
　　　calcicolous and likes warm situations.
AI:　M; ♃
　　　Name relates to the helmet-like form of the flower. The tuber contains
　　　mucilages which have occasionally been used in medicine.

---

❸

20 — 50 cm

Early Purple Orchid *(Orchis mascula; O. masculus)*
Orchidaceae
　　　See p. 264

---

❹

15 — 30 cm

Spider Orchid *(Ophrys sphegodes; O. aranifera)*
Orchidaceae
　　　See p. 262

---

❺

15 — 30 cm

Bumblebee Orchid *(Ophrys fuciflora)*
Orchidaceae
IM:　Labellum without spur, large, hairy and resembling the abdomen of a
　　　bumblebee.
D:　　Spike with few flowers. Outer petals spreading, white or reddish in colour.
　　　Labellum as broad as long, with an outwardly curved appendage at the
　　　distal end, brownish purple with a yellow pattern.
H:　　Semi-dry turf. Likes a deep, chalky or loess soil, rich in humus. Prefers warm
　　　situations.
AI:　M
　　　This plant owes its name to the shape of its labellum. For pollination see Fly
　　　Orchid, p. 264. Not only do the species of this genus show considerable variation
　　　in colour and pattern of their flowers but there are many hybrids between
　　　them, particularly *Ophrys insectifera* x *O. fuciflora*, *O. fuciflora* x *O. apifera* and
　　　also *O. sphegodes* x *O. insectifera*. Such hybrids can be expected wherever their
　　　parental species share the same habitat as usually all *Ophrys* species share the
　　　same pollinating insects.

---

❻

15 — 30 cm

Bee Orchid *(Ophrys apifera)*
Orchidaceae
IM:　Labellum without spur, large, hairy, longer than broad.
D:　　Spike with few flowers. Outer petals spreading, white or pinkish in colour.
　　　Labellum with a backwardly directed appendage, brownish red, with a yellow
　　　pattern.
H:　　Semi-dry turf and light, dry woodland thickets. Likes a deep, porous, chalky
　　　soil in warm situations.
AI:　M; ♃
　　　Pollination: see Fly Orchid, p. 264. Hybrids: see Bumblebee Orchid, above.

242

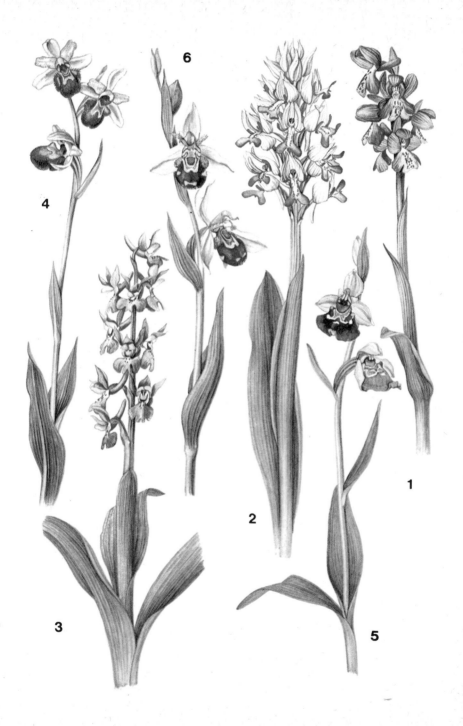

❶ **Fly Orchid** *(Ophrys insectifera; O. muscifera)*
Orchidaceae
10—30 cm   See p. 264

❷ **Fragrant Orchid** *(Gymnadenia conopsea; G. conopea)*
Orchidaceae
10—60 cm   IM: Flower spur twice as long as the ovary (appears as flower stalk). Flowers sweetly scented.
     D: Long spikes of numerous flowers. Flowers rather small. Labellum broader than long, trilobed. Leaves linear-lanceolate to broadly lanceolate.
     H: Semi-dry turf, reed beds, moorland and fens, occasionally in light thickets and woodland.
     AI: M; ♃
     The nectar of this group of orchids is found in the tips of the long spurs. Pollination is brought about by butterflies and day-flying moths.

❸ **Spotted Orchid** *(Dactylorhiza maculata; Dactylorchis maculata; Orchis maculata; O. maculatus)*
Orchidaceae
20—60 cm   See p. 336

❹ **Bitter Milkwort** *(Polygala amara)*
Polygalaceae
5—15 cm   IM: Plant tastes bitter.
     D: Racemes with numerous flowers. Flowers mainly blue or pale blue. Stem decumbent or erect. Lower leaves form a rosette, invert-ovoid, larger than the linear stem leaves.
     H: Semi-dry turf and damp meadows. Likes a chalky soil which is damp in winter and dry in summer.
     AI: P; ♃
     Name: see Common Milkwort, p. 306.
     Bitter Milkwort contains abundant saponin and polygalic acid. An old medicinal plant. At one time was fed to cattle in the belief that it would increase the milk flow (cf. Common Milkwort, p. 306).

❺ **Tufted Milkwort** *(Polygala comosa)*
Polygalaceae
5—25 cm   IM: Bracts about as long as the open flower. Immediately before the opening of the flowers, the inflorescence forms a tuft or head at the top of the stem.
     D: Racemes of many flowers. Flowers usually pink, sometimes blue. Stem decumbent or erect. Leaves usually alternate, narrowly spatulate or invert-ovoid.
     H: Dry and semi-dry turf. Likes a friable loamy soil.
     AI: P; ♃
     Name: see Common Milkwort, p. 306.
     Tufted Milkwort is usually pollinated by butterflies.

❻ **Common Milkwort** *(Polygala vulgaris)*
Polygalaceae
15—25 cm   See p. 306

❶

15—40 cm

Mountain *or* **Tuberous Pea** *(Lathyrus montanus)*
Fabaceae (Leguminosae)
   See p. 304

---

❷

30—60 cm

Common Sainfoin *(Onobrychis viciaefolia)*
Fabaceae (Leguminosae)
IM: Racemes. Flowers deep rose, with yellow stripes. Leaves pinnate.
D: Multiflorous racemes. Stem decumbent or erect. Flowers with 19—25 leaflets. Leaflets linear-lanceolate.
H: Semi-dry turf, meadows, roadsides.
AI: P; ♃
    The scientific name of the genus is of Greek origin and means 'donkey food'. Sainfoin is occasionally used as a protein-rich fodder plant.

---

❸

30—130 cm*

Pink Sicklewort, Pink Coronilla *(Coronilla varia)*
Fabaceae (Leguminosae)
   See p. 266

---

❹

30—50 cm

Zigzag *or* **Meadow Clover** *(Trifolium medium)*
Fabaceae (Leguminosae)
IM: Flowers in a spherical to ovoid head, 2—3 cm long, sessile or on a short stalk. Calyx glabrous, except for the ciliate teeth, and possessing 10 veins. Stem hairy.
D: Stem geniculate in a zigzag manner. Leaflets elliptical. A similar species is Purple Clover *(Trifolium rubens)* with a cylindrical flower head 3—7 cm long, 20 veins on the calyx and a glabrous stem. It occurs in similar localities to the Zigzag Clover.
H: Semi-dry turf, dry meadows, thickets, wood margins, light, dry woodland. Likes a porous, loamy soil.
AI: P; ♃
    The fruits of the Zigzag Clover are sometimes dispersed by ants.

---

❺

15—30 cm

Red Clover *(Trifolium pratense)*
Fabaceae (Leguminosae)
IM: Usually 2 flower heads on one stem, each 2—3.5 cm long. Calyx hairy, with 10 veins, half as long as the petals. Stem usually hairy.
D: Flowers fragrant. Stem decumbent or erect. Similar species: Alpine Clover *(Trifolium alpestre; T. alpester)* with 20 veins to the calyx, occurring in dry turf and thickets, on sandy soils. *T. incarnatum*, with a cylindrical flower head and dark red flowers. A cultivated species which is occasionally found wild on semi-dry turf.
H: Dry to moderately damp meadows. Likes a deep soil, rich in nutrients. Often sown with meadow grass seed, or sown by itself to produce fodder for cattle.
AI: P; ♃
    An important, protein-rich fodder plant.

---

❻

10—60 cm

Marsh Woundwort *(Stachys palustris)*
Lamiaceae (Labiatae)
   See p. 280

❶ **Betony** *(Betonica officinalis; Stachys officinalis; S. betonica)*
Lamiaceae (Labiatae)

30—60 cm   IM: Flowers in dense, terminal spikes. Basal leaves form a rosette.
D: Dense spikes with a single whorl of flowers separate from the rest of the spike. Stem quadrangular and, like the leaves, with rough hairs. Leaves petiolate, opposite and decussate, ovoid-lanceolate, crenate.
H: Dry and damp meadows, open mixed and deciduous woodland. Likes a sandy or loamy soil which is dry in summer but otherwise damp.
AI: G; ⌄
An ancient medicinal plant. Contains tannins.

❷ **Viper's Bugloss** *(Echium vulgare)*
Boraginaceae

30—120 cm   See p. 228

❸ **Hedge Hyssop** *(Gratiola officinalis)*
Scrophulariaceae

15—40 cm   See p. 280

❹ **Wall Germander** *(Teucrium chamaedrys)*
Lamiaceae (Labiatae)

15—30 cm   See p. 268

❺ **Common Thyme** *(Thymus serpyllum)*
Lamiaceae (Labiatae)

5—30 cm   IM: 3—6 flowers in the axils of leaves and at the end of the stem in small heads.
D: Stem prostrate or decumbent, woody at the base, round or slightly angular. Leaves small, 3 or 4 times as long as broad, opposite and decussate, rather leathery, elliptical or linear. On rubbing the leaves they give off a strong scent.
H: Roadside verges, edges of paths, slopes, dry and semi-dry turf. Likes a porous, often sandy or stony soil, but occurs also on loams.
AI: G; ⌄
This plant is extraordinarily variable. Many forms have been regarded as separate species. An old medicinal plant, containing ethereal oils (smell), tannins and an alkaloid.

❻ **Wild Marjoram** *(Origanum vulgare)*
Lamiaceae (Labiatae)

30—60 cm   IM: Inflorescence an umbellate panicle. Upper leaves with a reddish tinge. Leaves almost glabrous.
D: Flowers purplish red or mauve. Stem erect, round, hairy. Leaves opposite and decussate, ovoid, pointed.
H: Mountain woodland, dry woods and thickets, edges of woods, semi-dry turf, roadside verges. Likes a calcareous soil, rich in nutrients, and a warm situation.
AI: G; ⌄
An old medicinal plant which contains ethereal oil (smell) and tannins.

❶ **Rosebay Willowherb, Fireweed** *(Chamaenerion angustifolium; Epilobium angustifolium)*
Onagraceae (Oenotheraceae)
60—140 cm
IM: Petals 1.2—1.5 cm long. Stem mainly glabrous or very slightly hairy. Leaves lanceolate, 1—2.5 cm wide, undersides with conspicuous veins.
D: Loose racemes; flowers slightly bilaterally symmetrical.
H: Deciduous and mixed woodland, coniferous forest, mainly in clearings and on the edge of woodland. Likes a porous soil, rich in nitrogen.
AI: P; ♃
It was in this species that the botanist Sprengel discovered self-pollination in 1790. The plant contains tannins and mucilage, particularly in its root. Seed hairs: see Great Willowherb, p. 214.

❷ **Broad-leaved Willowherb** *(Epilobium montanum)*
Onagraceae (Oenotheraceae)
30—100 cm
IM: Petals 8—12 mm long, emarginated. Stem glabrous, leaves often alternate.
D: Loose racemes. Leaves lanceolate, serrate, dentate.
H: Deciduous and coniferous woodland, canyon forest, mainly in clearings, along woodland paths and at the edge of woods. Likes a moist, rather stony soil.
AI: P; ♃
Seed hairs: see Great Willowherb, p. 214.

❸ **Pale Willowherb** *(Epilobium roseum)*
Onagraceae (Oenotheraceae)
15—100 cm
See p. 270

❹ **Common Enchanter's Nightshade** *(Circaea lutetiana)*
Onagraceae (Oenotheraceae)
20—60 cm
IM: Peduncles without any subtending leaflets or bracts. Leaves hairy, dull.
D: Terminal racemes. Flowers white or faintly pink. Stem erect or decumbent, hairy. Leaves ovoid-lanceolate.
H: Fen woodland, damp mixed, deciduous and coniferous woodland, particularly in clearings. Likes a moist, loamy, nitrogenous soil.
AI: P; ♃
The origin of the scientific generic name and the common name is not clear. Both refer to magic or witchcraft (Circe — a witch in Greek mythology). Possibly the plant is so named because its fruits attach themselves to everything which passes by means of their hooked hairs.

❺ **Alpine Enchanter's Nightshade** *(Circaea alpina)*
Onagraceae (Oenotheraceae)
8—25 cm
IM: Peduncles with setaceous bracts at the base. Leaves hairy and glossy.
D: Terminal racemes. Flowers white or faintly pink. Stem decumbent, glabrous. Leaves opposite, almost ovoid.
H: Canyon and mountain forest; deciduous, mixed and coniferous forest. Likes a stony soil, rich in loam and saturated with ground water.
AI: P; ♃
Name: see Common Enchanter's Nightshade, above.

❻ **Lungwort** *(Pulmonaria officinalis)*
Boraginaceae
15—30 cm
See p. 340

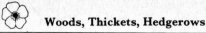

❶

10 — 50 cm

Creeping Gromwell *(Lithospermum purpureo-coeruleum)*
Boraginaceae
IM: Flowers first red, then blue, 1 — 1.5 cm in diameter.
D: Stem erect. Leaves lanceolate, pointed, with rough hairs.
H: Deciduous, dry woodland, dry thickets. Likes a porous, calcareous soil, rich in humus in warm situations. Abundant in those localities where it does occur.
AI: G; ♃
     For flower colour change see Mountain Pea, p. 304.

---

❷

30 — 100 cm

Common Comfrey, Knitbone *(Symphytum officinale)*
Boraginaceae
See p. 274

---

❸

30 — 120 cm

Bistort, Snakeweed *(Polygonum bistorta)*
Polygonaceae
See p. 232

---

❹

30 — 50 cm

Water Avens *(Geum rivale)*
Rosaceae
IM: No possibility of confusion with other species.
D: Stem multiflowered, drooping. Some of flowers with 6 petals. Calyx reddish brown, petals reddish yellow. Leaves pinnate; terminal leaflet large, lateral leaflets smaller, serrate or pinnate.
H: Wet meadows, moorland, fen woodland, damp mountain pastures. Likes a soil saturated with ground water.
AI: P; ♃ ; (†)
     The rhizome of Water Avens smells of clove oil. The flowers are usually pollinated by bumblebees, but the short-tongued species may often bite through the petals to get at the rich supply of nectar. The rhizome contains the slightly poisonous substance eugenol. An old medicinal plant.

---

❺

30 — 100 cm

Red Campion *(Silene dioica; Melandrium rubrum; M. diurnum)*
Caryophyllaceae
IM: Petals deeply cleft into two. Calyx inflated, hairy with 10 veins.
D: Loose cymes. Flowers unisexual. Stem limp, branched at the top. Leaves opposite, the upper ones ovoid. Plant dioecious.
H: Fen woodland, damp places in mixed and deciduous woodland, or in coniferous forest, damp meadows. Likes a rich, nitrogenous soil, saturated with ground water. An indicator of wetness.
AI: P; ☉ — ♃
     Red Campion is pollinated by bumblebees and butterflies. It is day-flowering, in contrast to the other two common species of the genus. The stamens are occasionally infected by a smut fungus.

---

❻

15 — 50 cm

Viscid Campion *(Lychnis viscaria; Viscaria vulgaris)*
Caryophyllaceae
IM: Stem sticky as a result of rings of viscid secretion below the lower nodes.
D: Flowers in panicles. Leaves opposite, lanceolate, glabrous.
H: Semi-dry turf, heaths, dry meadows, dry woodland and thickets. An indicator of acid, sandy soils.
AI: P; ♃
     The plant contains saponin. It is pollinated by both bees and butterflies.

252

❶ 30—100 cm

Splendid Pink *(Dianthus superbus)*
Caryophyllaceae
See p. 234

❷ 5—15 cm

Wall Gypsy Weed *(Gypsophila muralis)*
Caryophyllaceae
See p. 220

❸ 25—50 cm

Herb Robert *(Geranium robertianum)*
Geraniaceae
IM: Stem with distinct red tinge. Leaf composed of 3 fully distinct leaflets, which are pinnately lobed. On rubbing the plant gives off an unpleasant smell.
D: Flowers in twos, rose pink. Petals with 3 longitudinal white stripes. Stem creeping or decumbent, hairy.
H: Mixed and deciduous woodland, coniferous and mountain forest, screes, walls. Likes a nitrogenous soil and thrives in humidity.
AI: P; ⊙
Generic name: see Meadow Crane's-bill, p. 300. The specific and common name are in honour of Pope Robert. For fruit-dispersal mechanism see Marsh Crane's-bill, p. 272. Herb Robert contains ethereal oil (smell), tannins, and an unknown alkaloid. An old medicinal plant.

❹ 8—15 cm

Umbellate Wintergreen *(Chimaphila umbellata)*
Pyrolaceae
IM: 2—7 flowers in an umbel. Petals 5—6 mm long.
D: Stem erect or decumbent, quadrangular. Leaves petiolate, opposite and decussate, crenate, heart-shaped at the base.
H: Mixed and coniferous woodland, particularly in pine-woods. Likes a soil overgrown with moss, sandy, loamy and rather calcareous.
AI: G; ♃
A medicinal plant, which contains alkaloids (arbutin and ursone) in its leaves.

❺ 10—50 cm

Bloody Crane's-bill *(Geranium sanguineum)*
Geraniaceae
IM: Flowers 2.5—3.5 cm in diameter, carmine, solitary.
D: Petals crenate. Stem and peduncle hairy. Leaves palmate, divided into 5—7 segments. Lobes of leaves linear.
H: Light woodland, edges of woods, semi-dry turf, in warm situations. Abundant in those localities where it occurs.
AI: P; ♃
Contains tannins in its rootstock which have styptic properties. At one time the plant was used to stop the flow of blood from wounds. The name refers to this and not to the colour of the flowers, which are far from blood red. Also contains an alkaloid.

❻ 5—50 cm

Wood Sanicle *(Sanicula europaea)*
Apiaceae (Umbelliferae)
See p. 74

❼ 50—200 cm

Wood Angelica *(Angelica sylvestris)*
Apiaceae (Umbelliferae)
See p. 76

❶ **Common Wintergreen, Lesser Wintergreen** *(Pyrola minor; Pirola minor)*
10—20 cm Pyrolaceae
See p. 68

❷ **Greater Wintergreen** *(Pyrola rotundifolia; Pirola rotundifolia)*
15—30 cm Pyrolaceae
IM: 10—30 flowers in a raceme. Style projecting well beyond the campanulate flower.
D: Flowers drooping. Stem obtuse-angled. Leaves round, finely crenate, leathery, evergreen, forming a rosette.
H: Mixed and coniferous woodland. Likes a damp, slightly acid, loamy soil.
AI: G; ♃
Name: see One-flowered Wintergreen, p. 68.
Although the flowers of the Greater Wintergreen are scented they are not much visited by insects. Seed formation results mainly from self-pollination. An old medicinal plant containing arbutin in the leaves.

❸ **Lesser** *or* **Common Centaury** *(Centaurium minus; C. umbellatum; Erythraea centaurium)*
8—50 cm Gentianaceae
See p. 236

❹ **Common** *or* **Lesser Dodder** *(Cuscuta epithymum)*
10—60 cm Cuscutaceae
See p. 236

❺ **Orpine, Livelong** *(Sedum telephium; S. maximum)*
20—50 cm Crassulaceae
See p. 176

❻ **Marsh Valerian** *(Valeriana dioica)*
10—30 cm Valerianaceae
IM: Lower leaves undivided, upper leaves pinnate.
D: Cymes. Plants often dioecious. Flowers rose coloured or flesh pink. Stem single, erect, grooved, glabrous.
H: Moorland, wet meadows, ditches, river banks, marshes, wet deciduous, mixed and coniferous woodland, fen woodland. Likes a rich soil saturated with ground water.
AI: G; ♃

❼ **Common Valerian, All-Heal** *(Valeriana officinalis)*
30—170 cm Valerianaceae
IM: All leaves unpaired pinnate.
D: Terminal umbel-like panicles. Flowers flesh pink to very pale, whitish pink. Stem simple, grooved, hollow. Leaves opposite with 15—21 leaflets. Upper leaves with entire leaflets, lower ones with dentate leaflets. Flowers scented, although some people have difficulty in detecting the scent.
H: Damp deciduous, mixed and coniferous woodland, clearings and woodland paths, damp meadows, moorland and ditches. Likes a rich loamy soil, wet with ground water.
AI: G; ♃; (†)
A medicinal plant containing ethereal oils and alkaloids in the root. The scent of the plant attracts cats.

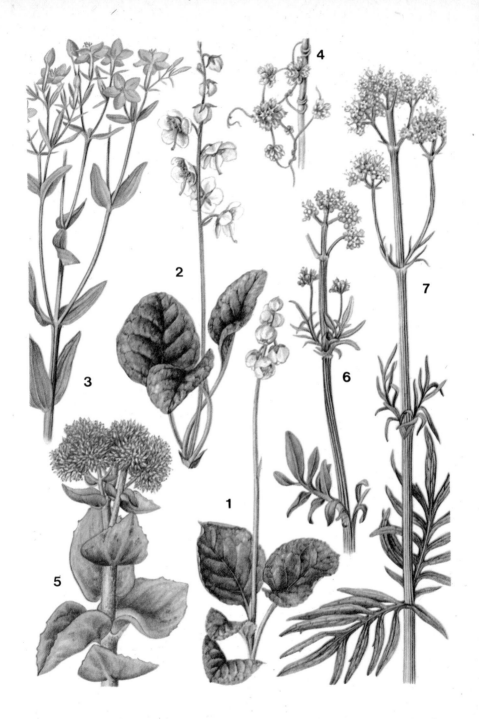

❶ **Martagon Lily** *(Lilium martagon)*
Liliaceae
30—120 cm
IM: Leaves form whorls. Flowers drooping, turban-like, spotted.
D: Loose racemes. Plant grows from a large, golden bulb.
H: Deciduous and mixed woodland, canyon forest. Prefers a damp, porous soil, rich in humus and nutrients, particularly calcium.
AI: M; ♃
The bulb of the Martagon Lily regulates the depth at which it occurs by means of contractile roots. The spotting of the flowers is genetically controlled, but not the pattern which the spots form. No petal is therefore exactly identical with another in terms of spotting. The pigment spots are produced as a result of pigments of low solubility developing in cells lying next to each other. As the pigment diffuses a little way from where it is produced the spots often have a kind of halo around them.

❷ **Crow Garlic** *(Allium vineale)*
Liliaceae
30—60 cm
See p. 222

❸ **Red Hare's Lettuce** *(Prenanthes purpurea)*
Cichoriaceae (Compositae)
60—160 cm
See p. 334

❹ **Hemp Agrimony** *(Eupatorium cannabinum)*
Asteraceae (Compositae)
70—150 cm
See p. 278

❺ **Marsh Thistle** *(Cirsium palustre)*
Asteraceae (Compositae)
90—200 cm
See p. 276

❻ **Sawwort** *(Serratula tinctoria)*
Asteraceae (Compositae)
30—100 cm
IM: Flowers in capitula arranged in umbel-like racemes. Only disc florets present. The outside florets no bigger than bracts without their membranous points.
D: Capitulum small, 0.6—1.2 cm in diameter. Stem erect, branched at the top and bearing leaves. Leaves undivided to pinnate, deeply serrate.
H: Light deciduous and mixed woodland, wet meadows, ditches. Likes a loamy soil. Abundant in those localities where it occurs.
AI: G; ♃
Contains in the leaves a precursor of a yellow pigment which under the influence of alkali develops into a yellow dye.

❼ **Mountain Everlasting, Mountain Cat's-ear** *(Antennaria dioica; Gnaphalium dioicum)*
Asteraceae (Compositae)
8—25 cm
IM: 3—12 small capitula in terminal, cymose racemes. Only disc florets present. Involucral bracts membranous, glabrous. Leaves undivided.
D: Flowers mostly purplish pink, filamentous. Stem unbranched, decumbent or erect. Basal leaves form a rosette, spatulate, invert-ovoid. Stem leaves linear-lanceolate. Leaves glabrous above, with whitish felt-like hairs below.
H: Semi-dry turf, dry thickets, light dry woodland. Likes a porous, sandy soil.
AI: G; ♃

❶ **Purple Loosestrife** *(Lythrum salicaria)*
50 — 160 cm   Lythraceae
     See p. 240

❷ **Spotted Deadnettle** *(Lamium maculatum)*
Lamiaceae (Labiatae)
30 — 80 cm   IM: Plant nettle-like but without stinging hairs. Lower lip of corolla with a single middle lobe, divided into 2 parts, and 2 lateral lobes. Flowers 2 — 3 cm long. Leaves 3 — 5 cm long.

    D: 3 — 5 flowers in axillary false whorls. Lower lip of corolla flecked with white. Stem erect or decumbent. Leaves opposite and decussate, petiolate, ovoid to heart-shaped, often spotted.
    H: Deciduous and mixed woodland, edges of woods, thickets, banks of rivers. Likes a damp soil, rich in nutrients and usually calcareous.
    AI: G; ♃
    The flowers are mainly pollinated by long-tongued bumblebees and day-flying moths or butterflies. The seeds are dispersed by ants.

❸ **Autumn Crocus** *(Colchicum autumnale)*
Liliaceae
5 — 20 cm   See p. 240

❹ **Toothwort** *(Lathraea squamaria)*
Scrophulariaceae
10 — 25 cm   IM: Whole plant pinkish red in colour without any green leaves.
    D: Dense racemes, with the flowers on one side, initially drooping. Stem erect, fleshy, with pallid scales.
    H: Canyon and mountain forest, damp mixed and deciduous woodland, fen woodland. Likes a porous, damp soil, rich in loam.
    AI: G; ♃
    A parasitic plant devoid of chlorophyll. The roots of the host plants (deciduous trees) are penetrated by haustoria of Toothwort. Flowering does not take place until the plant is about 10 years old.

❺ **Hollow Wort, Hollow Corydalis, Hollow Fumitory** *(Corydalis cava)*
Papaveraceae
15 — 30 cm   See p. 224

❻ **Fingered Fumitory** *or* **Corydalis** *(Corydalis solida)*
Papaveraceae
15 — 30 cm   IM: Upper leaves dissected in a digitate manner. Tuber not hollow.
    D: Terminal racemes. Flowers usually dull red, more rarely mauve or white. Spur horizontal or slightly tilted upwards. Stem with two leaves. Leaves double ternate, deeply dissected, fragile, glabrous.
    H: Deciduous woodland and thickets, edges of woods. Likes a non-chalky, loamy soil.
    AI: P; ♃; †
    The seeds of this plant are dispersed by ants. Fingered Fumitory contains an alkaloid, particularly in the tuber, and is therefore poisonous.

❼ **Mountain** *or* **Tuberous Pea** *(Lathyrus montanus)*
15 — 40 cm   Fabaceae (Leguminosae)
    See p. 304

❶   **Spring Pea** *or* **Vetchling** (*Lathyrus vernus*)
20—60 cm   Fabaceae (Leguminosae)
        See p. 316

❷   **Lady's Slipper** (*Cypripedium calceolus*)
15—80 cm   Orchidaceae
IM: No possibility of confusion with other species.
D: Large slipper-like, yellow labellum. Outer petals lanceolate, mostly brownish purple, more rarely lemon yellow. Stem with 1 or 2 (rarely more) flowers. Leaves large, elliptical.
H: Mixed, deciduous woodland, beechwood and coniferous forest, also in mountain-pine brushwood. Likes a calcareous, loamy soil in warm situations.
AI: M; ♃
The flower of the Lady's Slipper may be easily recognized, not only because of its unique shape, but also because of its large size. With a diameter of 8 cm it is among the largest of the central European flowers. The labellum functions as a fly-trap. It succeeds as such because the curvature of the peduncle ensures that the opening of the labellum is directed upwards. Flies are able to fly through the opening but once inside they can only crawl and are trapped because of the steepness and smoothness of the walls which allows them to proceed in one direction only, viz. towards the stamens and stigma. They thus bring about self-pollination. The labellum contains no food for the trapped insects.

❸   **Red Helleborine** (*Cephalanthera rubra*)
20—80 cm   Orchidaceae
IM: Flowers without spur. Labellum pointed.
D: Spike with few flowers (the 'peduncle' is really the compressed ovary). Petals 15—20 mm long, spreading. Leaves lanceolate.
H: Dry, deciduous woodland, also light coniferous forest. Likes a porous, calcareous soil rich in nutrients and in a warm situation.
AI: M; ♃

❹   **Fragrant Orchid** (*Gymnadenia conopsea; G. conopea*)
10—60 cm   Orchidaceae
        See p. 244

❺   **Spider Orchid** (*Ophrys sphegodes; O. aranifera*)
15—30 cm   Orchidaceae
IM: Labellum without a spur, large, hairy and similar to the body of a spider. Outer petals spreading, greenish or yellowish green.
D: Spikes of few flowers. Labellum broad, swollen, undivided, and with 2—4 longitudinal lines, purple red generally but yellowish towards the edge. Stem leaves confined to the lower part.
H: Semi-dry turf and light woodland. Likes a porous, calcareous soil, containing humus, in warm situations.
AI: M; ♃
The Spider Orchid owes its name to the shape of the labellum.
Fertilization: see Fly Orchid, p. 264. Hybrids: see Bumblebee Orchid, p. 242.

❻   **Bee Orchid** (*Ophrys apifera*)
15—30 cm   Orchidaceae
        See p. 242

❶ **Fly Orchid** *(Ophrys insectifera; O. muscifera)*
Orchidaceae

10—40 cm
IM: Labellum without spur, large, with velvety hairs. The flower as a whole resembles a fly.
D: Spikes of few flowers. Outer petals spreading, greenish or yellowish green. Labellum deeply cleft into 3 parts, purplish red, with a quadrangular blue spot in the middle. Leaves confined mainly to the lower part of the stem.
H: Semi-dry turf and light, dry woodland, in warm situations.
AI: M; ♃
Not only do the flowers appear to resemble insects to the human eye but they also appear to deceive the males of certain hymenoptera. The latter fly to the flowers and attempt to mate with the labellum. Apparently both the hairiness and the smell of the flower is involved in the deception. As a result of their activities the male insects carry pollinia from flower to flower and thus assist in pollination. This activity ceases, however, when there are sufficient female insects about.

❷ **Spotted Orchid** *(Dactylorhiza maculata; Dactylorchis maculata; Orchis maculata; O. maculatus)*
Orchidaceae

20—60 cm
See p. 336

❸ **Early Purple Orchid** *(Orchis mascula; O. masculus)*
Orchidaceae

20—50 cm
IM: Labellum with a single, backwardly directed spur. Bracts membranous. Leaves with their maximum width in the middle.
D: Long, loose spikes of many flowers. Flowers purple with darker flecks. Labellum trilobed. Leaves linear-lanceolate, not usually spotted. Tuber undivided.
H: Semi-dry turf, meadows, deciduous woodland. Likes a porous, loamy soil.
AI: M; ♃
The scientific name of this species refers to the fact that the undivided tuber resembles the testicles of the human male. The tuber contains mucilage which has been used in medicine.

❹ **Military Orchid** *(Orchis militaris)*
Orchidaceae

25—50 cm
See p. 242

❺ **White Dittany, Burning Bush** *(Dictamnus albus)*
Rutaceae

50—100 cm
IM: Plant has a lemon-like smell. Petals unequal, pink with darker veins.
D: Leaves unpaired pinnate. Leaflets finely serrate, with transparent spots.
H: Dry thickets, edges of woods, clearings. Likes a rather stony, porous, chalky soil in warm situations.
AI: P; ♃; †
The scientific name is derived from the Cretan mountain Dikte. Dittany contains alkaloid, saponins and ethereal oils. The latter evaporate so strongly on hot days that in still air they can be ignited, hence 'Burning Bush'.

❻ **Zigzag** *or* **Meadow Clover** *(Trifolium medium)*
Fabaceae (Leguminosae)

30—50 cm
See p. 246

264

❶   **Pink Sicklewort, Pink Coronilla** *(Coronilla varia)*

30—130 cm   Fabaceae (Leguminosae)

IM: 10—20 flowers (1—1.5 cm long) in a bright-pink umbel. Stem angular, prostrate or decumbent.

D: Leaves usually with long petioles, and 11—25 leaflets which have a short stalk and are invert-ovoid to linear.

H: Semi-dry turf, roadside verges, dry thickets. Likes a dense soil, rich in nutrients and prefers warm situations.

AI: P; ♃; †

This plant contains in its foliage a poisonous glycoside, similar in its action to digitalis.

---

❷   **Red Foxglove** *(Digitalis purpurea)*

30—150 cm   Scrophulariaceae

IM: No possibility of confusion with other species.

D: Unilateral racemes. Flowers with spots in the throat. Stem erect. Basal leaves form a rosette, ovoid-lanceolate, crenate, with grey felt-like undersides.

H: Clearings in woods, light mixed, deciduous and coniferous woodland, edges of woods. Likes a sandy, loamy soil, rich in nitrogen. Calcifugous. Very numerous where it occurs.

AI: G; ⊙; †

For spotting of flowers see Martagon Lily, p. 258.

An important medicinal plant, containing numerous poisonous glycosides.

---

❸   **Common Calamint** *(Calamintha clinopodium; C. vulgaris; Satureja vulgaris; S. clinopodium; Clinopodium vulgare)*

30—60 cm   Lamiaceae (Labiatae)

IM: 10—20 flowers in dense whorls. Up to 4 whorls one above the other. Stem with rough hairs. Leaves ovoid or linear.

D: Calyx aristate. Stem erect. Leaves petiolate, ovoid, crenate or serrate, with shaggy hairs.

H: Dry woodland and thickets, wayside verges. Likes a porous soil which is rich in nutrients and rather chalky.

AI: G; ♃

---

❹   **Wild Marjoram** *(Origanum vulgare)*

30—60 cm   Lamiaceae (Labiatae)

See p. 248

---

❺   **Betony** *(Betonica officinalis; Stachys officinalis; S. betonica)*

30—60 cm   Lamiaceae (Labiatae)

See p. 248

---

❻   **Hedge Woundwort** *(Stachys sylvatica)*

60—120 cm   Lamiaceae (Labiatae)

IM: About 6 flowers in false axillary whorls and in a terminal spike.

D: Corolla twice as long as calyx. Stem erect, often branched at the top, with rough hairs. Leaves opposite and decussate, heart-shaped, serrate and bearing rough hairs.

H: Deciduous and mixed woodland, mountain and canyon forest, fen woodland. Likes a porous nitrogenous soil, moist with ground water.

AI: G; ♃

❶ **Common Hempnettle** *(Galeopsis tetrahit)*
Lamiaceae (Labiatae)
10—80 cm
IM: Upper lip helmet-shaped. Lower lip with a hollow tooth on each side. Stem swollen below the nodes.
D: Inflorescence consists of several round, multiflorous false whorls. Stem simple or branched, hairy at the nodes. Leaves with long petioles, ovoid-lanceolate. There are several similar species which are difficult to distinguish.
H: Weedy places in fields, along waysides, on wasteland and embankments; also on the edges of woods and in clearings. Likes a rather stony soil, rich in nutrients, particularly nitrogen.
AI: P; ☉—⊙
The Common Hempnettle is derived from two other species of the same genus as a result of hybridization followed by doubling of the chromosomes. This was demonstrated by the Swedish botanist A. Müntzing, who produced the 'synthetic' individuals of *Galeopsis tetrahit* by appropriate experimental crosses.

❷ **Narrow-leaved Everlasting Pea** *(Lathyrus sylvestris)*
Fabaceae (Leguminosae)
90—210 cm
IM: 3—10 flowers in a raceme. Peduncle winged. Stamens fused in a tube with a straight border. Leaves compound pinnate with 2—6 leaflets.
D: Stem very tough, prostrate, decumbent or climbing, quadrangular with two flanges or wings. Leaves with a branched tendril.
H: Deciduous or mixed woodland, clearings and the edges of woods. Likes a rather calcareous soil, rich in nutrients.
AI: P; ♃
Within this species there are several races which have been distinguished from time to time.

❸ **Wall Germander** *(Teucrium chamaedrys)*
Lamiaceae (Labiatae)
15—30 cm
IM: Flowers without any upper lip. Lower lip with 5 lobes. Flowers as long as the bracts.
D: Flowers axillary or terminal, reddish brown. Stem decumbent or erect. Leaves linear-cuneate, with a crenate margin.
H: Dry or semi-dry turf, dry thickets, light woodland, more rarely on chalk cliffs. Likes a chalky soil, rich in humus.
AI: G; ♃
The rootstock of this plant carries throughout the year two generations of leafy stems, of which only the second bears flowers.

Stony Slopes, Rocks **Red or Pink**

❹ **Cheddar Pink** *(Dianthus gratianopolitanus; D. caesius)*
Caryophyllaceae
10—25 cm
See p. 232

❺ **Orpine, Livelong** *(Sedum telephium; S. maximum)*
Crassulaceae
20—50 cm
See p. 176

❶

10—300 cm

Spiked Water Milfoil *(Myriophyllum spicatum)*
Haloragaceae
IM: Upper bracts and subtending leaves undivided.
D: Erect spikes of many flowers. Stem usually reddish and branched. Leaves much divided in a pectinate manner, mostly in whorls of 4. Similar species: Whorled Water Milfoil *(Myriophyllum verticillatum)* with its upper subtending leaves divided and the submerged leaves in whorls of 5—6. 10—200 cm. Same habitats as Spiked Water Milfoil, but in non-calcareous waters.
H: Plant communities of stagnant water; submerged. Likes warm waters rich in nutrients and dissolved calcium salts.
AI: P; ⑭

❷

10—100 cm

Common Water Plantain *(Alisma plantago-aquatica)*
Alismataceae
IM: 6 styles, longer than the ovaries.
D: Whorled panicles. Flowers pedunculate. Petals markedly deciduous, white or pink, yellowish at the base. Stem erect. Leaves on long petioles, forming a rosette. Submerged leaves narrower.
H: Banks of slow-running or stagnant water, also in reed beds or along river banks which are sometimes submerged.
AI: M; ⑭
The juice of this plant has an acrid, burning taste and is poisonous to cattle. By contrast goats readily eat the plant without ill effects. The active principle of the Common Water Plantain is still not defined, although sometimes termed an 'alkaloid'. However, no true alkaloids or cyanide compounds have been recovered from the plant.

❸

15—80 cm

Hoary Willowherb *(Epilobium parviflorum)*
Onagraceae (Oenotheraceae)
IM: Petals 5—10 mm long, bright pink. Stem, at least near the base, markedly hairy.
D: Loose racemes. Stem erect or decumbent. Leaves linear-lanceolate, the lower and middle leaves opposite, the upper ones alternate.
H: Banks of running, less usually still, waters, ditches, reed beds, also in woods, particularly woodland clearings. Likes loamy soils, rich in nutrients and wet with ground water.
AI: P; ⑭
Seed hairs: see Great Willowherb, p. 214.

❹

90—140 cm

Great *or* **Hairy Willowherb, Codlins-and-Cream** *(Epilobium hirsutum)*
Onagraceae (Oenotheraceae)
See p. 214

❺

15—100 cm

Pale Willowherb *(Epilobium roseum)*
Onagraceae (Oenotheraceae)
IM: Petals 5—6 mm long, strongly emarginated. Stem glabrous below, slightly hairy above. Leaves linear-lanceolate, on rather long petioles, serrate.
D: Loose racemes. Peduncles droop after flowering is over. Stem usually branched.
H: Banks of streams and brooks, ditches. Likes a porous, calcareous soil, wet from seepage and which contains humus and other nutrients.
AI: P; ⑭
Seed hairs: see Great Willowherb, p. 214.
The plant contains tannins and mucilage, particularly in the roots.

270

❶ **Bird's-eye Primrose** (*Primula farinosa*)

5—30 cm

Primulaceae
IM: Underside of leaves floury white.
D: Erect umbels. Flowers purplish violet to pink. Leaves form a rosette, linear to invert-ovoid, crenate, slightly wrinkled.
H: Moorland, springs, moist alpine mat.
AI: G; ♃
    Name: see Oxlip, p. 170. The plant contains saponin in the rootstock.

❷ **Buckbean, Bogbean, Marsh Trefoil** (*Menyanthes trifoliata*)

15—30 cm

Gentianaceae
IM: Leaves like those of Clover, but much bigger.
D: Flowers in dense racemes, with white hairs on the margins. Leaves basal.
H: Moorland, fen, reed beds, marshes, the edges of dykes. Likes a slightly acid, usually peaty soil, more rarely grows from mud. Abundant in those localities where it occurs.
AI: G; ♃
    An old medicinal plant, containing an alkaloid in the root and leaves.

❸ **Common Valerian, All-Heal** (*Valeriana officinalis*)

30—170 cm

Valerianaceae
  See p. 256

❹ **Marsh Valerian** (*Valeriana dioica*)

10—30 cm

Valerianaceae
  See p. 236

❺ **Marsh Cinquefoil** (*Potentilla palustris; Comarium palustre*)

10—50 cm

Rosaceae
IM: No possibility of confusion with other species.
D: Cymes. Stem prostrate, decumbent or erect. Basal axis woody. Leaves palmate, divided into 7 segments or leaflets.
H: Moorland, fens or marshes. Likes an acid soil, which is at least occasionally submerged.
AI: P; ♃

❻ **Marsh Crane's-bill** (*Geranium palustre*)

20—100 cm

Geraniaceae
IM: Flowers in twos.
D: Flowers 2.5—3 cm in diameter. Petals only slightly crenate, stem branched, decumbent, with rough hairs. Leaves palmate, with 7 leaflets.
H: Banks of streams, damp meadows. Likes a soil wet with ground water, loamy or gravelly. Usually occurs in small numbers in a given locality.
AI: P; ♃
    Name: see Meadow Crane's-bill, p. 300.
    The Marsh Crane's-bill contains tannins in its rootstock. An interesting feature of the plant is its method of seed dispersal. The awns of the seeds are twisted and in this position under tension. In a particular stage of maturity this tension is lost suddenly and the seeds are ejected violently. The seeds of Marsh Crane's-bill (5 mg in weight) can be ejected over a distance of 2.5 m.

❶

20—80 cm

Pale Polygonum, Pale Persicaria, Pale Knotgrass *(Polygonum lapathifolium)*
Polygonaceae
IM: Leaf sheaths either non-ciliated or with short cilia.
D:　Spikes on the main and lateral branches. Stem erect, richly branched, with thickened nodes and well provided with leaves. Leaves at their broadest over the basal third, often with dark spots.
H:　Weedy places, particularly in vegetable fields, less often along paths, but also on the banks of rivers and ponds and even in the water. Likes a soil rich in nutrients.
AI: P; ⊙—⊙

❷

10—80 cm

Persicaria *(Polygonum persicaria)*
Polygonaceae
See p. 220

❸

30—60 cm

Common Soapwort *(Saponaria officinalis)*
Caryophyllaceae
IM: Petals slightly crenate, with 2 small teeth in the throat of the corolla.
D:　Flowers mainly in dense, terminal clusters on the main stem and its branches. Stem erect, finely pubescent, often with a reddish or purplish tinge. Leaves opposite, linear-lanceolate, with 3 veins, pointed.
H:　Weedy places on walls and on gravel banks of valley bottoms. Likes a moist, porous soil.
AI: P; ♃
The plant is rich in saponin. This produces a lather if the plant is rubbed in water, hence the scientific and common names for the plant. An old medicinal plant.

❹

5—15 cm

Wall Gypsy Weed *(Gypsophila muralis)*
Caryophyllaceae
IM: Calyx with membranous stripes. Flowers only 6—15 mm long.
D:　Panicles. Stem stiffly erect, with forked branches. Leaves opposite, linear, barely 1 mm wide.
H:　Weedy places in fields, along woodland paths and on muddy river banks. Rather calcifugous. An indicator of wetness.
AI: P; ⊙
The name *Gypsophila* refers to a species of the genus which likes soils containing gypsum.

❺

30—100 cm

Common Comfrey, Knitbone *(Symphytum officinale)*
Boraginaceae
IM: Leaves distinctly decurrent. Plant with rough hairs.
D:　Inflorescence drooping, cymose. Flowers a dirty purple, pinkish violet or yellowish white. Stem richly branched at the base. Stem leaves furrowed.
H:　River banks, ditches, fen woodland, wet meadows, also on damp wasteland and waysides. Likes a moist, nitrogenous soil.
AI: G; ♃; (†)

❻

5—25 cm

Marsh Pennywort, White Rot *(Hydrocotyle vulgaris)*
Apiaceae (Umbelliferae)
See p. 96

1

2

3

4

5

6

** Marshes, Moorland, Shore and Aquatic Vegetation   Red or Pink**

❶

50—200 cm

Wood Angelica *(Angelica sylvestris)*
Apiaceae (Umbelliferae)
   See p. 220

---

❷

30—60 cm

Butterbur *(Petasites hybridus; P. officinalis)*
Asteraceae (Compositae)
IM: Flowers in capitula arranged in a racemose manner. Plant without leaves
     during the flowering period, only leaf scales being present on the stem. The
     whole plant during the flowering period is covered in a cobweb-like mass of
     hairs.
D: Ray and disc florets dirty purple or pale pink, with a pleasant smell. Leaves
     appear towards the end of the flowering period. They are very large (rhubarb-
     like) and have a dense woolly covering to the underside.
H: Banks of rivers, ditches, water meadows, edges of woods. Likes a stony,
     calcareous, damp soil.
AI: G; ♃
     The plant contains ethereal oils, an alkaloid and tannins in its rootstock.
     An old medicinal plant.

---

❸

50—150 cm

Flowering Rush *(Butomus umbellatus)*
Butomaceae
IM: An umbellate inflorescence. Flowers with 6 petals.
D: Terminal, false umbel. Petals pink, with darker veins. Leaves basal, stiffly
     erect, reed-like, triangular in section.
H: Banks of still or slow-running water in warm situations. Likes a soil rich in
     nutrients. Indicator of muddy conditions.
AI: M; ♃

---

❹

20—50 cm

Angular Garlic *(Allium angulosum)*
Liliaceae
IM: Stem leafless, markedly angular at the top. Leaves flat, but with a definite
     keel on the underside.
D: False umbels of flowers and no bulbils. Leaves basal.
H: Wet meadows and places with rushes, particularly on the banks of lakes
     and rivers. Likes a loamy soil with humus, but little nitrogen. The plant
     will withstand some drying out of the soil during the summer months and
     therefore shows the level of moisture in the ground.
AI: M; ♃

---

❺

50—160 cm

Purple Loosestrife *(Lythrum salicaria)*
Lythraceae
   See p. 240

---

❻

90—200 cm

Marsh Thistle *(Cirsium palustre)*
Asteraceae (Compositae)
IM: Flowers in capitula arranged in a cymose manner. Only disc florets present.
     Carpels with pinnate hairs (use a magnifying glass). Stem with prickly
     flanges. Leaves prickly.
D: Stem with leaves right to the top and a covering of dense hairs.
H: Moorland, wet meadows, fens, clearings in wet woodland. Likes a wet, rather
     muddy or peaty soil and avoids markedly calcareous soils.
AI: G; ☉

276

❶

Downy *or* **Felted Burdock** *(Arctium tomentosum)*
Asteraceae (Compositae)

50—150 cm
- IM: Flowers in spherical capitula, very hairy, 2—3 cm in diameter and arranged in a paniculate manner. Only disc florets present. Bracts of involucre hooked (burs).
- D: Stem bearing leaves. Leaves very large, petiolate, rounded or heart-shaped at the base.
- H: Weedy places on waysides, also on waste ground and by streams. Likes a calcareous, loamy soil, rich in nitrogen.
- AI: G; ⊙
  Hybrids and chemical constituents: see Lesser Burdock, p. 224.

❷

Hemp Agrimony *(Eupatorium cannabinum)*
Asteraceae (Compositae)

70—150 cm
- IM: Flowers in capitula which are arranged in a cymose manner. Leaves in part opposite, mostly divided into 3 leaflets. Leaflets lanceolate, coarsely serrate.
- D: Capitula small. Flowers inconspicuous, dark or pale pink. Stem erect.
- H: Light mixed or deciduous woodland, fen woodland, clearings or the edges of woods, river banks. Likes a damp, calcareous soil, rich in nutrients. An indicator of soil moisture.
- AI: G; ⊙—2↓; (†)
  Scientific generic name: see Common Agrimony, p. 128. An old medicinal plant. Contains a bitter chemical substance which has not so far been identified.

❸

Spotted Deadnettle *(Lamium maculatum)*
Lamiaceae (Labiatae)

30—80 cm
See p. 260

❹

Lousewort *(Pedicularis sylvatica)*
Scrophulariaceae

5—15 cm
- IM: Lower lip clearly shorter than the upper lip.
- D: Spikes. Flowers bright rose pink. Stem prostrate or decumbent. Leaves pinnate, with leaflets which are themselves pinnate.
- H: Moorland, marshes, reed beds, damp mountain pastures, woodland paths. Likes a soil wet with ground water, acid, peaty or sandy.
- Al: G; ⊙—2↓; (†)
  Hemiparasite. Name and chemical constituents see Red Rattle, below.

❺

Red Rattle, Marsh Lousewort *(Pedicularis palustris)*
Scrophulariaceae

10—40 cm
- IM: Lower and upper lips of corolla equally long.
- D: Flowers solitary in the leaf axils, rose pink. Stem hollow, branched, stiffly erect, glabrous. Leaves pinnate, with crenate leaflets.
- H: Moorland, reed beds. Likes a rather peaty soil, wet with ground water.
- AI: G; ⊙; (†)
  Hemiparasite on grasses and sedges. An extract of the plant was at one time used against animal lice, hence the name Lousewort. The species contains the acrid glycoside aucubin, which is certainly poisonous to insects and is possibly so for warm-blooded animals.

❶

Broad-leaved Marsh Orchid (*Dactylorhiza majalis; Dactylorchis latifolia; Orchis impudica; O. latifolia; O. majalis*)
Orchidaceae

25—30 cm

IM: Labellum with a cylindrical, backwardly directed spur. Petals spread out laterally. Bracts leaf-like, longer than the dark red flowers. Leaves with their maximum width in the middle, usually spotted or blotched.

D: Dense spikes of many flowers. Labellum clearly divided. Stem broadly tubular. 4—6 lanceolate or broadly lanceolate leaves. Tubers palmately divided.

H: Fens, moorland, damp meadows. Likes a slightly acid soil, rich in nutrients. Less sensitive to nitrogenous material than other species of the same genus.

AI: M; ♃

---

❷

Spotted Orchid (*Dactylorhiza maculata; Dactylorchis maculata; Orchis maculata; O. maculatus*)
Orchidaceae

20—60 cm

See p. 336

---

❸

Meadow Orchid (*Dactylorhiza incarnata; Orchis strictifolia; O. strictifolius; O. incarnatus; O. incarnata*)
Orchidaceae

20—40 cm

IM: Labellum with a cylindrical, backwardly directed spur. Lateral petals spreading. Bracts leaf-like, longer than the flesh-coloured flowers. Leaves broadest at the base, drawn together into a hood at the distal end; no spotting.

D: Dense spikes of many flowers. Spur shorter than ovary. Labellum completely undivided. Stem usually hollow with 3—6 leaves which are lanceolate.

H: Fens, moorland, wet meadows. Occurs equally on calcareous and acid, clay soils.

AI: M; ♃

---

❹

Fragrant Orchid (*Gymnadenia conopsea; G. conopea*)
Orchidaceae

10—60 cm

See p. 244

---

❺

Marsh Woundwort (*Stachys palustris*)
Lamiaceae (Labiatae)

10—60 cm

IM: Flowers in whorls in the axils of the upper leaves continuous with those of the terminal spike. Corolla twice as long as the calyx. Leaves sessile for the most part, but with the lower ones on short petioles, linear.

D: Whorls consisting of 6—12 flowers. Lower lip spotted. Stem with stiff hairs. Leaves opposite and decussate, with stiff hairs, serrate.

H: Wet meadows and pastures, roadside verges. Likes a damp, loamy soil.

AI: G; ♃

---

❻

Hedge Hyssop (*Gratiola officinalis*)
Scrophulariaceae

15—40 cm

IM: No possibility of confusion with other species.

D: Flowers solitary, in the axils of leaves. Petals whitish or pink, corolla tube yellowish. Stem erect or decumbent. Leaves opposite and decussate, sessile, lanceolate, serrate and glabrous.

H: Margins of stagnant or slow-flowing water, river banks, damp meadows. Likes a muddy, somewhat calcareous, dense soil. Withstands summer drought.

AI: G; ♃; †
Constituents: see p. 100.

1

2

3

4

5

6

❶

50—150 cm

Mezereon *(Daphne mezereum)*
Thymelaeaceae
IM: Flowers borne directly on woody stem. Plants without leaves at flowering time, or only with a bunch of leaves at the ends of the twigs.
D: Flowers rose pink or rose violet, with a strong scent. Fruit a berry. Stem branched, erect, with a wrinkled bark.
H: Mixed and deciduous woodland. Likes a rich, calcareous soil.
AI: P; †
All organs of the plant contain the acrid and poisonous substance mezerine.

❷

5—35 cm

Striped Daphne *(Daphne striata)*
Thymelaeaceae
IM: Flowers rose pink, glabrous externally, smelling of lilac.
D: Terminal clusters of 8—10 flowers. Twigs glabrous. Leaves linear-cuneate, leathery, clustered at the ends of the twigs.
H: Mountain pastures and rocky screes in alpine and subalpine localities.
AI: P
All organs of the plant contain the acrid and poisonous substance mezerine.

❸

10—30 cm

Rosemary Daphne *(Daphne cneorum)*
Thymelaeaceae
IM: Flowers purple red, hairy externally, smelling of cloves or pinks.
D: Terminal clusters of 6—10 flowers. Twigs pubescent. Leaves entire, about 1.5 cm long, evergreen, and evenly distributed along the twigs.
H: Light, dry woodland, semi-dry turf, rocky outgrowths in the mountains and in subalpine localities. Likes a shallow, calcareous soil in warm situations.
AI: P; †
All organs of the plant contain the acrid and poisonous substance mezerine.

❹

Up to 30 m

Pedunculate Elm *(Ulmus laevis; U. diffusa)*
Ulmaceae
IM: Flowers in small, pendulous clusters, with long peduncles. Winged fruit ciliated.
D: Leaves alternate, obliquely set, double serrate, 5—8 cm long. Buds glabrous.
H: Marshy woodland. Likes a deep soil, wet with ground water.
AI: P

❺

10—30 m

Dwarf Elm *(Ulmus minor; U. carpinifolia)*
Ulmaceae
IM: Flowers in small clusters, without peduncles, with white hairs. Seed near the indentation of the wing of the fruit. Buds glabrous.
D: Leaves alternate, obliquely set, double serrate, 5—8 cm long.
H: Mixed and fen woodland. Likes a wet, calcareous, loamy soil.
AI: P

❻

10—30 m

Wych Elm *(Ulmus glabra; U. scabra; U. montana)*
Ulmaceae
IM: Flowers in small clusters, without peduncles, with rust-coloured hairs. Seed in the middle of the winged fruit. Buds with rusty-red hairs.
D: Leaves alternate, obliquely set, double serrate, 8—10 cm long.
H: Canyon forest, mountain forest and fen woodland. Likes a calcareous, stony soil. Often occurs on ledges of cliffs and other habitats with dripping water.
AI: P

❶

30—50 cm

Crowberry *(Empetrum nigrum)*
Empetraceae
IM: Flowers inconspicuous. Leaves needle-like, white underneath, keeled, rolled
at the edges.
D: Plant dioecious. Male flowers pink, female flowers purple, small. Branches
decumbent or erect. Leaves alternate or in whorls, with very short petioles,
glossy.
H: Heaths, moorland, dunes, alpine mat. Likes an acid, porous soil. Very
abundant in those localities where it does occur.
AI: P; (†)
Crowberry contains the poison andrometoxin.

❷

Up to 80 cm
long

Cranberry *(Oxycoccus palustris; Vaccinium oxycoccus)*
Ericaceae
IM: Stem creeping. Leaves small, pointed and rolled at the edges.
D: Flowers small, drooping, on long peduncles. Leaves dark green, glossy.
H: Moorland, peaty open woodland. Likes a wet, acid, peaty soil. Very abundant
where it does occur.
AI: G
The fruit of the Cranberry is rich in vitamin C. It is edible and tastes particu-
larly nice after it has been subjected to at least one frost.

❸

10—50 cm

Cross-leaved Heath *(Erica tetralix)*
Ericaceae
IM: Leaves needle-like, 4—7 mm long in whorls of 3—4, fringed with stiff hairs.
D: Flowers in terminal, umbellate heads; each flower shaped like an urn, flesh
pink in colour. Stem branches erect, with rough hairs. Plant evergreen.
H: Heaths and moorland. Likes a damp or wet, sandy or peaty, acid soil. Forms
conspicuous clumps.
AI: G
Where it occurs in masses, it provides abundant nectar for bees. The tongues
of the collecting insects must be at least 7 mm long, in order to get to the
base of the corolla where the nectar lies.

❹

60—150 cm

Common Cotoneaster *(Cotoneaster integerrima)*
Rosaceae
IM: Flowers axillary, 2—10 in an axil. Petals 2—3 mm long. Leaves entire, except
that they may be finely serrate at the tip; upper side glabrous, underside with
a dense covering of hairs.
D: Umbellate racemes. Flowers small, campanulate, pale pink. Young twigs
often with a felt-like covering of hairs. Leaves rounded-ovoid, pointed or
crenate.
H: Dry thickets and woodland, mainly on steep, rocky, south-facing slopes. Likes
a stony, calcareous soil, but may occasionally occur on sandy soils in warm
situations.
AI: P
The Common Cotoneaster is pollinated particularly by wasps. Its seeds
contain an organic cyanide compound.

❺

Up to 10 m

Wild Apple, Crab Apple *(Malus sylvestris; M. communis, ssp. acerba)*
Rosaceae
See p. 104

Shrubs and Trees **Red or Pink**

❶ Apple Rose, Downy Rose *(Rosa villosa; R. pomifera)*
Rosaceae
1—2 m
IM: Flowers bright red. Sepals remain attached to the fruit. Stem with straight, narrow spines. Leaves pinnate.
D: Flowers solitary, about 7 cm in diameter. Leaves consist of 5—7 leaflets, hairy on the underside, 1—4 cm long.
H: Rocky slopes, thickets and dry woodland. Likes warm situations and is largely confined to sunny, south-facing slopes.
AI: P
The fruit contains very little vitamin C (cf. Dog Rose, below).

❷ Dog Rose *(Rosa canina)*
Rosaceae
1.3—2.8 m
IM: Flowers pale pink to bright pink. The calyx segments fall off after flowering is over. Stem prickly. Leaves pinnate.
D: Flowers in groups of 1—3, scented. Petals 2—2.5 cm long. Stem covered with spines. Leaves unpaired pinnate, alternate, consisting of 5—7 leaflets which are ovoid or elliptical and markedly serrate. The genus consists of many species, rich in races, all of which are difficult to distinguish.
H: Deciduous woodland, hedges, edges of woods and thickets. Likes a porous soil.
AI: P
The fruit of the Dog Rose (hips) is extremely rich in vitamin C (up to 1,700 mg per 100 g fresh fruit). It also contains provitamin A (carotene), vitamins of the B group, vitamin K and vitamin P. The best way to exploit the high vitamin content of rose hips is to make them into jam.

❸ Cowberry, Red Whortleberry *(Vaccinium vitis-idaea)*
Ericaceae
10—30 cm
See p. 106

❹ Bog Whortleberry *(Vaccinium uliginosum)*
Ericaceae
30—90 cm
IM: Twigs round, greyish brown. Leaves entire, blue green below, with blue stripes.
D: Several terminal flowers. Stem decumbent or erect. Leaves up to 4 cm long and 2 cm wide, blunt, almost sessile and rolled at the edges.
H: Moorland, bogs, peaty woodlands, alpine mats. Likes a damp, acid soil. Abundant in those localities where it occurs.
AI: G; (†)
The berries contain a substance, not yet identified, which can produce intoxication if they are eaten in large amounts. Possibly this poison is not produced by the berries themselves but by some fungus which parasitizes them. The leaves contain arbutin and can be used to make a tea.

❺ Marsh Tea *(Ledum palustre)*
Ericaceae
50—130 cm
IM: Flowers not campanulate. Leaves with rust-red hairs on the undersides.
D: Terminal umbels of many flowers. Stem with whorls of lateral branches. Leaves only 3 mm broad, upper sides glossy. The bush has an unpleasant smell.
H: Moorland, marshes, peaty woodland. Likes a wet, peaty soil.
AI: G; †
The leaves contain an ethereal oil (smell) and the poisonous substance ledol.

286

❶ **Marsh Andromeda, Bog Rosemary** *(Andromeda polifolia)*
Ericaceae
15—30 cm
IM: Leaves lanceolate, undersides bluish white, markedly rolled up at the edges, 1—3 mm wide.
D: 1—4 terminal flowers. Stem erect or decumbent.
H: Moorland. Likes a wet, acid, peaty soil. Abundant where it does occur.
AI: G; †
The scientific generic name refers to Andromeda, the daughter of King Cepheus and Queen Cassiopeia in Greek mythology. The leaves of the plant contain the poisonous andrometoxin.

❷ **Hairy Alpenrose** *(Rhododendron hirsutum)*
Ericaceae
40—120 cm
IM: Leaves green on both sides (except for a few rust-coloured spots), hairy at the edges.
D: Multiflorous umbels. A very twiggy shrub, thickly covered with leaves. Leaves elliptical or linear, invert-ovoid, not rolled.
H: Woods in alpine areas, more rarely mountain forest in subalpine districts, alpine thickets. Likes a porous, calcareous, stony soil, which is rather damp. Forms extensive stands in those localities where it does occur.
AI: G

❸ **Rusty Alpenrose** *(Rhododendron ferrugineum)*
Ericaceae
40—120 cm
IM: Leaves rusty yellow or red on the underside, not hairy, rolled at the edges.
D: Multiflorous umbels. Shrubs with few leaves at the base. Leaves linear-lanceolate.
H: Woods in alpine areas, more rarely in subalpine districts, alpine thickets. Likes a non-calcareous, porous, stony and rather moist soil, rich in humus.
AI: G

❹ **Heather, Ling** *(Calluna vulgaris)*
Ericaceae
10—50 cm
IM: Leaves needle-like, 1—3 mm long, arranged in fours, but opposite.
D: Approaching unilaterally directed racemes. Flowers small on short peduncles.
H: Heaths, moorland, deciduous, mixed and coniferous woods, roadside verges, mountain pastures. Likes an acid, sandy soil.
AI: G
A rich source of nectar for bees, also an old medicinal plant. Contains flavones, tannins and arbutin.

❺ **Spiny Restharrow** *(Ononis spinosa)*
Fabaceae (Leguminosae)
30—60 cm
IM: Hairs on stem in 1 or 2 rows.
D: Flowers 1—3 in the leaf axils, often joined together into racemose inflorescences with many leaves. Leaves composed of 3 leaflets, sessile or with short petioles. Similar species: Creeping Restharrow *(Ononis repens)*, in which the hairs form rings around the stem, which is usually prostrate. Habitats and distribution similar to those of *O. spinosa*.

H: Semi-dry turf; roadside verges, meadows. Likes a stony, calcareous, loamy soil in warm situations.
AI: P

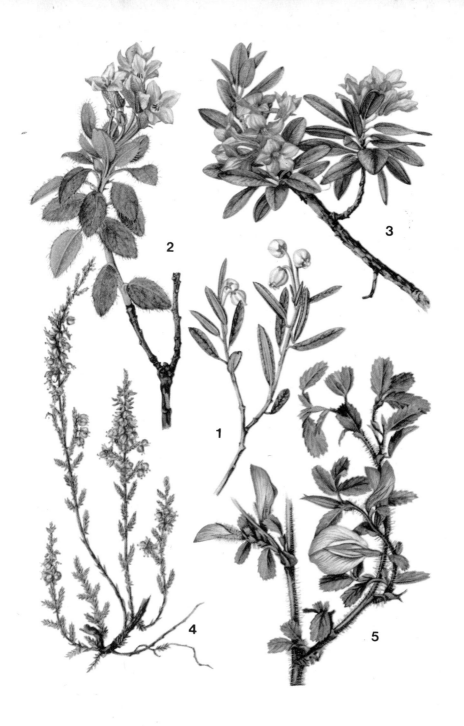

2

3

1

4

5

❶

10—40 cm

Buxbaum's Speedwell *(Veronica persica ; V. tournefortii)*
Scrophulariaceae
IM: Flowers solitary in the axils of leaves, 8—12 mm in diameter. Leaves heart-shaped, crenate. Capsel 8—10 mm broad.
D: Flowers on long peduncles, sky blue with a yellowish throat to the corolla. Stem prostrate or decumbent, simple or branched, with curled hairs.
H: Weedy places in vegetable fields, gardens and vineyards, more rarely on wayside verges and on wasteland. Likes a rather loamy soil, rich in nutrients.
AI: G; ☉ — ☉
Originally a native of Asia Minor. Today it is a very common garden weed.

❷

5—30 cm

Ivy-leaved Speedwell *(Veronica hederifolia)*
Scrophulariaceae
See p. 308

❸

5—15 cm

Fingered Speedwell *(Veronica triphyllos)*
Scrophulariaceae
IM: Terminal, loose racemes. Peduncle longer than calyx. Bracts not clearly different from the stem leaves. Middle and upper leaves composed of 3—5 leaflets.
D: Peduncle, at least as long as, and usually longer than the calyx. Flowers dark blue. Stem erect or decumbent, branched at the base. Lower leaves ovoid, middle leaves digitate with 3—5 leaflets, upper leaves lanceolate.
H: Weedy places in cornfields, but also in vegetable fields, gardens, vineyards and along waysides. Likes a porous, sandy soil. Somewhat calcifugous.
AI: G; ☉

❹

10—25 cm

Wall Speedwell *(Veronica arvensis)*
Scrophulariaceae
See p. 308

❺

15—30 cm

Germander Speedwell *(Veronica chamaedrys)*
Scrophulariaceae
IM: Hairs on stem in two rows.
D: Loose, axillary racemes (usually only 2). Petals fall off readily, blue in colour, with darker veins. Stem prostrate or decumbent. Leaves opposite, on short petioles, crenate, hairy.
H: Meadows, mixed and deciduous woodland, dry thickets, roadside verges. Likes a porous, nitrogenous soil.
AI: G; ♃ ; (†)
The Germander Speedwell contains the glycoside aucubin (see Red Rattle, p. 278).

❻

15—50 cm

Greater Speedwell *(Veronica teucrium)*
Scrophulariaceae
See p. 296

290

1

2

3

5

4

6

❶   **Lamb's Lettuce, Corn Salad** *(Valerianella locusta ; V. olitoria)*

5—20 cm
Valerianaceae
IM: ·No possibility of confusion with other species.
D: Cymes. Flowers inconspicuous, pale blue. Stem erect, forked. Lower leaves spatulate, upper leaves lanceolate. Several very similar species, all difficult to distinguish.
H: Weedy places in vegetable fields, along waysides, in gardens and vineyards, also in meadows and on semi-dry turf.
AI: G; ⊙
Used as a salad plant, a practice possibly dating from the Middle Ages.

❷   **Field Speedwell** *(Myosotis arvensis ; M. intermedia)*

20—40 cm
Boraginaceae
IM: Flowers 4—6 mm in diameter. Peduncles erect, 1—2 mm long at the time of flowering. The stalk of the mature fruit is 2—3 times as long as the calyx. Fructification about as long as the residual length of the stem.
D: Inflorescence racemose, multiflorous. Stem round, erect, branched. Basal leaves invert-ovoid, petiolate, grey green in colour, forming a rosette. Stem leaves linear-lanceolate, sessile.
H: Weedy places in fields and along field paths. Likes a loamy soil and is rather calcifugous. Its presence indicates some slight acidity in the soil.
AI: G; ⊙; ⊖

❸   **Scarlet Pimpernel** *(Anagallis arvensis)*

8—15 cm
Primulaceae
See p. 220

❹   **Field Bugloss** *(Anchusa arvensis ; Lycopsis arvensis)*

15—45 cm
Boraginaceae
IM: Corolla tube bent in the middle.
D: Inflorescence loose and consisting of both flowers and leaves. Flowers with short peduncles. Stem angular, erect. Leaves lanceolate, undulating, with stiff hairs.
H: Weedy places in fields and along waysides. Likes a porous, sandy soil. Rather calcifugous and likes a warm situation.
AI: G; ⊙

❺   **Common Bugloss** *or* **Alkanet** *(Anchusa officinalis)*

30—100 cm
Boraginaceae
See p. 322

❻   **Common Grape Hyacinth** *(Muscari racemosum)*

10—30 cm
Liliaceae
See p. 302

❼   **Cornflower, Bluebottle** *(Centaurea cyanus)*

30—90 cm
Asteraceae (Compositae)
IM: Flowers in large, solitary capitula. Only disc florets present. Leaves no more than 5 mm wide, alternate.
D: Stem erect, leaves not decurrent.
H: Weedy places in cornfields, more rarely on old compost heaps, wasteland or rubbish tips. Likes a porous soil rich in nutrients.
AI: G; ⊙

❶ **Chicory, Wild Succory** *(Cichorium intybus)*

30—130 cm
Cichoriaceae (Compositae)
IM: Flowers in large capitula. Only ray florets present. Carpels usually without a pappus of hairs. Stem strongly branched.
D: Stem geniculate, branched. Lower leaves coarsely toothed, upper leaves linear, undivided, clasping the stem.
H: Weedy places on wayside verges, on wasteland, embankments, more rarely in or around the edge of fields. Tolerates most types of soil, providing it is nitrogenous.
AI: G; ♃
The flowers of Chicory open at 6 a.m. and close about midday. Chicory, as used as a flavouring, has been extracted from the root of the plant since the 17th century. An old medicinal plant.

❷ **Forking Larkspur** *(Consolida regalis; Delphinium consolida)*

10—50 cm
Ranunculaceae
IM: No possibility of confusion with other species.
D: Raceme of few flowers. Flowers with long spurs and long peduncles. Stem strongly branched. Leaves divided into narrow segments.
H: Weedy places, particularly in cornfields, more rarely on compost heaps. Likes a loamy, chalky soil.
AI: P; ☉; (†)

❸ **Viper's Bugloss** *(Echium vulgare)*

30—120 cm
Boraginaceae
See p. 228

❹ **Meadow Sage** *or* **Clary** *(Salvia pratensis)*

20—60 cm
Lamiaceae (Labiatae)
See p. 326

❺ **Geneva Bugle** *(Ajuga genevensis)*

5—30 cm
Lamiaceae (Labiatae)
IM: Flowers without an upper lip to the corolla. Lower lip trilobed. Bracts deeply cleft into 3. Plant without runners.
D: 6—12 flowers in axillary whorls and in a terminal spike. Stem and leaves very hairy. Only a few basal leaves which soon shrivel up. Stem leaves strongly crenate.
H: Light woodland, dry and semi-dry turf, roadside verges. Likes a porous, calcareous soil in warm situations.
AI: G; ♃
Geneva Bugle propagates itself by seeds and root buds.

❻ **Field Scabious** *(Knautia arvensis)*

30—70 cm
Dipsacaceae
See p. 324

❶ **Germander Speedwell** (*Veronica chamaedrys*)
Scrophulariaceae
15—30 cm IM: Hairs on stem in two rows.
D: Loose, axillary racemes (usually only 2). Petals fall off readily, blue in colour, with darker veins. Stem prostrate or decumbent. Leaves opposite, on short petioles, crenate, hairy.
H: Meadows, mixed and deciduous woodland, dry thickets, roadside verges. Likes a porous, nitrogenous soil.
AI: G; ♃; (†)
The Germander Speedwell contains the glycoside aucubin.

❷ **Greater Speedwell** (*Veronica teucrium*)
Scrophulariaceae
15—50 cm IM: Racemes. Stem decumbent or erect. Leaves ovoid or lanceolate, sessile, usually only the lower ones with petioles.
D: Flowers 1—1.3 cm in diameter, azure blue. Peduncle hairy.
H: Dry and semi-dry turf, dry thickets, light woodland, roadside verges. Likes a rather stony, calcareous soil, although one which is far from shallow.
AI: G; ♃

❸ **Common Speedwell** (*Veronica officinalis*)
Scrophulariaceae
15—30 cm IM: Racemes. Flower pale blue, with darker veins. Calyx with 4 segments. Leaves invert-ovoid.
D: Racemes erect, axillary. Stem creeping, decumbent towards the tip. Leaves with short petioles, stout, serrate.
H: Heaths, sparse meadows, deciduous, mixed and coniferous woodland. Likes a sandy, loamy and rather acid soil and is an indicator of surface acidity.
AI: G; ♃; (†)
An old medicinal plant. Contains aucubin, tannins and an alkaloid.

❹ **Devil's-bit Scabious** (*Succisa pratensis*)
Dipsacaceae
30—110 cm IM: Marginal flowers no larger than the inner ones. Stem hairy below the capitulum. Leaves undivided.
D: Flowers in terminal, hemispherical capitula, usually dark blue, more rarely bluish violet. Leaves opposite, ovoid or lanceolate.
H: Wet meadows, moorland, mountain pastures, light damp woodland. Likes a slightly acid soil, which is damp at least part of the time.
AI: G; ♃
The name Devil's-bit refers to the rootstock, which in the autumn looks as though it has been bitten. An old medicinal plant, containing saponin in the rootstock, together with tannins and the glycoside, scabioside.

❺ **Fringed Gentian** (*Gentianella ciliata* ; *Gentiana ciliata*)
Gentianaceae
10—25 cm IM: Segments of the corolla fringed.
D: Flowers mainly solitary, more rarely with flowering side branches. Leaves linear, or less often linear-lanceolate, with a single vein.
H: Semi-dry turf, roadside verges, light woodland and thickets. Likes a porous, stony soil in warm situations.
AI: G; ☉—♃

❶ **Spring Gentian** *(Gentiana verna)*
Gentianaceae

3—15 cm IM: Stem uniflorous. Petals spreading in a saucer-like manner. Plant with non-
flowering shoots.

D: Flowers terminal, 1.8—3 cm in diameter. Stem erect, with 1—3 pairs of small,
opposite leaves. Basal leaves form a rosette, variable in size, elliptical to
lanceolate.

H: Semi-dry turf, dry meadows, mountain pastures. Likes a calcareous, stony soil,
rich in humus. Forms extensive masses where it does occur.

AI: G; ♃

The Spring Gentian may occasionally flower a second time in the autumn.
This happens particularly in warm years.

❷ **Marsh Gentian** *(Gentiana pneumonanthe)*
Gentianaceae

15—40 cm See p. 318

❸ **Milkweed Gentian** *(Gentiana asclepiadea)*
Gentianaceae

30—70 cm IM: Flowers axillary. Corolla segments not spread out in a flat, saucer-like manner.
Leaves ovoid or lanceolate, with 5 veins.

D: 1—3 flowers in each axil. Stem erect or drooping, thickly covered with leaves,
which are opposite and decussate.

H: Damp woodland in alpine and subalpine regions, damp mountain pastures,
alpine mat. Likes a calcareous, damp, loamy soil, rich in humus.

AI: G; ♃

The name Milkweed Gentian refers to the similarity between the leaves
of this plant and those of many Milkweeds. The flowers of the Milkweed Gentian
open between 8 and 9 a.m. and close between 5 and 6 p.m. The plant contains
an alkaloid in the leaves and roots.

❹ **Spreading Campanula, Bellflower** *or* **Harebell** *(Campanula patula)*
Campanulaceae

30—60 cm See p. 330

❺ **Clustered Bellflower** *(Campanula glomerata)*
Campanulaceae

15—70 cm IM: Flowers in a terminal cluster. Lower stem leaves rounded or heart-shaped
at the base. Plant covered with soft hairs.

D: Flowers 1.5—3 cm long. Stem simple, erect. A similar species is the Setaceous
Bellflower *(Campanula cervicaria)*, which is covered in stiff hairs and whose
lower stem leaves are not rounded. In thickets and meadows.

H: Semi-dry turf, meadows. Likes a porous, rather stony, calcareous, loamy soil.

AI: G; ♃

❻ **Common Harebell** *(Campanula rotundifolia)*
Campanulaceae

15—50 cm See p. 312

❶

15—50 cm

Wood Forget-me-not *(Myosotis sylvatica)*
Boraginaceae
IM: Flowers 6—10 mm in diameter. Calyx with spreading hairs.
D: Inflorescence racemose. Leaves entire, lanceolate, with rough hairs.
H: Mixed, deciduous and coniferous woodland, fen woodland, mountain pastures, alpine mats. Likes a porous, damp soil, rich in loam.
AI: G; ♃
Flower buds often deep pink. During the period of flowering, the colour of the corolla changes from pink to blue, a colour change which reflects changes in the acidity of the cells of the petals (see Mountain Pea, p. 304).

❷

30—60 cm

Meadow Crane's-bill *(Geranium pratense)*
Geraniaceae
IM: Flowers 2.5—4 cm in diameter. Peduncle bends round after flowering.
D: Flowers in twos. Stem erect. Leaves large, palmate, with 7 lobes or segments.
H: Meadows of all kinds. Likes a deep, calcareous, loamy soil. Often blooms a second time after the meadow has been mown.
AI: P; ♃
The common name draws attention to the form of the fruit which resembles the bill of a crane. The peduncle of the plant undergoes a slow movement during the period of flowering; this is due to very unequal growth in the cells on the two sides of the peduncle. The buds are first erect, then droop over. As the flower opens, it stands erect but then the flower axis assumes a horizontal position. The flowers droop at night and during rain. Often it is possible to see flowers in different developmental phases and different relative positions on the same plant. For seed-dispersal mechanism see Marsh Crane's-bill, p. 272.

❸

10—40 cm

Sea Holly *(Eryngium maritimum)*
Apiaceae (Umbelliferae)
IM: Flowers in spherical umbels. Involucral bracts of umbel spiny. Leaves with spines like those of Holly.
D: Stem strong, markedly branched, so as to form a hemispherical 'bush'. Basal leaves with long petioles, stem leaves with short petioles. Topmost leaves sessile. The whole plant with a bluish tinge.
H: Dunes. Likes a saline, sandy soil. Quite abundant where it does occur.
AI: P; ☉—♃
Constituents see Field Eryngo, p: 32.

❹

15—40 cm

Water Forget-me-not *(Myosotis palustris; M. scorpioides)*
Boraginaceae
See p. 310

❺

30—60 cm

Common *or* **Wild Columbine** *(Aquilegia vulgaris)*
Ranunculaceae
See p. 310

❻

5—20 cm

Lamb's Lettuce, Corn Salad *(Valerianella locusta; V. olitoria)*
Valerianaceae
See p. 292

❶ **Spiked Rampion** *(Phyteuma spicatum)*
Campanulaceae
30—100 cm See p. 48

❷ **Round-headed Rampion** *(Phyteuma orbiculare)*
Campanulaceae
15—50 cm
IM: Flower head spherical, deep blue.
D: Flower buds curved like claws. Stem erect, with leaves scattered over its
length. Leaves crenate or serrate; the lower ones with long petioles and ovoid
or heart-shaped, the upper ones linear.
H: Semi-dry turf, mountain pastures. Likes a porous, rather stony, calcareous
soil in warm situations. Occasionally occurs on moorland soils if they are
well aerated.
AI: G; ♃

❸ **Sheep's-bit** *(Jasione montana)*
Campanulaceae
15—50 cm
IM: Flowers in a flattened, terminal head. Flowers and flower buds straight,
sky blue in colour. Leaves entire, small, corrugated at the edge, with rough
hairs.
D: Stem decumbent or erect. Leaves alternate, linear, the lower ones invert-
ovoid or linear.
H: Dunes, stony turf. Likes a dry, sandy soil; calcifugous.
AI: G; ☉

❹ **Lesser Grape Hyacinth** *(Muscari botryoides)*
Liliaceae
10—30 cm See p. 314

❺ **Common Grape Hyacinth** *(Muscari racemosum)*
Liliaceae
10—30 cm
IM: 4—6 leaves, only 2—3 mm wide, flabby. Leaves appear first in the autumn.
D: Flowers in dense racemes, each one spherical, scented. Stem without leaves
at flowering time.
H: Weedy places in vegetable fields, vineyards and on semi-dry turf. Likes
a calcareous, loamy or loess soil. Abundant in those localities where it occurs.
AI: M; ♃
This plant was at one time grown in cottage gardens as an ornamental species
and its occurrence in the wild is therefore as a garden escape.

❻ **Mountain Knapweed** *(Centaurea montana)*
Asteraceae (Compositae)
30—60 cm
IM: Flowers in large, solitary capitula. Only tubular florets present. Leaves at
least 1 cm wide.
D: Involucral bracts with a black border, fringed. Inner florets violet.
H: Canyon forest, mountain forest, deciduous and mixed woodland (particularly
in light spots, along woodland paths and clearings), mountain pastures. Likes
a calcareous soil, rich in humus. Abundant in those places where it does occur.
AI: G; ♃

❶   **Dog Violet** (*Viola canina*)
Violaceae

5—15 cm   IM: Peduncle bearing leaves, also small basal leaves present. Flowers 4—5 mm long.
D: Flowers solitary, axillary. Spur mostly yellowish. Stem decumbent or erect. Leaves ovoid or heart-shaped.
H: Heaths, dry turf, light mixed and deciduous woodland. Avoids chalky soils, preferring a sandy loam.
AI: P; ♃

❷   **Mountain** *or* **Tuberous Pea** (*Lathyrus montanus*)
Fabaceae (Leguminosae)

15—40 cm   IM: Loose racemes of 2—5 flowers which are 11—22 mm long. Flowers red at first, then a dirty blue. Stamens fused together by their stalks into a tube. Stem winged. Leaves compound, pinnate, with 4—6 leaflets. Undersides of leaves blue green.
D: Leaflets linear-lanceolate, glabrous.
H: Deciduous and mixed woodland, more rarely coniferous forest or heath and sparse mountain pastures. Likes a sandy or loamy soil. Calcifugous.
AI: P; ♃
The change in colour of the flowers is due to the change in acidity of the cell sap during the period of flowering. In the young flower the cell sap is acid and the pigment is red. In older flowers the cell sap is neutral or alkaline and the pigment is blue. Similar changes in colour occur in other flowers, e.g. Forget-me-not and Viper's Bugloss. It is possible to demonstrate experimentally that red and blue colours result from the same pigment at different acidities. If one takes a blue flower, e.g. Harebell, and places it on an ants' nest, the inhabitants will spray formic acid on it. Where the acid comes into contact with the flower, red splashes will result.

❸   **Blue Monkshood, Blue Aconite** (*Aconitum napellus*)
Ranunculaceae

50—180 cm   See p. 316

❹   **Geneva Bugle** (*Ajuga genevensis*)
Lamiaceae (Labiatae)

5—30 cm   See p. 294

❺   **Creeping** *or* **Common Bugle** (*Ajuga reptans*)
Lamiaceae (Labiatae)

15—30 cm   IM: Flowers without an upper lip. Lower lip of 3 lobes. Upper leaves and bracts undivided. Plant possesses runners. Basal leaves spatulate, slightly crenate, forming a rosette.
D: 6—12 flowers in whorls in the leaf axils. Stem square, with 2 rows of hairs or almost glabrous. Upper stem leaves opposite and decussate.
H: Mixed, deciduous and coniferous woodland, meadows. Likes a rather moist, loamy soil, rich in nutrients.
AI: G; ♃
Occasionally white or pink mutant forms of this plant are found. Seeds are dispersed by ants. An old medicinal plant containing tannins.

❻   **Meadow Sage** *or* **Clary** (*Salvia pratensis*)
20—60 cm   Lamiaceae (Labiatae)
        See p. 326

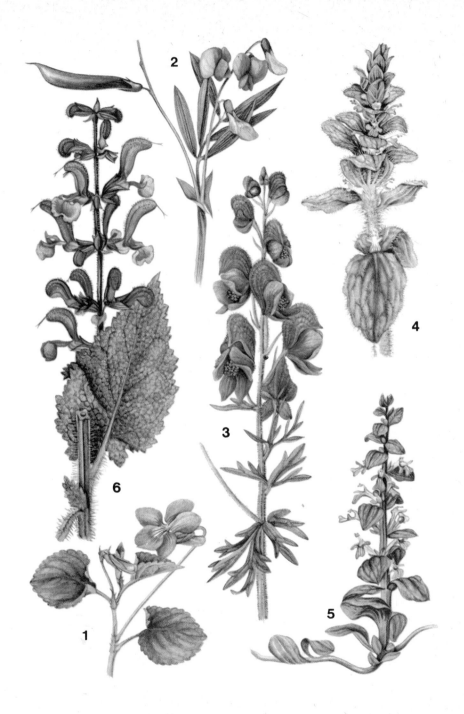

❶

30—120 cm

Viper's Bugloss *(Echium vulgare)*
Boraginaceae
See p. 228

---

❷

5—25 cm

Tufted Milkwort *(Polygala comosa)*
Polygalaceae
See p. 244

---

❸

5—15 cm

Bitter Milkwort *(Polygala amara)*
Polygalaceae
See p. 244

---

❹

15—25 cm

Common Milkwort *(Polygala vulgaris)*
Polygalaceae

IM: Bracts shorter than the flowers. The bracts do not grow over the inflorescence just before the flowers open.

D: Loose racemes of 4 flowers, which are usually blue but may be pink. Stem erect or decumbent. Leaves alternate; the upper ones narrow and lanceolate, the lower ones smaller and elliptical.

H: Meadows, mountain pastures. Likes a rather sandy soil, rich in humus. Calcifugous, and where it occurs in chalky areas it denotes surface acidity.

AI: P; ♃

The scientific name *Polygala* is derived from Greek and means 'much milk'. In olden days it was believed that cattle which ate this plant would give more milk. The plant contains saponin.

---

❺

5—30 cm

Globe Daisy *(Globularia elongata; G. aphylanthes; G. willkommii; G. vulgaris)*
Globulariaceae

IM: No possibility of confusion with other genera.

D: Flowers in solitary, spherical, terminal heads, 1—1.5 cm wide and violet blue in colour. Stem erect, unbranched. Basal leaves spatulate, forming a rosette. Stem leaves ovoid to lanceolate. There are a few similar species, which are rare and difficult to distinguish from this species.

H: Dry and semi-dry turf. Likes a shallow, stony or rocky soil. Calcareous.

AI: G; ♃; †

The scientific and common names refer to the spherical or globe-like form of the inflorescence. The Globe Daisy contains a glycoside, globularine. A medicinal plant.

---

❻

30—70 cm

Field Scabious *(Knautia arvensis)*
Dipsacaceae

IM: Stem below the inflorescence with spreading hairs. The upper leaves are usually pinnate.

D: Flowers in terminal heads. Outer flowers usually larger than the inner ones, bluish violet in colour. Leaves opposite, greyish green.

H: Meadows, semi-dry turf, roadside verges, occasionally also weedy places in fields. Likes a porous, rather calcareous, loamy soil.

AI: G; ♃

An old medicinal plant. Contains tannins and an alkaloid.

❶　　　　　　**Common Speedwell** *(Veronica officinalis)*
　　　　　　Scrophulariaceae
15 — 30 cm　　　See p. 296

---

❷　　　　　　**Ivy-leaved Speedwell** *(Veronica hederifolia)*
　　　　　　Scrophulariaceae
5 — 30 cm　　IM: Flowers solitary, axillary. Leaves with 3 — 7 lobes.
　　　　　　D: Flowers 2 — 5 mm in diameter, blue or bluish violet, more rarely white. Stem prostrate or decumbent, branched. Leaves hairy.
　　　　　　H: Weedy places in fields and gardens, along waysides and on wasteland, also in woods, particularly woodland clearings. Likes a porous, loamy soil, which is rather damp.
　　　　　　AI: G; ⊙
　　　　　　The seeds of this plant are dispersed by ants. Because of oil-containing tissue in the seeds, the ants carry them to their nests.

---

❸　　　　　　**Greater Speedwell** *(Veronica teucrium)*
　　　　　　Scrophulariaceae
15 — 50 cm　　See p. 296

---

❹　　　　　　**Germander Speedwell** *(Veronica chamaedrys)*
　　　　　　Scrophulariaceae
15 — 30 cm　　See p. 290

---

❺　　　　　　**Fringed Gentian** *(Gentianella ciliata ; Gentiana ciliata)*
　　　　　　Gentianaceae
10 — 25 cm　　See p. 296

---

❻　　　　　　**Devil's-bit Scabious** *(Succisa pratensis)*
　　　　　　Dipsacaceae
30 — 110 cm　IM: Marginal flowers no larger than the inner ones. Stem hairy below the capitulum. Leaves undivided.
　　　　　　D: Flowers in terminal, hemispherical capitula, usually dark blue, more rarely bluish violet. Leaves opposite, ovoid or lanceolate.
　　　　　　H: Wet meadows, moorland, mountain pastures, light damp woodland. Likes a slightly acid soil, which is damp at least part of the time.
　　　　　　AI: G; ♃
　　　　　　For name and constituents: see p. 296.

---

❼　　　　　　**Wall Speedwell** *(Veronica arvensis)*
　　　　　　Scrophulariaceae
10 — 25 cm　IM: Racemes. Peduncle shorter than the calyx. Bracts and upper leaves not clearly distinguishable from the stem leaves. Leaves heart-shaped or ovoid, crenate, hairy.
　　　　　　D: Racemes of few flowers, which are small and sky blue in colour. Peduncle shorter than the calyx. Stem erect or decumbent, richly branched. Leaves crenate, the lower ones heart-shaped or ovoid, the upper ones lanceolate and usually entire.
　　　　　　H: Weedy places in fields, gardens and vineyards, also on wasteland and in woodland clearings. Likes a porous soil.
　　　　　　AI: G; ⊙
　　　　　　The seeds of Wall Speedwell are dispersed by ants (see Ivy-leaved Speedwell, above).

❶   **Creeping Gromwell** (*Lithospermum purpureo-coeruleum*)
10—50 cm   Boraginaceae
          See p. 252

---

❷   **Wood Forget-me-not** (*Myosotis sylvatica*)
15—50 cm   Boraginaceae
          See p. 300

---

❸   **Water Forget-me-not** (*Myosotis palustris ; M. scorpioides*)
15—40 cm   Boraginaceae
        IM: Flowers 4—10 mm in diameter. Calyx with adpressed hairs.
        D: Inflorescence racemose, leafless. Stem angular. Leaves linear and lanceolate, sessile, hairy.
        H: Wet meadows, banks of streams, ditches, wet woodlands. Likes a loamy soil containing nitrogen and wet with ground water. Found also on mud. Indicator of soil moisture.
        AI: G; ♃
           Flower buds bright pink. For colour change see Mountain Pea, p. 304.

---

❹   **Lesser Periwinkle** (*Vinca minor*)
Up to 60 cm Apocynaceae
        IM: Flowers solitary, axillary. Corolla mostly flat, with its segments sharply truncated. Stem creeping, flowering stem decumbent. Stem woody at the base.
        D: Segments of corolla saucer-shaped collectively, flat and sharply truncated. Leaves opposite, lanceolate or elliptical, leathery, evergreen.
        H: Mixed and deciduous woodland, more rarely in light coniferous forest. Likes a porous, rather calcareous, loamy soil. Susceptible to frost.
        AI: G; ♃
           Common in gardens and often planted in cemeteries. The plant spreads mainly by means of runners.

---

❺   **Common** or **Wild Columbine** (*Aquilegia vulgaris*)
30—60 cm   Ranunculaceae
        IM: No possibility of confusion with other species.
        D: Flowers on long peduncles. Spurs to corolla bent into a hook at the end. Leaves on long petioles, doubly divided into 3, upper leaves sessile. Leaflets 3-lobed, crenate.
        H: Dry woodland, mountain forest, deciduous and mixed woods, mountain pastures. Likes a calcareous soil, rich in loam.
        AI: P; ♃;(†)
           The flowers of the Columbine are pollinated by bumblebees. Short-tongued bumblebees and honey bees often bite through the corolla spurs to get to the nectar inside. An old medicinal plant. It is slightly poisonous due to the presence in its tissues of a cyanogenic glycoside and an unknown alkaloid.

---

❻   **Spreading Campanula, Bellflower** or **Harebell** (*Campanula patula*)
30—60 cm   Campanulaceae
          See p. 330

❶   **Common Harebell** *(Campanula rotundifolia)*
Campanulaceae
15—50 cm   IM: Flowers in panicles, bell-shaped. Stem leaves narrow, lanceolate, entire.
        D: Flowers usually drooping, 1.5—2 cm long, with the free segments of the corolla only about ⅓ the total length of the flower. Basal part of stem downy. Basal leaves with long petioles, kidney-shaped, round, ovoid or heart-shaped.
        H: Meadows, heaths, semi-dry turf, light woodland. Likes a rather sandy soil and is somewhat calcifugous.
        AI: G; ♃

❷   **Peach-leaved Campanula** *(Campanula persicifolia)*
Campanulaceae
70—120 cm   IM: Unilateral racemes of few flowers. Flowers 2.5—4 cm in diameter. Stem leaves linear, at most 1 cm wide.
        D: Flowers hemispherical, sky blue. Lower leaves finely serrate, linear and ovoid.
        H: Dry woodland and thickets, mixed and deciduous woods, edges of woodland. Likes a porous, calcareous soil, rich in humus and nutrients, in warm situations.
        AI: G; ♃

❸   **Nettle-leaved Campanula** *(Campanula trachelium)*
Campanulaceae
50—100 cm   IM: Multilateral racemes. Stem angular, hairy. Lower stem leaves heart-shaped with long petioles.
        D: Inflorescence contains leaves. Flowers 3.5—4.5 cm long with small hairs on the edge. Leaves coarsely double-serrate, with stiff hairs. Upper leaves sessile.
        H: Deciduous and mixed woodland, more rarely coniferous forest, canyon forest and fen woodland. Likes a porous, often rather stony soil, but one containing humus and of the consistency of a damp loam.
        AI: G; ♃

❹   **Spiked Rampion** *(Phyteuma spicatum)*
Campanulaceae
30—100 cm   See p. 48

❺   **Milkweed Gentian** *(Gentiana asclepiadea)*
Gentianaceae
30—70 cm   IM: Flowers axillary. Corolla segments not spread out in a flat, saucer-like manner. Leaves ovoid or lanceolate, with 5 veins.
        D: 1—3 flowers in each axil. Stem erect or drooping, thickly covered with leaves which are opposite and decussate.
        H: Damp woodland in alpine and subalpine regions, damp mountain pastures, alpine mat. Likes a calcareous, damp, loamy soil, rich in humus.
        AI: G; ♃
        The name Milkweed Gentian refers to the similarity between the leaves of this plant and those of many Milkweeds. The flowers of the Milkweed Gentian open between 8 and 9 a.m. and close between 5 and 6 p.m. The plant contains an alkaloid in the leaves and roots.

❶   **Two-leaved Squill** *(Scilla bifolia)*
Liliaceae
10—20 cm   IM: No possibility of confusion with other species.
       D: Racemes of 2—8 flowers. Stem round, usually with only 2 accompanying leaves. Bulbous plant.
       H: Beechwood, mixed deciduous woodland, fen woodland, occasionally also in damp meadows. Likes a particularly chalky soil, rich in humus and nutrients, in warm situations. Occurs in masses in those localities where it is found.
       AI: M; ♃
       The seeds are dispersed by ants.

❷   **Lesser Grape Hyacinth** *(Muscari botryoides)*
Liliaceae
10—30 cm   IM: 2—3 leaves.
       D: Flowers in dense racemes, spherical, with a white edge. No scent. Stem stiffly erect, 5—10 mm wide, and widening towards the top.
       H: Mountain pastures, thickets and light woodland. Likes a calcareous, loamy soil.
       AI: M; ♃

❸   **Trilobed Anemone** *(Hepatica nobilis ; Anemone hepatica ; Hepatica triloba)*
Ranunculaceae
8—25 cm   IM: No possibility of confusion with other species.
       D: Flowers up to 4 cm in diameter, with 6—10 petals which readily drop off. Leaves basal, on long petioles and 3-lobed, the lobes being entire.
       H: Deciduous woodland. Likes a moist, calcareous, loamy soil, rich in humus. Abundant where it does occur.
       AI: P; ♃;(†)
       The flowers of this plant droop towards evening and in wet weather shut completely. During the 8 days of the flower's existence, the petals increase to double their length when the flower first opens. The seeds are dispersed by ants. At one time the plant was used in folk medicine against liver disorders (cf. scientific generic name: Greek *heparatos* (liver)). This species contains protoanemonine and is therefore slightly poisonous.

❹   **Siberian Iris** *(Iris sibirica)*
Iridaceae
30—90 cm   See p. 352

❺   **Mountain Knapweed** *(Centaurea montana)*
Asteraceae (Compositae)
30—60 cm   See p. 302

❻   **Dog Violet** *(Viola canina)*
Violaceae
5—15 cm   See p. 304

❶

20—60 cm

Spring Pea *or* **Vetchling** *(Lathyrus vernus)*
Fabaceae (Leguminosae)
IM: 2—5 flowers in one raceme. Flowers pink at first, then dirty blue. Stamens form
     a tube, with a straight margin. Stem angular. Leaves compound pinnate,
     with 4—6 leaflets, grass green on the underside.
D: Stem square. Leaves without tendrils, only short points present.
H: Deciduous woodland and mixed woodland. Likes a soil rich in nutrients.
AI: P; ♃
     For flower colour change see Mountain Pea, p. 304.

❷

15—40 cm

Mountain *or* **Tuberous Pea** *(Lathyrus montanus)*
Fabaceae (Leguminosae)
See p. 304

❸

50—180 cm

Blue Monkshood, Blue Aconite *(Aconitum napellus)*
Ranunculaceae
IM: No possibility of confusion with other species.
D: Dense, terminal racemes. Flowers consist of coloured sepals. Petals transformed
     into nectaries, which occur within the hood. Stem erect. Leaves petiolate,
     divided into 5 or 7 leaflets. Each segment of leaf narrowly linear, dark green
     above, light green below, glossy.
H: Marshy woodland at high altitudes, banks of brooks and springs, damp alpine
     pastures. Likes a porous soil, rich in humus, and with water draining through
     it. Indicator of nitrogen. Occurs in limestone areas at high altitudes.
AI: P; ♃; †
     Contains large amounts of the alkaloid aconitine and is therefore poisonous.
     Medicinal plant.

❹

5—30 cm

Geneva Bugle *(Ajuga genevensis)*
Lamiaceae (Labiatae)
See p. 294

❺

15—30 cm

Creeping Bugle, Common Bugle *(Ajuga reptans)*
Lamiaceae (Labiatae)
See p. 304

 Marshes, Moorland, Shore and Aquatic Vegetation   **Blue**

❻

20—60 cm

Brooklime *(Veronica beccabunga)*
Scrophulariaceae
IM: Leaves on short petioles, rounded at the end. Stem round.
D: Loose axillary racemes. Flowers 4—9 mm in diameter, deep blue in colour.
     Stem decumbent to erect. Leaves glabrous, glossy.
H: Margins of flowing, more rarely of stagnant, water, banks of streams, brooks
     and springs. Likes fairly fast flowing water, rich in nutrients and with a muddy
     soil.
AI: G; ♃; (†)
     An old medicinal plant containing aucubin (see Red Rattle, p. 278), an
     alkaloid and tannins.

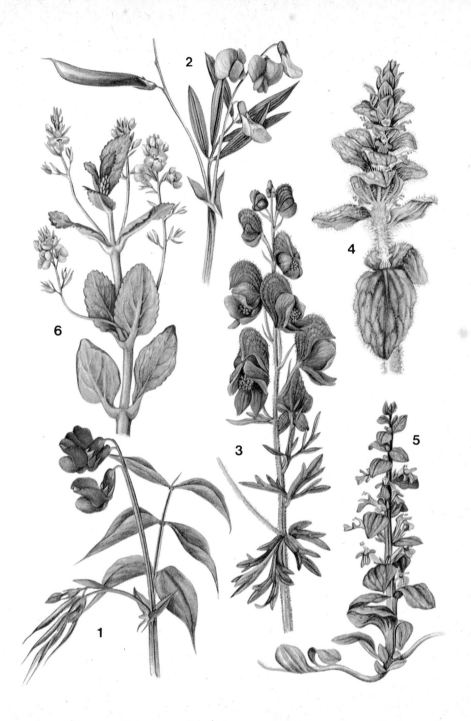

❶ **Water Speedwell** *(Veronica anagallis-aquatica)*
Scrophulariaceae
15—50 cm
- IM: Leaves pointed, and tending to clasp the stem. Stem quadrangular.
- D: Opposite, axillary racemes. Flowers dark blue, with even darker veins. Leaves faintly serrate.
- H: Margins of running, more rarely of stagnant, water, banks of streams. Likes a muddy soil, rich in nitrogen. Often associated with village streams.
- AI: G; ♃

❷ **Devil's-bit Scabious** *(Succisa pratensis)*
Dipsacaceae
30—110 cm
See p. 308

❸ **Water Forget-me-not** *(Myosotis palustris; M. scorpioides)*
Boraginaceae
15—40 cm
See p. 310

❹ **Marsh Gentian** *(Gentiana pneumonanthe)*
Gentianaceae
15—40 cm
- IM: Flowers usually terminal, erect, with 5 green stripes on the outside.
- D: Mostly 1—10 flowers at the end of the stem, more rarely in the axils of the upper leaves. Leaves opposite, linear and lanceolate, obtuse and rolled up at the edges.
- H: Reed beds, marshes, fens. Likes a peaty soil, moist with water containing dissolved calcium salts, but which dries out in summer.
- AI: G; ♃
  An old medicinal plant, containing an alkaloid.

❺ **Common Skullcap** *(Scutellaria galericulata)*
Lamiaceae (Labiatae)
10—40 cm
- IM: Flowers 1—1.8 cm long. Calyx with a dorsal scale.
- D: 1—8 axillary flowers, facing the same way, violet blue in colour. Leaves crenate.

- H: Banks of rivers and ponds, reed beds. Likes a sandy or peaty soil.
- AI: G; ♃
  Name: see Lesser Skullcap, p. 352.

❻ **Blue Monkshood, Blue Aconite** *(Aconitum napellus)*
Ranunculaceae
50—180 cm
See p. 316

Shrubs and Trees **Blue**

❼ **Alpine Clematis** *(Clematis alpina)*
Ranunculaceae
2—4 m
- IM: No possibility of confusion with other species.
- D: Flowers solitary, drooping, on long peduncles, axillary. Flowers consist only of coloured sepals (4—5). Petals form small, whitish nectaries. Leaves opposite, pinnate or double pinnate. Leaflets ovoid or lanceolate, serrate, with hairs on the undersides. Petioles tendril-like.
- H: Thickets and mountain forest of the Alps. Likes a rather stony, calcareous soil, rich in humus and other nutrients.
- AI: P

❶

15—30 cm

Hoary Plantain *(Plantago media)*
Plantaginaceae
IM: Stem 2—5 times as long as the flower spike. Leaf blades at least 4 times as long as the petioles.
D: Short, thick spikes. Flowers inconspicuous. Anthers reddish violet, long. Leaves form a rosette, margins entire.
H: Semi-dry turf, meadows, pastures, paths, verges, sports fields. Likes a rather calcareous, loamy soil, rich in nutrients.
AI: G; ♃
An old medicinal plant containing mucilage.

❷

15—30 cm

Greater Plantain *(Plantago major)*
Plantaginaceae
See p. 378

❸

15—50 cm

Corn Mint *(Mentha arvensis)*
Lamiaceae (Labiatae)
IM: Plant without a terminal inflorescence. Flowers in axillary whorls. Leaves rounded or linear.
D: Stem quadrangular. Leaves opposite and decussate, petiolate. Plant with an aromatic smell.
H: Banks of rivers, margins of running and still waters, ditches, wet fields and meadows. Likes a damp soil containing nitrogen.
AI: G; ♃
The plant contains ethereal oils (smell).

❹

30—75 cm

Horse Mint *(Mentha longifolia)*
Lamiaceae (Labiatae)
See p. 328

❺

30—100 cm

Water Mint *(Mentha aquatica)*
Lamiaceae (Labiatae)
IM: Plant with terminal flowers in a rounded head. Leaves ovoid to elliptical.
D: Below the terminal inflorescence there are at most 2 axillary whorls of flowers. Stem angular. Leaves opposite and decussate, serrate.'
H: Margins of running and still waters, river banks, ditches, wet fields and meadows. Likes a rather acid, muddy soil. Calcifugous. An indicator of wetness in fields.
AI: G; ♃
Contains ethereal oils (smell) and tannins.

❻

90—200 cm

Wild Teasel *(Dipsacus sylvestris)*
Dipsacaceae
IM: Leaves crenate, glabrous along the edges.
D: Flowers in a whitish or purplish head. Stem prickly but without hairs. Leaves sessile, fused together in pairs at the base, with prickly or glabrous borders.
H: Weedy places along paths, on slopes and wasteland, also on the edges of woods and thickets. Likes a rather stony, calcareous soil, containing nitrogen.
AI: G; ☉
Contains a glycoside believed to be scabioside. As the bracts of the inflorescence are flexible and not stiff, the fruits cannot be used, like those of the Cultivated Teasel, for teasing cloth.

❶ **Field Madder** *(Sherardia arvensis)*
Rubiaceae
5—30 cm   IM: Flowers in terminal cymes.
  D: Flowers only 4—5 mm long. Stem prostrate or decumbent, square in section. Leaves with one vein, rough at the edges. Lower leaves invert and ovoid, in whorls of 4; upper leaves lanceolate, in whorls of 5—6.
  H: Weedy places, particularly in cornfields, more rarely in gardens, vineyards, along roadsides or in vegetable fields. Likes a porous, sandy and chalky soil in warm situations.
  AI: G; ⊙
    The scientific generic name is in honour of the English botanist W. Sherard (1659—1728). The plant is the source of a red dye, madder.

❷ **Common Bugloss** *or* **Alkanet** *(Anchusa officinalis)*
Boraginaceae
30—100 cm   IM: All flowers in the axils of subtending leaves at the top of the flowering stem. Corolla tube not bent.
  D: Inflorescence loose, with many leaves. Stem angular, bearing stiff hairs. Leaves hairy, lanceolate or tongue-shaped, the upper ones sessile.
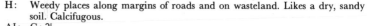
  H: Weedy places along margins of roads and on wasteland. Likes a dry, sandy soil. Calcifugous.
  AI: G; ♃
    An old medicinal plant. Contains an alkaloid poisonous to warm-blooded animals and tannin.

❸ **Creeping Campanula** *or* **Bellflower** *(Campanula rapunculoides)*
Campanulaceae
30—60 cm   IM: Racemes of many flowers pointing in the same direction. Stem round or slightly obtuse-angled. Stem leaves heart-shaped or ovoid to linear-ovoid, with short petioles, often bent slightly downwards.
  D: Flowers 2—3.5 cm long, ciliated along the edges of the corolla segments, pale violet. Basal leaves shrivel at the time of flowering.
  H: Weedy places in fields, along waysides, in thickets and on the edge of woodland. Likes a deep, calcareous, loamy soil, with nitrogenous material.
  AI: G; ♃

❹ **Common Comfrey, Knitbone** *(Symphytum officinale)*
Boraginaceae
30—100 cm   IM: Leaves distinctly decurrent. Plant with rough hairs.
  D: Inflorescence drooping, cymose. Flowers a dirty purple, pinkish violet or yellowish white. Stem richly branched at the base. Stem leaves furrowed.
  H: River banks, ditches, fen woodland, wet meadows, also on damp wasteland and waysides. Likes a moist, nitrogenous soil.
  AI: G; ♃; (†)
    Name and constituents: see p. 178.

❺ **Common Vervain** *(Verbena officinalis)*
Verbenaceae
30—60 cm   IM: Spikes. Flowers pale lilac. Inflorescence sparingly branched.
  D: Stem leaves with 3 segments, crenate.
  H: Weedy places, particularly along waysides. Likes a nitrogenous soil.
  AI: G; ⊙ — ♃
    An old medicinal plant, containing glycoside.

1

2

3

5

4

❶

60—130 cm

Field Thistle *(Cirsium arvense)*
Asteraceae (Compositae)
IM: Flowers in 1—1.5 cm wide capitula arranged in a paniculate manner. Only tube florets present. Carpels with long, pinnate hairs (use a magnifying glass). Stem strongly branched, with some non-flowering branches. Leaves prickly.
D: Leaves somewhat decurrent, linear-lanceolate, undivided or coarsely pinnate, somewhat wavy along the edges.
H: Weedy places in fields, gardens and vineyards, also on waysides and wasteland. Likes a deep, loamy soil.
AI: G; ♃

❷

15—30 cm

Common, Bitter *or* **Blue Fleabane** *(Erigeron acer)*
Asteraceae (Compositae)
See p. 238

❸

30—60 cm

Small Scabious, Dove Scabious *(Scabiosa columbaria)*
Dipsacaceae
IM: Marginal flowers larger than the inner flowers. The inflorescence contains blackish brown hairs (sepals). Stem below the inflorescence with decurrent hairs. Leaves pinnate.
D: Flowers in terminal heads, violet blue. Lower stem leaves lyre-shaped, upper leaves pinnate.
H: Dry and semi-dry turf, also on roadside verges. Likes a dry, calcareous, loamy soil.
AI: G; ☉ — ♃

The common and scientific names denote the use of this plant as a remedy against scabies. The Small Scabious contains the glycoside, scabioside.

❹

30—70 cm

Field Scabious *(Knautia arvensis)*
Dipsacaceae
IM: Stem below the inflorescence with spreading hairs. The upper leaves are usually pinnate.
D: Flowers in terminal heads. Outer flowers usually larger than the inner ones, bluish violet in colour. Leaves opposite, greyish green.
H: Meadows, semi-dry turf, roadside verges, occasionally also weedy places in fields. Likes a porous, rather calcareous, loamy soil.
AI: G; ♃
An old medicinal plant. Contains tannins and an alkaloid.

❺

10—30 cm

Persian Clover *(Trifolium resupinatum)*
Fabaceae (Leguminosae)
IM: The flowers appear to be 'upside down'. The standard is directed downwards and the keel upwards.
D: Flowers whitish purple, rose pink or violet, smelling of honey. Stem prostrate or decumbent, but never rooting at the nodes. Pinnate leaflets finely toothed.
H: Roadside verges, wasteland. Likes a porous soil rich in nutrients, but will also grow on clay in warm situations.
AI: P; ☉

1

2   3

4

5

❶

30—60 cm

Bush Vetch *(Vicia sepium)*
Fabaceae (Leguminosae)
  See p. 348

---

❷

20—60 cm

Smooth Tare *(Vicia tetrasperma)*
Fabaceae (Leguminosae)
IM: 1—3 flowers in racemes on long peduncles, pale violet in colour. Filaments of
     stamens form a tube which is obliquely truncate. Pods with 4 (cf. scientific
     specific name), or more rarely 5 seeds. Leaves pinnate, with 6—8 leaflets and
     a terminal tendril.
D: Frequently there are only 1—2 flowers to the inflorescence. Stem very slender,
     slightly angular, decumbent or climbing with the help of tendrils.
H: Weedy places in cornfields. Likes a non-chalky, sandy soil.
AI: P; ☉

---

❸

30—150 cm

Tufted Vetch *(Vicia cracca)*
Fabaceae (Leguminosae)
  See p. 348

---

❹

10—20 cm

Heart's-ease, Field *or* **Wild Pansy** *(Viola tricolor)*
Violaceae
  See p. 160

---

❺

1—10 cm

Sweet Violet *(Viola odorata)*
Violaceae
IM: Flowers scented, deep violet. All the leaves basal and usually slightly hairy.
     Stipules broadly ovoid, up to 4 mm wide, entire or slightly fringed.
D: Peduncle arises directly from the basal rosette of leaves. Corolla spur long.
     Leaves broadly ovoid or kidney-shaped, crenate. Plant with stolons.
H: Dry thickets and woodland verges. Likes a soil rich in nutrients, particularly
     nitrogen. Common on waysides near villages, where it has escaped from culti-
     vation.
AI: P; ⚄
     The seeds of the Sweet Violet are dispersed by ants. In the past this plant has
     had particular significance in folklore. The Greeks regarded it as a symbol of
     death. An old medicinal plant, containing saponin in the root.

---

❻

20—60 cm

Meadow Sage *or* **Clary** *(Salvia pratensis)*
Lamiaceae (Labiatae)
IM: No possibility of confusion with other species.
D: Flowers in false whorls of 6. Stem square in section, rather sticky at the top.
     Leaves ovoid, doubly crenate, undivided or trilobed, wrinkled.
H: Semi-dry turf, mountain pastures, roadside verges. Likes a porous, rather
     calcareous soil, rich in nutrients. Prefers warm situations. Tolerates dryness as
     the roots often go down to a depth of 1 m.
AI: G; ⚄
     The stamens and style of Meadow Clary are flexible, so that an insect entering
     the flower can effect pollination.

❶ **Cuckoo Flower, Lady's Smock, Milkmaids** *(Cardamine pratensis)*
Brassicaceae (Cruciferae)
30—60 cm   See p. 42

---

❷ **Columbine-leaved Meadow Rue** *(Thalictrum aquilegifolium)*
Ranunculaceae
50—150 cm
- IM: No possibility of confusion with other species.
- D: Umbellate panicles. Flowers tightly packed. Petals fall off very readily. Stamens violet, thickened towards the top. At the base of the branched petiole are membranous stipules.
- H: Fen woodland, deciduous woodland, moorland. Likes a damp, loamy soil.
- AI: P; ♃
    The leaves contain a yellow pigment which was formerly used to dye wool.

---

❸ **Hoary Plantain** *(Plantago media)*
Plantaginaceae
15—30 cm   See p. 320

---

❹ **Greater Plantain** *(Plantago major)*
Plantaginaceae
15—30 cm
- IM: Stem about as long as the flower spike. Leaf blade at most twice as long as the petiole.
- D: Long, dense spikes of inconspicuous flowers. Stamens yellowish white, anthers pale violet. Leaves entire, forming a basal rosette.
- H: Weedy places along paths and verges, on wasteland, sports fields, meadows and pastures. Likes a rather moist, sandy or loamy soil, rich in nitrogen. Resistant to trampling.
- AI: G; ♃
    The seeds of Greater Plantain become attached to shoes and are dispersed in this way. An old medicinal plant containing mucilage.

---

❺ **Horse Mint** *(Mentha longifolia)*
Lamiaceae (Labiatae)
30—75 cm
- IM: Stem bears an ovoid flowering spike. Plant densely covered in grey hairs. Leaves 5—10 cm long and 1.5—3 cm broad.
- D: Flowers pale reddish violet. Leaves opposite and decussate, almost sessile, linear-lanceolate, not wrinkled.
- H: Banks of streams, ditches, wet meadows, mountain pastures, damp field paths. Likes a moist, calcareous soil, which is rich in nitrogen, hence it often occurs near village streams.
- AI: G; ♃
    Horse Mint often hybridizes with related species and the hybrids are difficult to identify. Contains ethereal oils and tannins.

---

❻ **Corn Mint** *(Mentha arvensis)*
Lamiaceae (Labiatae)
15—50 cm   See p. 320

---

❼ **Water Mint** *(Mentha aquatica)*
Lamiaceae (Labiatae)
30—100 cm   See p. 320

❶

15—70 cm

Clustered Bellflower (*Campanula glomerata*)
Campanulaceae
  See p. 298

---

❷

30—60 cm

Spreading Campanula, Bellflower *or* **Harebell** (*Campanula patula*)
Campanulaceae
IM: Inflorescence a panicle of few flowers, 1.2—2.5 cm long. Corolla segments spreading, pale violet in colour. Stem leaves linear.
D: Flowers cleft down to the middle of the bell. Stem with short hairs towards the base. Basal leaves linear-ovoid, crenate.
H: Damp meadows, clearings in woods. Likes a moist, sandy or loamy soil.
AI: ⊙; ⊖

---

❸

30—60 cm

Meadow Crane's-bill (*Geranium pratense*)
Geraniaceae
  See p. 300

---

❹

30—60 cm

Wood Crane's-bill (*Geranium sylvaticum*)
Geraniaceae
IM: Flowers 3—3.5 cm in diameter. Peduncles erect after flowering is over.
D: Flowers in twos. Stem erect. Leaves large, palmate, divided into 7 segments or leaflets. Leaf segments deeply serrate.
H: Fen woodland, damp mixed and deciduous woodland, damp mountain pastures and alpine meadows. Likes a moist, loamy soil, rich in humus.
AI: P; ♃
    Seed dispersal: see Marsh Crane's-bill, p. 272.
    Name: see Meadow Crane's-bill, p. 300.
    Wood Crane's-bill contains tannin, particularly in the rootstock.

---

❺

30—100 cm

Common Comfrey, Knitbone (*Symphytum officinale*)
Boraginaceae
IM: Flowers distinctly decurrent. Plant with rough hairs.
D: Inflorescence drooping, cymose. Flowers a dirty purple, pinkish violet or yellowish white. Stem richly branched at the base. Stem leaves furrowed.
H: River banks, ditches, fen woodland, wet meadows, also on damp wasteland and waysides. Likes a moist, nitrogenous soil.
AI: G; ♃; (†)
    Name and constituents: see p. 178.

---

❻

20—40 cm

Sea Pink, Common Thrift (*Armeria maritima; A. vulgaris*)
Plumbaginaceae
IM: Leaves form a rosette, grass-like.
D: Dense, compact, umbellate heads. Stem erect. Leaves no more than 3 mm wide, ciliated at the edge.
H: Sandy turf, dunes. Likes a sandy, slightly acid, dry soil. Occurs in masses in certain localities.
AI: G; ♃

❶ **Purple Crocus** *(Crocus neapolitanus; C. albiflorus,* ssp. *neapolitanus)*
Iridaceae
8—15 cm IM: Petals only twice or three times as long as they are broad.
D: Flowers with hairy throats, appearing before leaves. Stigma extends beyond the anthers. Grows from a corm.
H: Mountain meadows, but in most localities occurs as an escape from cultivation.
AI: M; ♃
Like the closely related White Crocus, this species maintains its correct depth in the soil by contractile roots.

❷ **White Crocus, Spring Crocus** *(Crocus albiflorus)*
Iridaceae
8—15 cm IM: Petals 4—5 times as long as they are broad.
D: Flowers only slightly hairy in their throats, appearing before leaves. Stigma shorter than the stamens. Grows from a corm.
H: Mountain meadows. Likes a calcareous soil, rich in nutrients and moist in spring. Occurs in large numbers in certain localities.
AI: M; ♃
The violet-flowered form of this species is very much rarer than the white (about 97% of all flowers are white); however, the proportion of white to violet flowers can vary from year to year in the same locality.

❸ **Spring Anemone** *(Pulsatilla vernalis; Anemone vernalis)*
Ranunculaceae
5—35 cm See p. 344

❹ **Field Anemone** *(Pulsatilla pratensis; Anemone pratensis)*
Ranunculaceae
10—50 cm IM: Flowers drooping, campanulate. Petals with apices somewhat curved back.
D: Flowers solitary, dark purple to light purplish red (the inside of the petals somewhat yellowish). Carpels with long styles. The peduncle bears a whorl of fused stem leaves, or bracts, which are calyx-like and deeply dissected. Basal leaves appear first during the time of flowering and are bi- or tripinnate.
H: Semi-dry turf. Likes a well-aerated, rather sandy soil, which is warm in summer. Numerous in those localities where it does occur.
AI: P; ♃; †
The Field Anemone contains protoanemonine and anemonine and is therefore poisonous. An old medicinal plant. As in all other anemones the peduncle above the whorl of bracts grows substantially after flowering is over.

❺ **Pasque Flower** *(Pulsatilla vulgaris; Anemone pulsatilla)*
Ranunculaceae
5—40 cm See p. 344

❶ **Finger Anemone** *(Pulsatilla patens; Anemone patens)*
Ranunculaceae
5—40 cm   IM: Flowers more or less erect. Petals open in a campanulate manner. Leaves
              digitately divided, developing first during the flowering period.
       D: Flowers bluish violet. A quadripartite whorl of bracts below the flower.
       H: Dry and semi-dry turf, more rarely in thickets and dry woodland. Likes
              a calcareous soil in warm situations.
       AI: P; ♃; †

❷ **Autumn Crocus** *(Colchicum autumnale)*
Liliaceae
5—20 cm   IM: Flowers on a white 'stalk', which is actually the base of the corolla tube. No
              leaves present at flowering time.
       D: Flowers solitary. 6 stamens, 3 styles. Leaves appear first the following spring.
              They are fleshy, like those of a tulip, and enclose the large capsular fruit.
       H: Damp meadows and fen woodland. Likes a deep clay and loam soil, rich in
              nutrients, particularly nitrogen.
       AI: M; ♃; †
       See also p. 240

❸ **Mountain Aster** *(Aster amellus)*
Asteraceae (Compositae)
20—60 cm   IM: Flowers in capitula, consisting of an outer row of violet or mauve ray florets
              and inside, the yellow disc florets. Inflorescence branched, each branch with
              one capitulum. Leaves serrate or entire, hairy.
       D: Capitula arranged in a cymose fashion, each one 3—5 cm in diameter. Stem
              erect, branched at the top. Leaves with 3 veins. Flowers have a faint scent of
              vanilla.
       H: Dry and semi-dry turf, light dry thickets and woodland. Likes a shallow,
              porous, calcareous and often stony soil. Where it does occur the plant may be
              abundant.
       AI: G; ♃
       The name Aster comes from the Greek for a star and refers to the star-shaped
       arrangement of the ray florets.

❹ **Red Hare's Lettuce** *(Prenanthes purpurea)*
Cichoriaceae (Compositae)
60—160 cm   IM: Only 3—5 ray florets to a capitulum. Capitula arranged in panicles.
       D: Stem branched upwards. Leaves glabrous, clasping the stem at their bases,
              undersides blue green. Lower leaves linear-lanceolate, sinuous. Upper leaves
              lanceolate, usually entire.
       H: Mixed, deciduous and coniferous woodland, mountain forest, alpine mat.
              Likes a soil rich in humus. Rather calcifugous.
       AI: G; ⊙

❺ **Blue, Common** *or* **Bitter Fleabane** *(Erigeron acer)*
Asteraceae (Compositae)
15—30 cm   See p. 238

4

1

2

5

3

❶ **Green-winged Orchid** *(Orchis morio)*
Orchidaceae
8—40 cm
IM: Labellum with horizontally directed spur. All the petals, except for the labellum, bend inward to form a helmet-shaped structure. Labellum broader than long, trilobed.
D: Loose spikes of 4—12 flowers, purple in colour. Leaves linear-lanceolate. Stem angular.
H: Semi-dry turf, meadows, pastures. Likes a soil rich in nutrients.
AI: M; ♃
The tuber of this orchid contains mucilage, which occasionally finds a use as a medicament.

❷ **Spotted Orchid** *(Dactylorhiza maculata; Dactylorchis maculata; Orchis maculata; O. maculatus)*
Orchidaceae
20—60 cm
IM: Labellum with a cylindrical, backwardly directed spur. Lateral petals spreading. Bracts green and leaf-like, about as long as the ovary (appears to be peduncle). Leaves usually spotted.
D: Spike initially pyramidal. Flowers bright purple, pink or white, sometimes pale violet. Labellum trilobed, with the middle lobe narrowest. Stem a narrow tube or medullated. Tubers divided into finger-like processes.
H: Poor turf, heaths, moorland, light woodland. Occurs on both acid and calcareous soils. Abundant in some localities.
AI: M; ♃
Species of the genera *Orchis* and *Dactylorchis* are pollinated by various nectar-seeking insects (bumblebees, honey bees), although their flowers contain no nectar. The insects seek in vain for nectar at the bottom of the spurs, thrusting their probosces down and bringing about pollination in the process.

❸ **Dog Violet** *(Viola canina)*
Violaceae
5—15 cm
See p. 304

❹ **Heart's-ease, Field** *or* **Wild Pansy** *(Viola tricolor)*
Violaceae
10—20 cm
See p. 160

❺ **Tufted Vetch** *(Vicia cracca)*
Fabaceae (Leguminosae)
30—150 cm
IM: 5—30 flowers (8—11 mm long) in a long-stemmed raceme; bluish violet in colour. Raceme as long as its subtending leaf or longer. Stamens fused into a tube with a truncated edge. Leaves compound pinnate, with 16—20 leaflets.
D: Stem climbs with the help of leaf tendrils, slender with soft hairs. Leaflets linear-lanceolate, tendrils branched.
H: Meadows, thickets, edges of woodland, weedy places in cornfields. Likes a deep, loamy soil containing nitrogen.
AI: P; ♃

❻ **Bush Vetch** *(Vicia sepium)*
Fabaceae (Leguminosae)
30—60 cm
See p. 348

❶

10—30 cm

Basil Calamint *(Calamintha acinos ; Satureja acinos)*
Lamiaceae (Labiatae)
IM: Whorls of few (2—7) flowers, which are 7—10 mm long. Upper lip flat, longer than the stamens. Leaves 3—10 mm wide.
D: 2—5 flowers in axillary whorls. Stem prostrate, decumbent or erect. Leaves almost sessile, entire or sparingly toothed, somewhat rolled at the edges.
H: Dry and semi-dry turf. Likes a porous, often rather sandy or soil in warm situations.
AI: G; ⊙—♃

❷

20—60 cm

Meadow Sage *or* **Clary** *(Salvia pratensis)*
Lamiaceae (Labiatae)
IM: No possibility of confusion with other species.
D: Flowers in false whorls of 6. Stem square in section, rather sticky at the top. Leaves ovoid, doubly crenate, undivided or trilobed, wrinkled.
H: Semi-dry turf, mountain pastures, roadside verges. Likes a porous, rather calcareous soil, rich in nutrients. Prefers warm situations. Tolerates dryness as the roots often go down to a depth of 1 m.
AI: G; ♃
Pollination mechanism: see p. 326.

❸

10—20 cm

Common Self-Heal *(Prunella vulgaris ; Brunella vulgaris)*
Lamiaceae (Labiatae)
IM: Flowers 8—15 mm long. Upper lip helmet-shaped. Calyx with 2 lips, about half as long as the corolla.
D: Inflorescence directly attached to the leaves. Stem square in section. Leaves opposite and decussate, linear-ovoid, slightly crenate or entire.
H: Semi-dry turf, meadows, woodland clearings. Likes a rather moist, loamy soil, containing nitrogen.
AI: G; ♃
Old medicinal plant. Contains tannins, an alkaloid and an ethereal oil. At one time used as a remedy against diphtheria and throat infections.

❹

5—25 cm

Large-flowered Self-Heal *(Prunella grandiflora)*
Lamiaceae (Labiatae)
IM: Flowers 20—25 mm long. Upper lip helmet-shaped. Calyx with 2 lips, about $\frac{1}{3}$ as long as the corolla.
D: Inflorescence clearly above and separate from the uppermost stem leaves. Stem erect, hairy. Leaves entire or weakly crenate.
H: Dry and semi-dry turf. Likes a porous, somewhat stony soil, rich in humus.
AI: G; ♃

❺

30—70 cm

Field Scabious *(Knautia arvensis)*
Dipsacaceae
See p. 324

❻

30—60 cm

Small Scabious, Dove Scabious *(Scabiosa columbaria)*
Dipsacaceae
See p. 324

❶

30—60 cm

Cuckoo Flower, Lady's Smock, Milkmaids (*Cardamine pratensis*)
Brassicaceae (Cruciferae)
IM: Ovaries more than 3 times as long as broad. Leaves pinnate.
D: Racemes. Stem hollow, almost circular in section. Basal leaves form a rosette, unpaired pinnate. Leaflets round; terminal leaflet often larger than the others. Stem leaves pinnate with linear segments.
H: Damp meadows, moist places in deciduous, mixed and coniferous woodland, fen woodland, mountain pastures. Likes a loamy soil, saturated with ground water. Very common, giving a characteristic appearance to damp meadows at the end of April.
AI: P; ♃
This plant is often covered with 'cuckoo spit' or 'frog spit', which is produced by leaf-hopper larvae. These suck juice from the stem and this, when mixed with air, gives the familiar froth. See also Ragged Robin, p. 230. The plant is rich in mustard oil and vitamin C.

❷

30—150 cm

Honesty (*Lunaria rediviva*)
Brassicaceae (Cruciferae)
IM: Fruit 3—5 cm long, at most 3 times as long as broad.
D: Cymose racemes. Flowers with a pleasant smell. Stem erect. Leaves petiolate, heart-shaped, serrate.
H: Canyon forest. Prefers a stony soil, rich in humus. Requires a high humidity, so that it is often found near the bottom of narrow crevices, in the vicinity of waterfalls, or in the spray zone of mountain brooks.
AI: P; ♃
At one time Honesty was commonly grown in cottage gardens, its silvery fruits being used for decoration.

❸

50—150 cm

Columbine-leaved Meadow Rue (*Thalictrum aquilegifolium*)
Ranunculaceae
See p. 328

❹

90—200 cm

Wild Teasel (*Dipsacus sylvestris*)
Dipsacaceae
IM: Leaves crenate, glabrous along the edges.
D: Flowers in a whitish or purplish head. Stem prickly but without hairs. Leaves sessile, fused together in pairs at the base, with prickly or glabrous borders.
H: Weedy places along paths, on slopes and wasteland, also on the edges of woods and thickets. Likes a rather stony, calcareous soil, containing nitrogen.
AI: G; ⊙
Constituents and use: see p. 320.

❺

15—30 cm

Lungwort (*Pulmonaria officinalis*)
Boraginaceae
IM: Leaves heart-shaped at the base or rounded, petiolate, often spotted.
D: Cymes of primula-like flowers. Stem rough at the top. Several similar species, all difficult to distinguish.
H: Deciduous and mixed woodland, dry thickets. Likes a porous, calcareous, loamy soil. Quite abundant where it does occur.
AI: G; ♃
The flowers of Lungwort undergo a colour change from red to blue (cf. Mountain Pea, p. 304).

❶   **Common Comfrey, Knitbone** *(Symphytum officinale)*
30—100 cm   Boraginaceae
        IM: Leaves distinctly decurrent. Plant with rough hairs.
        D: Inflorescence drooping, cymose. Flowers a dirty purple, pinkish violet or yellowish white. Stem richly branched at the base. Stem leaves furrowed.
        H: River banks, ditches, fen woodland, wet meadows, also on damp wasteland and waysides. Likes a moist, nitrogenous soil.
        AI: G; ♃; (†)
          Name and constituents: see p. 178.

❷   **Purple Columbine** *(Aquilegia atrata)*
30—70 cm   Ranunculaceae
        IM: No possibility of confusion with other species.
        D: Flowers on long peduncles, brownish or reddish violet. Spurs run more or less straight to the hooked end. Leaves on long petioles, doubly tridentate; upper leaves sessile. Leaflets with 3 lobes, crenate.
        H: Mixed woodland, dry pine forest. Likes a calcareous, gravelly soil.
        AI: P; ♃; (†)
          For poisonous content see Common or Wild Columbine, p. 310.

❸   **Spreading Campanula, Bellflower** *or* **Harebell** *(Campanula patula)*
30—60 cm   Campanulaceae
          See p. 330

❹   **Creeping Campanula** *or* **Bellflower** *(Campanula rapunculoides)*
30—60 cm   Campanulaceae
          See p. 322

❺   **Wood Crane's-bill** *(Geranium sylvaticum)*
30—60 cm   Geraniaceae
          See p. 330

❻   **Deadly Nightshade, Dwale** *(Atropa belladonna)*
50—150 cm   Solanaceae
        IM: No possibility of confusion with other species.
        D: Flowers solitary in the leaf axils, drooping. Berries similar to black cherries. Stem richly branched. Leaves ovoid, decurrent.
        H: Clearings and light places in woodland of various kinds, edges of woods. Likes a porous, somewhat chalky soil, rich in humus.
        AI: G; ♃; †
          The specific name *belladonna* (Latin: 'beautiful lady') refers to the fact that extract of the plant causes dilation of the pupils due to the presence in it of the alkaloid atropine. An old medicinal plant. Contains very poisonous alkaloids.

❼   **Trilobed Anemone** *(Hepatica nobilis; Anemone hepatica; Hepatica triloba)*
8—25 cm   Ranunculaceae
          See p. 314

❶

5—40 cm

Pasque Flower *(Pulsatilla vulgaris; Anemone pulsatilla)*
Ranunculaceae
IM: Flowers more or less erect, campanulate. Leaves bi- or tripinnate, first appearing at the time of flowering.
D: Flowers solitary, blue or violet in colour. The peduncle bears a whorl of bracts, divided into 4 segments.
H: Dry and semi-dry turf, more rarely dry thickets and woodland on south-facing slopes. Likes a chalky soil in warm situations. Occurs in considerable numbers in certain localities.
AI: P; ♃; †
The flowers of this plant bend over and droop in wet weather. The plant contains protoanemonine and anemonine and is therefore poisonous. An old medicinal plant.

❷

5—35 cm

Spring Anemone *(Pulsatilla vernalis; Anemone vernalis)*
Ranunculaceae
IM: Flowers more or less erect; violet outside, white inside. Petals open to give a bell. Leaves simply pinnate, fully developed at the time of flowering, leathery, evergreen.
D: Flowers solitary, with a dense covering of yellow, or more rarely white, hairs. Blue or reddish violet outside, yellowish white or white inside. The peduncle bears a whorl of bracts, divided into 4 segments.
H: Dry and semi-dry turf, dry light pine forests, alpine mats. Likes a porous, rather acid soil, rich in humus.
AI: P; ♃

❸

5—40 cm

Finger Anemone *(Pulsatilla patens; Anemone patens)*
Ranunculaceae
See p. 334

❹

60—160 cm

Red Hare's Lettuce *(Prenanthes purpurea)*
Cichoriaceae (Compositae)
IM: Only 3—5 ray florets to a capitulum. Capitula arranged in panicles.
D: Stem branched upwards. Leaves glabrous with a heart-shaped base, clasping the stem; undersides blue green. Lower leaves linear-lanceolate, sinuous. Upper leaves lanceolate, usually entire.
H: Mixed, deciduous and coniferous woodland, mountain forest, alpine mat. Likes a soil rich in humus. Rather calcifugous.
AI: G; ⊙

❺

20—60 cm

Mountain Aster *(Aster amellus)*
Asteraceae (Compositae)
See p. 334

❻

5—20 cm

Autumn Crocus *(Colchicum autumnale)*
Liliaceae
See p. 334

344

❶ **Spotted Orchid** *(Dactylorhiza maculata; Dactylorchis maculata; Orchis maculata; O. maculatus)*
Orchidaceae
20—60 cm   See p. 336

❷ **Hollow Wort, Hollow Corydalis, Hollow Fumitory** *(Corydalis cava)*
Papaveraceae
15—30 cm   See p. 224

❸ **Fingered Fumitory** *or* **Corydalis** *(Corydalis solida)*
Papaveraceae
15—30 cm   See p. 260

❹ **Sweet Violet** *(Viola odorata)*
Violaceae
1—10 cm

IM: Flowers scented, deep violet. All the leaves basal and usually slightly hairy. Stipules broadly ovoid, up to 4 mm wide, entire or slightly fringed.

D: Peduncle arises directly from the basal rosette of leaves. Corolla spur long. Leaves broadly ovoid or kidney-shaped, crenate. Plant with stolons.

H: Dry thickets and woodland verges. Likes a soil rich in nutrients, particularly nitrogen. Common on waysides near villages, where it has escaped from cultivation.

AI: P; ♃
The seeds of the Sweet Violet are dispersed by ants. In the past this plant has had a particular significance in folklore. The Greeks regarded it as a symbol of death. An old medicinal plant, containing saponin in the root.

❺ **Wood Violet** *(Viola reichenbachiana; V. silvestris)*
Violaceae
3—20 cm

IM: Peduncle bearing leaves, but basal leaves also present. Leaves heart-shaped. Stipules with long fringes. Leaves glabrous.

D: Flowers solitary, axillary. Stem prostrate or decumbent. Leaves crenate. According to the length and colour of the spurs, it is possible to recognize two subspecies, which are often indeed given specific rank; ssp. *silvestris* — spur violet, 5—6 mm long; ssp. *riviniana*, spur whitish, 3—4 mm long.

H: Deciduous and mixed woodland, coniferous forest, fen woodland. Likes a porous soil containing humus.

AI: P; ♃
The seeds of this species are dispersed by ants.

❻ **Hairy Violet** *(Viola hirsuta)*
Violaceae
Up to 10 cm

IM: Flowers scentless, pale violet. All leaves basal, usually slightly hairy. Stipules entire, or with only a short fringe, never ciliated.

D: Peduncles arise from the axils of the basal leaves. Spur slender. Leaves linear-ovoid, heart-shaped at the base, crenate.

H: Dry thickets and woodland. Likes a very porous, calcareous soil in warm situations.

AI: P; ♃
The seeds of this species are dispersed by ants.

❶ **Dog Violet** *(Viola canina)*
Violaceae
5 — 15 cm   See p. 304

---

❷ **Ground Ivy** *(Glechoma hederacea)*
Lamiaceae (Labiatae)
15 — 60 cm

IM: Upper lip of corolla flat. Stem creeping or decumbent.
D: Flowers in axillary whorls, few in number to each whorl. Leaves glabrous, petiolate, reniform or heart-shaped, crenate.
H: Fen woodland, damp deciduous, mixed or coniferous woodland, damp meadows. Likes a moist, nitrogenous soil.
AI: G; ♃
Ground Ivy was formerly used in the treatment of wounds. It contains an alkaloid and tannins. It is poisonous to animals.

---

❸ **Bush Vetch** *(Vicia sepium)*
Fabaceae (Leguminosae)
30 — 60 cm

IM: Flowers 2 — 5 in the axils of leaves. Stamens fused into a tube, with a truncated edge. Leaves compound pinnate, with 8 — 16 leaflets.
D: Stem climbing with the help of leaf tendrils, which are pinnately branched.
H: Meadows, roadside verges, hedgerows, weedy places in fields and woodland, thickets. Usually occurs on a loamy soil, rich in nitrogen.
AI: P; ♃
The Bush Vetch secretes nectar from the underside of its stipules, which are visited by ants. Because of its high protein content it is a valuable fodder plant.

---

❹ **Tufted Vetch** *(Vicia cracca)*
Fabaceae (Leguminosae)
30 — 150 cm

IM: 5 — 30 flowers (8 — 11 mm long) in a long-stemmed raceme; bluish violet in colour. Raceme as long as its subtending leaf or longer. Stamens fused into a tube with a truncated edge. Leaves compound pinnate, with 16 — 20 leaflets.
D: Stem climbs with the help of leaf tendrils, slender with soft hairs. Leaflets linear-lanceolate, tendrils branched.
H: Meadows, thickets, edges of woodland, weedy places in cornfields. Likes a deep, loamy soil containing nitrogen.
AI: P; ♃

---

❺ **Common Self-Heal** *(Prunella vulgaris ; Brunella vulgaris)*
Lamiaceae (Labiatae)
10 — 20 cm   See p. 338

---

❻ **Wood Scabious** *(Knautia sylvatica)*
Dipsacaceae
30 — 130 cm

IM: Stem beneath the inflorescence with spreading hairs. Leaves undivided.
D: Flowers in terminal heads. Marginal florets a little bigger than the inner ones, pinkish violet. Leaves elliptical, lanceolate or broadly ovoid.
H: Mountain forest, canyon forest, mixed and deciduous woodland, fen woodland. Likes a moist, loamy soil, rich in nutrients.
AI: G; ♃

2

3

6

5

4

1

Stony Slopes, Rocks   Violet

❶
5 — 15 cm

Common Butterwort *(Pinguicula vulgaris)*
Lentibulariaceae
IM: No possibility of confusion with other species.
D: Flowers solitary, bluish violet, 1 — 1.3 cm long, spurred, often with white flecks. Leaves basal, forming a rosette, yellowish, linear or elliptical, entire, bent upwards at the edges, sticky.
H: Moorland, wet rocks. Likes a peaty soil with water trickling through it, or wet screes and sometimes limestone. Widespread in suitable habitats.
AI: G; ♃
An insectivorous plant. Tiny insects running over the leaves become trapped on the sticky surface. The sticky secretion of the leaves contains a proteolytic and also a rennin-like enzyme. (Cf. Ladies' Bedstraw, p. 120.)

Marshes, Moorland, Shore and Aquatic Vegetation   Violet

❷
30 — 75 cm

Horse Mint *(Mentha longifolia)*
Lamiaceae (Labiatae)
See p. 328

❸
30 — 100 cm

Water Mint *(Mentha aquatica)*
Lamiaceae (Labiatae)
See p. 320

❹
15 — 50 cm

Corn Mint *(Mentha arvensis)*
Lamiaceae (Labiatae)
See p. 320

---

❺
30 — 100 cm

Common Comfrey, Knitbone *(Symphytum officinale)*
Boraginaceae
IM: Leaves distinctly decurrent. Plant with rough hairs.
D: Inflorescence drooping, cymose. Flowers a dirty purple, pinkish violet or yellowish white. Stem richly branched at the base. Stem leaves furrowed.
H: River banks, ditches, fen woodland, wet meadows, also on damp wasteland and waysides. Likes a moist, nitrogenous soil.
AI: G; ♃:(†)
Name and constituents: see p. 178.

---

❻
Up to 3 m

Bittersweet, Woody Nightshade *(Solanum dulcamara)*
Solanaceae
IM: Flowers similar to those of a potato.
D: Flowers in umbellate racemes. Stem woody at the base, erect, decumbent, sometimes prostrate or twining. Leaves linear-ovoid, glabrous, often deeply lobed. Flowers smell rather like mice.
H: Marshy woodland, weedy places on river banks and damp wasteland. Likes a damp soil, rich in nutrients, particularly nitrogen.
AI: G; †
Bittersweet contains a poisonous alkaloid. A medicinal plant.

❶

30 — 100 cm

Siberian Iris *(Iris sibirica)*
Iridaceae
IM: Outer petals spreading and devoid of hairs. All petals bluish violet, the inner ones darker than the outer. Stem round, longer than the leaves. Leaves 2 — 6 mm wide, grass-like.
D: Stem hollow. Uppermost leaves membranous.
H: Moorland pastures, often in places which are flooded in the early part of the year and even in summer remain damp. Likes a muddy, clay soil, which is somewhat calcareous and rich in nutrients, but not markedly alkaline. The plant only occurs on non-cultivated soils. May be numerous in favoured localities.
AI: M; 2↓

❷

20 — 60 cm

Spotted Orchid *(Dactylorhiza maculata; Dactylorchis maculata; Orchis maculata; O. maculatus)*
Orchidaceae
See p. 336

❸

8 — 15 cm

Marsh Violet *(Viola palustris)*
Violaceae
IM: Flowers pale violet. All leaves basal, glabrous.
D: Peduncles arise singly from the rootstock. Corolla spur short. Leaves round or kidney-shaped. Stipules with a fringe.
H: Reed beds, moorland. Likes a wet, rather peaty soil.
AI: P; 2↓
The seeds of the Marsh Violet are shed explosively from the capsule. They are not dispersed by ants.

❹

5 — 15 cm

Common Butterwort *(Pinguicula vulgaris)*
Lentibulariaceae
See p. 350

❺

5 — 25 cm

Lesser Skullcap *(Scutellaria minor)*
Lamiaceae (Labiatae)
IM: Flowers 6 — 8 mm long. Calyx with a scale dorsally.
D: Flowers pinkish violet, about 3 times as long as the calyx. Stem richly branched, decumbent or erect. Leaves 5 — 20 mm long, entire or with 1 — 2 teeth on each side.
H: Ditches, river banks, reed beds. Likes a peaty or sandy soil.
AI: G; 2↓
The generic name (Latin *scutellum* = shield) refers to the shape of the calyx with its scale at the time of fruiting.

1

4

3

5

2

❶ **Parsley Piert** *(Aphanes arvensis; Alchemilla arvensis)*
Rosaceae

5—10 cm
- IM: Flowers in axillary clusters. They measure 1.5—2 mm in diameter and are only represented by the calyx. Leaves with 3—5 lobes.
- D: Stem thin. Leaves wedge-shaped at the base, serrate, ciliated.
- H: Weedy places, particularly in cornfields. Calcifugous.
- AI: P; ⊙

❷ **Annual Mercury** *(Mercurialis annua)*
Euphorbiaceae

25—50 cm
- IM: Stem quadrangular, branched. Leaves opposite, serrate.
- D: Plant dioecious, up to 10 leaves in clusters or spikes. Stem erect. Leaves petiolate, ovoid-lanceolate. Plant has an unpleasant smell when crushed.
- H: Weedy places in vegetable fields, vineyards and gardens, also on wasteland. Likes a dry, porous soil in warm situations.
- AI: P; ⊙; †
  Name and poisonous constituents: see Dog's Mercury, p. 362. Annual Mercury is a wind-pollinated plant. Many male flowers shed their pollen at the same time, as a result of a turgor mechanism in the anthers (cells absorb water until they burst). This bursting of the anthers, which ejects the pollen over distances of more than 20 cm, can be observed by placing young male plants in a vase. The flowers usually burst open in the morning.

❸ **Reflexed Foxtail, Reflexed Amaranthus** *(Amaranthus retroflexus)*
Amaranthaceae

10—80 cm
- IM: Flowers in dense, spherical panicles arranged along a spike.
- D: Inflorescence like a fox's brush, branched at the base. Individual flowers inconspicuous, in clusters. Leaves on long petioles, rounded or rhomboid, bluish green, alternate. Several similar, but very rare species.
- H: Weedy places in vegetable fields and waste ground. Likes a sandy soil, containing humus and nitrogenous substances. Prefers warm situations.
- AI: P; ⊙

❹ **Small Nettle** *(Urtica urens)*
Urticaceae

15—60 cm
- IM: Lower leaves shorter than their petioles. Whole plant with stinging hairs.
- D: Flowering panicles short, horizontal or drooping. Plant monoecious. Leaves opposite and decussate, ovoid-elliptical.
- H: Waste ground, roadside verges, walls, compost heaps. An indicator of nitrogen and somewhat calcicolous.
- AI: P; ⊙; (†)
  Stinging hairs: see Common Nettle, p. 364.

❺ **Common Nettle** *(Urtica dioica)*
Urticaceae

60—150 cm
See p. 364

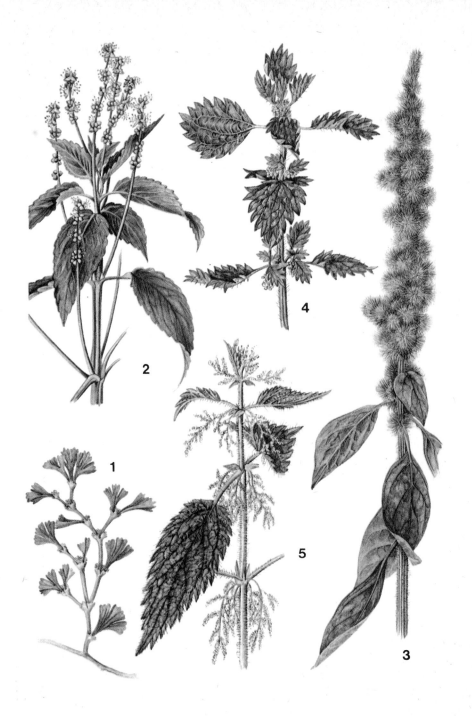

❶   **Salad Burnet** *(Poterium sanguisorba; Sanguisorba minor)*
                      Rosaceae
20—70 cm   See p. 360

❷   **Good King Henry, Allgood** *(Chenopodium bonus-henricus)*
                      Chenopodiaceae
10—60 cm   IM: Leaves spear-shaped or triangular.
                      D: Terminal spikes on main and lateral branches. Stem without definite nodes.
                           Leaves grass green on long petioles, entire, slightly wavy at the margins. Plant
                           with a floury appearance, somewhat sticky.
                      H: Weedy places on walls and in ditches, also in well-manured fields, on compost
                           heaps and dunghills. Likes a soil rich in humus and is a definite indicator of
                           nitrogenous conditions.
                      AI: P; ♃
                           Old medicinal plant. Contains saponin. Can be eaten as a wild vegetable.

❸   **White Goosefoot, Fat Hen** *(Chenopodium album)*
                      Chenopodiaceae
20—150 cm   IM: Inflorescence mealy white. Leaves bright bluish green, rhomboid to lanceolate,
                           serrate.
                      D: False panicle made up of clusters of flowers. Stem without definite nodes.
                           Several similar species, which are rare and difficult to distinguish from each
                           other.
                      H: Weedy places in fields and wasteland. Often one of the first plants to appear
                           on bare soil. Likes nitrogenous conditions.
                      AI: P; ⊙

❹   **Common Orache** *(Atriplex patula)*
                      Chenopodiaceae
30—100 cm   IM: Flowers with 2 rhomboid-oval bracts. Lower leaves lanceolate or linear-
                           lanceolate.
                      D: Flowers in clusters, unisexual. Lower leaves with a toothed margin on both
                           sides; upper leaves without teeth, lanceolate. Several similar species which
                           are rare and difficult to distinguish from each other.
                      H: Weedy places in vegetable fields and wasteland. Likes a porous, rather damp,
                           loamy soil, rich in humus. An indicator of nitrogenous conditions.
                      AI: P; ⊙
                           A species divisible into many races. Known as a weed of cultivation since
                           Neolithic times.

❺   **Spear Orache** *(Atriplex hastata)*
                      Chenopodiaceae
30—100 cm   IM: Flowers with 2 triangular bracts. Lower leaves triangular or hastate.
                      D: Flowers in clusters, unisexual. Lower leaves toothed, uppermost leaves
                           without teeth, lanceolate. Plant floury or glabrous. Several races occur,
                           varying particularly in the shape of their leaves.
                      H: Weedy places in fields and on roadside verges, also on waste ground, more
                           rarely on river banks; common in salt marshes and other maritime habitats.
                      AI: P; ⊙
                           A species divisible into many races. Known as a weed of cultivation since
                           Neolithic times. A halophytic species.

❶

50—120 cm

Broad-leaved Dock *(Rumex obtusifolius)*
Polygonaceae
IM: Basal leaves large, obtuse distally, heart-shaped proximally. Inflorescence only extends halfway along the subtending leaves.
D: False racemes made up of dense whorls of flowers. Stem often with a reddish tinge.
H: Weedy places along roadside verges, on compost heaps and around the edges of villages, occasionally also on wasteland and in woodland clearings.
AI: P; ♃
An old medicinal plant. The rootstock contains a purgative, the fruit an astringent.

❷

30—70 cm

Sharp *or* **Clustered Dock** *(Rumex conglomeratus)*
Polygonaceae
See p. 372

❸

30—100 cm

Curled Dock *(Rumex crispus)*
Polygonaceae
IM: Leaves with curly edges.
D: False racemes made up of dense whorls of flowers. Leaves stout, long and narrow.
H: Weedy places in fields, along roadside verges, also in meadows and on compost heaps. Likes a firm loamy soil, rich in nutrients. An indicator of nitrogen.
AI: P; ♃
An old medicinal plant, containing a purgative in the rootstock and an astringent in the fruits.

❹

8—20 cm

Annual Knawel *(Scleranthus annuus)*
Caryophyllaceae
IM: Flowers in crowded terminal or axillary cymes. Leaves without stipules. Flowers consist only of sepals. Sepals ovoid, pointed, green, with a membranous white margin.
D: Stem erect. Leaves opposite or clustered, linear or awl-shaped.
H: Weedy places in fields and gardens. Likes a porous, sandy soil. An indicator of surface acidity.
AI: P; ☉

❺

5—15 cm

Common Rupture-wort *(Herniaria glabra)*
Caryophyllaceae
IM: Flowers in crowded axillary cymes. Leaves with membranous stipules. Petals only about 1 mm long.
D: Stem prostrate or decumbent. Leaves small, opposite, glabrous, elliptical or oval, narrowing towards the base.
H: Weedy places, particularly on wasteland or roadside verges. Likes nitrogenous, sandy soils. Calcifugous.
AI: P; ☉
In medieval times the plant was used as a remedy for ruptures (hence name). It contains saponin and alkaloids.

❻

10—50 cm

Knotweed, Knotgrass *(Polygonum aviculare)*
Polygonaceae
See p. 30

358

❶

30—50 cm

Water Pepper *(Polygonum hydropiper)*
Polygonaceae
See p. 366

Meadows, Pastures, Grazing Land   Green

❷

20—70 cm

Salad Burnet *(Poterium sanguisorba ; Sanguisorba minor)*
Rosaceae
IM: No possibility of confusion with other species.
D: Flower heads spherical or ovoid. Flowers mostly unisexual; the lower ones male, the middle ones hermaphrodite and the upper ones female. Petals absent. Leaves 10—20 cm long, with 5—17 rounded, toothed leaflets.
H: Dry and semi-dry turf, wayside verges, dry woods and thickets. Likes a porous soil in warm situations. Calcicolous.
AI: P; ♃
An old medicinal plant. Salad Burnet contains tannins, particularly in the rootstock.

❸

15—50 cm

Common Lady's Mantle *(Alchemilla vulgaris)*
Rosaceae
IM: Flowers in terminal panicles, upper ones small and glabrous, consisting only of sepals. Leaves with 7—11 lobes, serrate.
D: Leaves round or reniform in outline. The species has recently been subdivided into several subspecies which are difficult to distinguish.
H: Meadows, more rarely in damp, grassy woodland and along woodland paths. Likes a deep, loamy, rather moist soil. Somewhat calcifugous.
AI: P; ♃
The name Lady's Mantle refers to the shape of the leaf which somewhat resembles the mantle covering the shoulders of the Virgin Mary in conventional portraits. On the serrated margin of the leaf are found glands which secrete water, particularly at night. The production of water may be so intense on warm, damp nights that the drops roll down into the funnel-like depression of the leaf and collect there. This plant is often mentioned in medieval books on magic. It was an essential requisite for the alchemist. Contains tannin in the leaf.

❹

50—180 cm

Alpine Dock *(Rumex alpinus)*
Polygonaceae
IM: Lowest leaves up to 50 cm long and 20 cm wide. Stem leaves lanceolate.
D: Inflorescence paniculate. Leaf blades wrinkled on the upper side.
H: Likes a deep, damp soil, rich in humus. Indicator of nitrogenous conditions. Abundant in localities where it does occur.
AI: P; ♃

❺

30—100 cm

Curled Dock *(Rumex crispus)*
Polygonaceae
See p. 358

❻

15—30 cm

Pyrenean Bastard Toadflax *(Thesium pyrenaicum ; T. pratense)*
Santalaceae
See p. 48

❶ **Spider Orchid** *(Ophrys sphegodes; O. aranifera)*
Orchidaceae
15—30 cm   See p. 262

❷ **Fly Orchid** *(Ophrys insectifera; O. muscifera)*
Orchidaceae
10—30 cm   See p. 264

❸ **Common Twayblade** *(Listera ovata)*
Orchidaceae
20—65 cm   See p. 368

Woods, Thickets, Hedgerows **Green**

❹ **Dog's Mercury** *(Mercurialis perennis)*
Euphorbiaceae
15—30 cm
IM: Either male or female flowers on the plant, never both. Stem round, un-branched. Leaves opposite, coarsely serrate.
D: Plant dioecious. Leaves in spiky axillary clusters. Stem usually erect. Leaves petiolate, ovoid-lanceolate, dark green. Plant smells faintly unpleasant when the leaves are rubbed.
H: Deciduous and mixed woodland, mountain forest, thickets, hedgerows, fen woodland. Likes a loamy soil which is rather stony but rich in nutrients.
AI: P; ♃; †
The scientific generic name recalls a Greek legend. According to the legend the Greek god Mercury discovered the healing properties of this plant. A medicinal plant containing saponin, ethereal oils, an alkaloid and tri-methylamine.

❺ **Common Lady's Mantle** *(Alchemilla vulgaris)*
Rosaceae
15—50 cm   See p. 360

❻ **Lords-and-Ladies, Wild Arum, Cuckoo-pint, Wake Robin,
Jack-in-the-Pulpit** *(Arum maculatum)*
Araceae
15—50 cm
IM: No possibility of confusion with other species.
D: Flowers occur at the base of the club-shaped spadix, which is enclosed within a greenish white bract — the spathe. The male flowers are above the female. Leaves sagittate, either dark green or dark green spotted with brown.
H: Damp mixed woodland or fen woodland, thickets, hedgerows. Likes a porous, loamy soil, rich in humus and plant nutrients, in warm situations.
AI: M; ♃; †
The inflorescence of this plant is a fly-trap. Flies are attracted by the smell of carrion which emanates from the spadix. The flies slip down the smooth sides of the spathe into the inside of the 'trap'. A crown of stiff hairs prevents them from escaping. At the bottom of the chamber enclosing the flies is some water which contains nectar. After the flowers have been pollinated the spathe shrivels and the flies can go free. The temperature inside the chamber is higher than that outside during the period when the female flowers are ready to be fertilized, because of high metabolic activity of the tissues. The whole plant is poisonous as it contains aroine.

1

5

2

3

4

6

❶ **Salad Burnet** *(Poterium sanguisorba; Sanguisorba minor)*
Rosaceae
20—70 cm   See p. 360

---

❷ **Sweet Spurge** *(Euphorbia dulcis)*
Euphorbiaceae
10—50 cm   IM: Umbel with 3—5 rays. Glands on the bracts yellow green, changing to reddish
yellow and purple.
D: Stem erect. Leaves 2.5—6 cm long and 1—2 cm wide, invert-ovoid or linear-
lanceolate, sessile or on short stalks. Plant exudes a white milky juice on injury.
H: Mixed and deciduous, dry woodland, fen woodland. Likes a porous, chalky
soil, rich in humus.
AI: P; ♃; †
Flowers: see Dwarf Spurge, p. 120. Sweet Spurge contains in its milky juice
the poison euphorbone.

---

❸ **Common Nettle** *(Urtica dioica)*
Urticaceae
60—150 cm   IM: Leaves longer than their petioles. Plant with stinging hairs.
D: Paniculate inflorescences long, pendulous. Plant dioecious. Leaves opposite
and decussate.
H: Wasteland, roadside verges, hedgerows, damp spots in deciduous and coniferous woodland. An indicator of nitrogen, and in woodlands an indicator
of damp conditions.
AI: P; ♃; (†)
The stinging hairs contain a so far unknown nettle poison and the substance
histamine. The two together evoke the characteristic nettle rash which results
from contact with the stinging hairs. The poison is destroyed by prolonged
cooking, so that young nettles are often used as a substitute for spinach
without any ill effects. Because of their high vitamin C and iron content they
are highly nutritious. The plant is the foodplant of the Small Tortoiseshell
(Aglais urticae) and Red Admiral *(Inachis io)* caterpillars.

---

❹ **Common Hop** *(Humulus lupulus)*
Cannabaceae
Up to 7 m   IM: A climbing plant.
D: Flowers in yellowish-green catkins. Plant dioecious. Stem twining in a right-
handed fashion, with stiff hairs. Leaves opposite, on long petioles, with 3—5
digitate lobes, coarsely serrate and covered with rough hairs.
H: Fen woodland, damp thickets, hedgerows, alder swamp. Likes a loamy soil,
saturated with ground water and rich in nitrogenous material. Prefers warm
habitats. Often an escape from hopfields.
AI: P; ♃
Hops contain a bitter substance which is an important constituent of beer.
Cultivation of the hop goes back at least to the 8th century.

---

❺ **Broad-leaved Dock** *(Rumex obtusifolius)*
Polygonaceae
50—120 cm   See p. 358

---

❻ **Sharp** *or* **Clustered Dock** *(Rumex conglomeratus)*
30—70 cm   Polygonaceae
See p. 372

1

2

3

4

5

6

❶

8 — 10 cm

Moschatel, Townhall Clock, Five-faced Bishop *(Adoxa moschatellina)*
Adoxaceae
IM: No possibility of confusion with other species.
D: Flowers in a stalked, terminal head. Individual flowers greenish yellow, inconspicuous. Stem erect. Basal leaves on long stalks, doubly trifid. Smell of flowers slightly unpleasant. Leaves have a musky smell.
H: Fen woodland, canyon forest, damp deciduous woodland and thickets. Likes a porous but rather damp soil, rich in loam and nitrogen. Somewhat calcicolous. Abundant where it does occur.
AI: G; ♃

❷

30 — 50 cm

Water Pepper *(Polygonum hydropiper)*
Polygonaceae
IM: Stem branched. Branches with loose spikes of flowers. Plant has an acrid taste.
D: Stem mainly erect. Leaves linear-lanceolate, narrowing towards the base and point.
H: Ditches, river banks, springs, also along damp woodland paths and wet field paths. Calcifugous. An indicator of nitrogen.
AI: P; ⊙; (†)

❸

50 — 250 cm

Wild Angelica *(Angelica archangelica)*
Apiaceae (Umbelliferae)
IM: Flowers in umbels. Stem at the base as broad as the human arm.
D: Umbels compound, with 20 — 30 rays. Upper part of umbel floury. Stem round, hollow, branched at the top. Leaves pinnate, sometimes bi- or tri-pinnate. Leaf sheaths inflated.
H: Weedy places on river banks and margins of both still and running water, marshy woodland. Likes a muddy soil rich in nitrogen.
AI: P; ⊙; (†)
Name: see Wood Angelica, p. 76. Angelica contains furocoumarin, which renders the skin sensitive to light, and thus skin stained with the juice of Angelica comes up in weals on exposure to sunlight.

❹

30 — 50 cm

Stinking Hellebore, Bear's-foot *(Helleborus foetidus)*
Ranunculaceae
IM: Flowers campanulate, in drooping cymose clusters. Leaves palmately divided. Stem with leaves except at base.
D: Petals converted to nectaries, so that flower consists only of petalloid sepals. Inflorescence of several flowers. Basal leaves absent. Lower leaves with petioles, compound with 7 — 9 segments. Upper leaves sessile, simple or divided into 3 lobes.
H: Dry woodland and thickets, particularly in clearings. Likes a porous, calcareous soil.
AI: P; ♃; †

❺

30 — 50 cm

Green Hellebore *(Helleborus viridis)*
Ranunculaceae
IM: Flowers expanded. Leaves palmately divided.
D: Petals converted to nectaries, so that flower consists of petalloid sepals. Inflorescence of 1 — 2 flowers. Leaflets serrate. Lower leaves curved back.
H: Deciduous and mixed woodland. Likes a soil rich in humus and nutrients, moist, calcareous. Mainly a garden escape.
AI: P; ♃; †

1

3

2

4

5

❶ Herb Paris *(Paris quadrifolia)*
Liliaceae
15—30 cm
IM: No possibility of confusion with other species.
D: Flowers consisting of a whorl of 4, more rarely 3 or 5 leaves. Fruit bluish black and cherry-like.
H: Deciduous woodland and stands of pine. Likes a moist, loamy soil, rich in humus and nutrients.
AI: M; ⅔; †
Herb Paris contains a poisonous saponin, which gives the fruit an unpleasant, bitter taste. The generic name recalls a Greek legend. The fruit of the plant symbolizes the apples around which Paris, Athene, Hera and Aphrodite gathered. The flowers of Herb Paris are scentless, but are nevertheless visited by small carrion flies.

❷ Spider Orchid *(Ophrys sphegodes; O. aranifera)*
Orchidaceae
15—30 cm
See p. 262

❸ Fly Orchid *(Ophrys insectifera; O. muscifera)*
Orchidaceae
10—40 cm
See p. 264

❹ Common Twayblade *(Listera ovata)*
Orchidaceae
20—65 cm
IM: Stem bears only 2 opposite, ovoid leaves. Labellum without a spur.
D: Raceme of many flowers. Labellum without a spur, long, deeply cleft. A similar species is Lesser Twayblade *(Listera cordata)* in which the racemes consist of only 5—15 flowers, the labellum has no spur, is deeply cleft, and is reddish purple in colour. The petals are usually green. Stem 4—20 cm. Coniferous and mixed woodland, particularly in mossy cushions.
H: Mixed and deciduous woodland, coniferous forest in the mountains, more rarely in damp meadows. Likes a rather calcareous, saturated soil.
AI: M; ⅔
The Twayblade is most usually pollinated by ichneumon wasps and beetles.

❺ Broad Helleborine *(Epipactis helleborine; E. latifolia)*
Orchidaceae
20—70 cm
IM: Labellum without a spur. Flowers slightly drooping. Petals spreading.
D: Racemes with flowers facing in a single direction. Labellum pointed. Ovary gradually tapering into the peduncle, both compressed. Stem only slightly hairy. Leaves alternate, broadly ovoid, clasping the stem at the base; hairs on the veins. Plant green, more rarely with a violet tinge when growing in shady places.
H: Mixed and deciduous woodland, coniferous forest. Likes a porous, calcareous, loamy soil, rich in nutrients.
AI: M; ⅔
The Broad Helleborine has its labellum split into 2 segments. Nectar is secreted in the swollen, hinder part of the flower. As the visiting insects (bumblebees and wasps) come in quest of the nectar, the pollinia attach themselves to the head of the insect. On visiting a second flower the pollen is transferred to the stigma.

1

4   2   3   5

❶ Ivy Duckweed *(Lemna trisulca)*
Lemnaceae
IM: Thalli pointed, 4—10 mm wide, arranged in the same plane but at right
    angles to each other, usually submerged, only floating at flowering time.
D: See illustration.
H: Zone of floating vegetation in stagnant water.
AI: M; ♃

❷ Lesser Duckweed *(Lemna minor)*
Lemnaceae
IM: Thalli flat on the underside, only 2—3 mm wide.
D: See illustration.
H: Zone of floating vegetation in stagnant water. Often occurs in such large
    masses as to constitute a green 'bloom' on the surface of ponds and ditches.
AI: M; ♃
    Lesser Duckweed is often fed to ducklings in order to speed their growth.

❸ Gibbous Duckweed *(Lemna gibba)*
Lemnaceae
IM: Thalli white on the underside and swollen, 2—3 mm wide.
D: See illustration.
H: Zone of floating vegetation in stagnant water. Likes water rich in dissolved
    nutrients and in warm situations.
AI: M; ♃

❹ Great Duckweed *(Spirodela polyrrhiza)*
Lemnaceae
IM: Each thallus has a cluster of roots. Thallus usually red on the underside,
    3—4 mm wide.
D: See illustration.
H: Zone of floating vegetation in stagnant water. Likes water rich in dissolved
    nutrients.
AI: M; ♃

❺ Broad-leaved Pondweed *(Potamogeton natans)*
Potamogetonaceae
50—150 cm
IM: Leaves ovoid, floating on the water surface; petioles long.
D: Flowers in terminal spikes; individual flowers inconspicuous. Peduncle to
    spike no thicker than stem. Floating leaves up to 12 cm long, somewhat
    heart-shaped at the base. Submerged leaves narrower, readily decomposable.
    Many allied species, all difficult to distinguish.
H: Zone of floating vegetation in stagnant or slowly flowing water, poor in
    nutrients.
AI: M; ♃

❻ Curled Pondweed *(Potamogeton crispus)*
Potamogetonaceae
30—200 cm
IM: Leaves markedly undulate at the edges, curly.
D: Flowers in a terminal spike; individual flowers inconspicuous. Stem square
    in section. Leaves all submerged.
H: Zone of floating vegetation in stagnant or slowly flowing water, submerged.
    Likes abundant dissolved nutrients. Indicator of muddy conditions.
AI: M; ♃

❶ **Sweet Flag** *(Acorus calamus)*
Araceae
90—160 cm   IM: Inflorescence obviously lateral.
D: Individual flowers inconspicuous. Stem compressed, grooved. Leaves linear, entire, reed-like. Rootstock creeping.
H: Margins of still or running water, also in reed beds or on shady, submerged, muddy soils.
AI: M; ♃
The root extract contains ethereal oils, alkaloids and choline, as a result of which it acts as a stimulant to appetite and digestion, Occasionally it is used in the liqueur and perfumery industry, also as an ingredient in toothpastes and mouthwashes.

❷ **Mare's-tail** *(Hippuris vulgaris)*
Hippuridaceae
10—200 cm   IM: No possibility of confusion with other species.
D: Flowers consist only of a single stamen and ovary and are axillary. Tops of the stems emerge above the water surface. Stem hollow. Leaves entire, in whorls of 6—12.
H: Submerged aquatic communities near the edge of slow-running or still water. Likes clear, somewhat calcareous water. Found in large numbers in certain localities.
AI: M; ♃

❸ **Common Hop** *(Humulus lupulus)*
Cannabaceae
Up to 7 m   See p. 364

❹ **Sharp** *or* **Clustered Dock** *(Rumex conglomeratus)*
Polygonaceae
30—70 cm   IM: Flowers in whorls. Inflorescence bearing leaves right up to the top.
D: Stem leaves heart-shaped to lanceolate. Basal leaves heart-shaped or ovoid.
H: Weedy places along waysides, in light woodland, and along the margins of slow-running or still water.
AI: P; ♃

❺ **Spear Orache** *(Atriplex hastata)*
Chenopodiaceae
30—100 cm   See p. 356

❻ **Glasswort, Marsh Samphire** *(Salicornia europaea; S. herbacea)*
Chenopodiaceae
5—45 cm   IM: No possibility of confusion with other species.
D: Flowers inconspicuous, usually in threes within the axils of sheath-like, subtending leaves. Stem apparently articulated, constricted at the nodes, glassy, green to dirty red, branched like a chandelier. No leaves present.
H: Mudbanks, saltmarsh. Frequents habitats exposed to flooding by the sea, therefore found on mudflats. Often planted to reclaim mudflats.
AI: P; ⊙ — ⊙
A definite halophyte, with a high salt content.

❶   **Water Pepper** *(Polygonum hydropiper)*
30—50 cm   Polygonaceae
         See p. 366

❷   **Wild Angelica** *(Angelica archangelica)*
50—250 cm   Apiaceae (Umbelliferae)
         See p. 366

❸   **Bladder Rush** *(Scheuchzeria palustris; S. palustre)*
   Scheuchzeriaceae
10—30 cm   IM: No possibility of confusion with other species.
      D: Flowers 3—8 in a loose raceme. Lower leaves with longer petioles than the
           upper ones. Stem erect. Leaves rush-like, grooved. Rootstock horizontal.

      H: Muddy, submerged peaty soils in warm situations.
      AI: M; ♃

❹   **Hornwort** *(Ceratophyllum demersum)*
   Ceratophyllaceae
10—120 cm   IM: Leaves singly or doubly furcate.
      D: Flowers inconspicuous, unisexual. Stem branched. Leaves stiff, singly or
           doubly furcate, hence with up to 4 segments. Similar species: Slender Hornwort
           (Ceratophyllum submersum), with leaves forked 3 or 4 times and therefore with
           at least 8 segments; soft.
      H: Submerged aquatic of still or slowly flowing water. Likes muddy water rich in
           nutrients.
      AI: P; ♃

Shrubs and Trees   Green

❺   **Common Spindle Tree** *(Euonymus europaea; Evonymus europaea)*
   Celastraceae
2—3 m   IM: Young twigs clearly quadrangular.
      D: Flowers in axillary panicles of less than 6 members, whitish green. Seeds with
           a bright red or orange seed coat. Leaves opposite and decussate, ovoid-
           lanceolate, dentate.
      H: Fen woodland, mixed and deciduous woodland, thickets. Likes a rather
           moist, deep loamy soil.
      AI: P; (†)
           Contains a poisonous alkaloid in the seeds. The shape of the seed coat recalls the
           cap of a Roman Catholic priest.

❻   **Common** *or* **Purging Buckthorn** *(Rhamnus cathartica)*
   Rhamnaceae
1—3 m   IM: Shoots and leaves opposite. Leaves with long petioles. Petiole 1—2.5 cm,
           leaf 3—6 cm.
      D: Plant often dioecious. Inflorescence a cyme of few flowers, axillary. Twigs
           squarrose, with terminal and lateral thorns.
      H: Dry woodland and thickets, margins of woods, fen woodland.
      AI: P; (†)
           The fruits contain numerous glycosides, which have markedly purging
           effects, hence its common and scientific specific names. An old medicinal
           plant.

❶

90—180 cm

Rock Currant *(Ribes petraeum)*
Saxifragaceae
IM: Pendulous racemes of flowers. Petals with red spots. Calyx with fine hairs.
D: Petiole longer than the leaf lamina. Leaves with 5 pointed lobes.
H: Canyon forest, mountain forest, mixed woodland. Likes a soil rich in humus.
AI: P

❷

120—150 cm

Black Currant *(Ribes nigrum)*
Saxifragaceae
IM: Pendulous racemes of flowers. Calyx densely covered with hairs.
D: Flowers in pendulous racemes of few flowers which are reddish on the inside of the corolla. Berries black. Leaves rounded, often heart-shaped at the base, on long petioles, with 5 lobes and yellow glands on the underside.
H: Marshy woodland. Somewhat calcifugous.
AI: P

❸

60—150 cm

Gooseberry *(Ribes uva-crispa; R. grossularia)*
Saxifragaceae
IM: Twigs with spines.
D: Flowers mostly solitary, more rarely in twos or threes. Spines mostly in threes, palmately spreading. Leaves in clusters, rounded, with 3—5 lobes.
H: Canyon forest, deciduous and mixed woodland, moist thickets, edges of woodland, hedges and scree. Likes a chalky and rather nitrogenous soil.
AI: P

❹

90—160 cm

Alpine Currant *(Ribes alpinum)*
Saxifragaceae
IM: Inflorescence erect. Flowers greenish yellow. Berries red, spherical, insipid, mucilaginous. Twigs hairy without any spines.
D: Leaves small, rounded, heart-shaped at the base with 3 lobes.
H: Canyon, mountain and coniferous forest. Likes a gravelly, calcareous soil.
AI: P

❺

15—30 cm

Bilberry, Whinberry, Whortleberry *(Vaccinium myrtillus)*
Ericaceae
IM: Twigs angular, green. Leaves slightly crenate, green on both sides.
D: Flowers singly in the leaf axils. Stem erect or decumbent, strongly branched. Leaves linear-ovoid, pointed, bright green.
H: Mixed and deciduous woodland, coniferous forest, moorland, heaths, alpine mat. Likes a porous, acid soil.
AI: G

❻

Up to 15 m

Common Ivy *(Hedera helix)*
Araliaceae
IM: Plant climbing by means of adventitious roots.
D: Flowers in semicircular umbellate racemes. Leaves of young plants with 3—5 lobes, those on the upper and flowering branches resemble the leaves of a pear tree.
H: Mixed and deciduous woodland, more rarely coniferous and fen woodland.
AI: P; †
Does not start flowering until 8—10th year. Contains a poisonous saponin, particularly in the berries. Old medicinal plant. Can live 400—500 years.

376

❶   **Greater Plantain** *(Plantago major)*
15—30 cm   Plantaginaceae
       See p. 328

---

❷   **Ribwort, Narrow-leaved Plantain** *(Plantago lanceolata)*
       Plantaginaceae
5—60 cm   IM: Spike short. Flowers inconspicuous. Stamens white, subsequently turning brown.
       D: Stem grooved. Leaves lanceolate, forming a rosette.
       H: Meadows, pastures, roadsides and paths, also on wasteland. Likes a sandy or loamy soil, rich in nutrients, particularly nitrogen.
       AI: G; ♃
       Constituents: see p. 26.

---

❸   **Asarabacca** *(Asarum europaeum)*
       Aristolochiaceae
5—10 cm   IM: No possibility of confusion with other species.
       D: Flowers on the soil surface or in leaf mould; greenish brown on the outside, purplish brown inside. Inflorescence arises directly from the rootstock. Leaves kidney-shaped, glossy. Plant has an acrid smell when the leaves are rubbed.
       H: Mixed and deciduous woodland, more rarely in coniferous forest and fen woodland. Likes a moist, calcareous soil, rich in humus.
       AI: P; ♃; †
       Contains a poisonous and burning ethereal oil, that has a pepper-like effect on the tongue.

---

❹   **Deadly Nightshade, Dwale** *(Atropa belladonna)*
       Solanaceae
50—150 cm   IM: No possibility of confusion with other species.
       D: Flowers solitary in leaf axils, drooping. Berries similar to black cherries. Stem richly branched. Leaves ovoid, decurrent.

       H: Clearings and light places in woodland of various kinds, edges of woods. Likes a porous, somewhat chalky soil, rich in humus.
       AI: G; ♃; †
       Name and constituents: see p. 342.

---

❺   **Lesser Reedmace** *(Typha angustifolia)*
       Typhaceae
90—220 cm   IM: Male part of spadix 1—15 cm above the female part of spadix.
       D: Male and female flowers in long cylindrical spadices. Individual flowers very small. Female spadix rusty brown. Grass-green leaves, 5—10 mm wide.
       H: Margins of still or slowly flowing water.
       AI: M; ♃
       The leaves are sometimes used to make vats waterproof.

❶   **Greater Reedmace** *(Typha latifolia)*

90 — 250 cm   Typhaceae

IM: The male spadix is directly above the female spadix and both are of approximately equal length.

D: Male and female flowers in long, cylindrical spadices. Individual flowers very small. Female spadix blackish brown. Bluish green leaves, 10 — 20 mm wide. A similar species is Shuttleworth's Reedmace *(Typha shuttleworthii)* : male spadix much shorter than the female spadix. Leaves 5 — 10 mm wide. 50 — 100 cm. Margins of still water.

H: Reed beds on margins of all still waters rich in nutrients. Pioneer of non-aquatic communities replacing aquatic ones.

AI: M; ♃

---

❷   **Great Burnet** *(Sanguisorba officinalis)*

60 — 150 cm   Rosaceae

IM: No possibility of confusion with other species.

D: Flowers brown or purplish black. Stem erect. Leaves unpaired pinnate. Leaflets heart-shaped or linear.

H: Fens and moorland, damp meadows. Likes a damp, peaty or loamy soil. Occurring in masses in suitable localities.

AI: P; ♃

The generic scientific name *Sanguisorba* ('blood ball') refers to the shape and colour of the inflorescence. The plant contains tannin in its rootstock, also saponin. An old medicinal plant.

---

❸   **Water Avens** *(Geum rivale)*

30 — 50 cm   Rosaceae

See p. 252

---

❹   **Common Figwort** *(Scrophularia nodosa)*

60 — 140 cm   Scrophulariaceae

IM: Stem square, but not winged.

D: Terminal panicles. Flowers brownish purple. Leaves opposite and decussate, undivided, ovoid-linear or heart-shaped, double serrate, glabrous.

H: Deciduous and mixed woodland, coniferous forest, fen woodland, clearings, more rarely in ditches and along river banks. Likes a porous, loamy soil, rich in nutrients and damp with ground water.

AI: G; ♃

The scientific name refers to the former use of the plant as a remedy against goitre (Latin *scrophula* = goitre). The plant contains saponin, flavones and small amounts of a digitalis glycoside. An old medicinal plant.

---

❺   **Winged Figwort** *(Scrophularia umbrosa ; S. alata)*

40 — 140 cm   Scrophulariaceae

IM: Stem broadly winged.

D: Cymose panicles. Flower brownish red, green at the base. Stem erect or decumbent. Leaves opposite, glabrous. Stem winged.

H: Margins of still or running water, ditches. Likes a muddy calcareous soil, at least occasionally submerged.

AI: G; ♃

The Winged Figwort contains saponin, flavones, and small amounts of a digitalis glycoside. An old medicinal plant.

Name: see Common Figwort above.

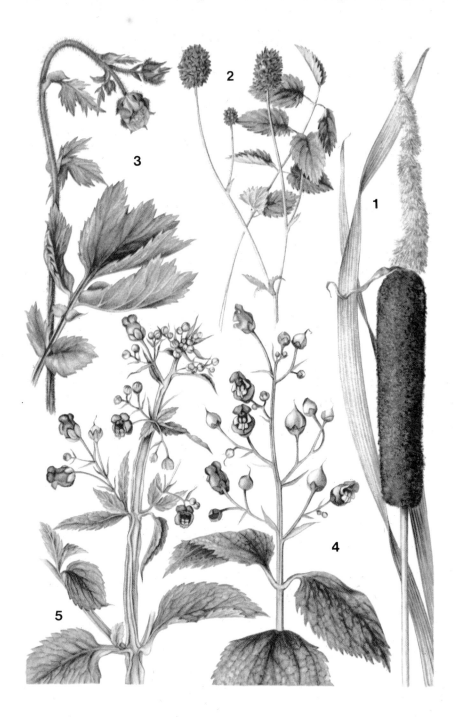

Bibliography

Butcher R. W.: *A New Illustrated British Flora*. 2 vols. London, 1961.

Cain S. A. and G. M. de Oliveira Castro: *Manual of Vegetation Analysis*. New York, 1959.

Clapham A. R., T. G. Tutin and E. F. Warburg: *Flora of the British Isles*. 2nd Edition. Cambridge, 1962.

Clapham A. R., T. G. Tutin and E. F. Warburg: *Excursion Flora of the British Isles*. 2nd Edition. Cambridge, 1968.

Cronquist A.: The Evolution and Classification of Flowering Plants. Boston, 1968.

Daubenmire R. F.: *Plants and Environment. A Textbook of Plant Auto-ecology*. New York, 1947.

Esau K.: *Plant Anatomy*. New York, 1953.

Fitter A. and R., M. Blamey: *Wild Flowers of Britain and Northern Europe*. London, 1974.

Hanson H.: *Dictionary of Ecology*. London, 1962.

Hutchinson J.: *Evolution and Phylogeny of Flowering Plants*. London and New York, 1969.

Kramer P. J.: *Plant and Soil Water Relationships*. New York, Toronto and London, 1949.

McClintock D. and Fitter R. S. R.: *The Pocket Guide to Wild Flowers*. London, 1956.

Morley B. D.: *Wild Flowers of the World*. London, 1974.

Oosting H. J.: *The Study of Plant Communities. An Introduction to Plant Ecology*. San Francisco, 1958.

Perring F. H. and S. M. Walters Ed.: *Atlas of the British Flora*. London, 1962.

Roles S. J.: *Illustrations for Flora of the British Isles by Clapham, Tutin and Warburg*. (4 vols). London, 1957-65.

Ross-Craig S.: *Drawings of British Plants*. London, 1951 to 1972 (published in separate parts at intervals).

Savile D. B. O.: *Collection and Botanical Specimens*. Ottawa, 1962.

Savonius M.: *All Colour Book of Flowers*. London, 1974.

Sinnott E. W. and K. S. Wilson: *Botany: Principles and Problems*. 5th Edition. New York, London and Toronto, 1955.

Slavík B.: *A Colour Guide to Familiar Wild Flowers*. London, 1974.

Tansley A. G.: *Introduction to Plant Ecology*. London, 1946.

Tansley A. G. and E. P. Evans: *Plant Ecology and the School*. London, 1946.

Van Dyne G. M., Ed.: *The Ecosystem Concept in Natural Resource Management*. New York and London, 1969.

Walker D. and R. G. West, Ed.: *Studies in the Vegetational History of the British Isles*. London, 1970.

Weisz P. B. and M. S. Fuller: *The Science of Botany*. New York, San Francisco, Toronto and London, 1962.

Index of common names

With plants that are included in several sections, the bold numbers refer to pages on which the detailed descriptions are given.

Index of scientific names

With plants that are included in several sections, the bold numbers refer to pages on which the detailed descriptions are given.